Systems of Order and Inquiry in Later Eighteenth-Century Fiction

ERIC ROTHSTEIN

Systems of
Order and Inquiry
in Later
Eighteenth-Century
Fiction

University of California Press
Berkeley Los Angeles London

University of California Press
Berkeley and Los Angeles, California

University of California Press, Ltd.
London, England

Copyright © 1975, by
The Regents of the University of California

ISBN 0-520-02862-7
Library of Congress Catalog Card Number: 74-16716
Printed in the United States of America

Contents

Acknowledgments

My discussion of *Caleb Williams* is an expanded version of my article "Allusion and Analogy in the Romance of *Caleb Williams*," UTQ 37 (1967): 18-30. I wish to thank the editors for their courtesy in permitting me to reprint this material.

This book has been a long time in the making. Among the deepest debts that I have accumulated over those years has been a debt to my students at the University of Wisconsin, whose energy, freshness, and skepticism have been invaluable. My research has been aided through the generosity of the Graduate School of the University of Wisconson. Mr. James L. Rhem and Professor Jeffrey Smitten have read portions of the manuscript and made suggestions from which I have profited. Ms. Jane Renneberg, Ms. Susan A. Gould, and Ms. Rhonda Nass typed the final manuscript (and one of its ancestors) fast and accurately.

Three people must be singled out in particular. Professor Howard Weinbrot has given me counsel, information, references, and insights; and has rescued me from careless, naive, and dogmatic lapses. Professor Edward W. Rosenheim, Jr., read the manuscript at a particular crisis in its composition; his advice, quite simply, saved it as a book. My wife, last but never least, has been, as Demosthenes said of Phocion, "the pruning hook of my periods," and a constant source of strength and perspective. To each of them I am profoundly grateful.

E. R.

Introduction

Writing in 1774, after the major novelistic achievements of the eighteenth century, John Ogilvie remarked that he did not "remember to have seen any regular attempt made to lay open the principles upon which a branch of Composition so universally popular, and susceptible of such high improvement, ought to be conducted." Joseph de la Porte had commented ten years earlier, despite a long tradition of French fiction, "nous n'avons aucun écrit en notre langue qui traite de la maniere de faire des Romans."[1] Both gentlemen tried briefly to make up for their colleagues' laxness, but neither they nor anyone else in the eighteenth century produced a body of theory about prose fiction like the shared body of theory about epic or lyric poetry, for example, or about the drama.

The most interesting discussions in England, at any rate, were Fielding's, which place his own novelistic practice within

---

1. John Ogilvie, *Philosophical and Critical Observations on the Nature, Characters, and Various Species of Composition*, 2 vols. (London, 1774), I: 349. Joseph de la Porte, *Ecole de littérature*, 2 vols. (Paris, 1764), 1: 204. At about the same time (1769) Mrs. Griffith knew "not whether novel, like the *epopee*, has any rules peculiar to itself"—see her preface to *The Delicate Distress*, in George L. Barnett, *Eighteenth-Century British Novelists on the Novel* (New York: Appleton-Century-Crofts, 1968), p. 119.

1

familiar contexts, such as the historian's and the playwright's.
He does not go far in clarifying the work of his contemporaries
or successors. Much of what he says does not apply to them,
because he conceives the genre in terms narrower than theirs.
If this most intellectual and articulate of novelists does not
throw sudden light on the work of other men, or even on any
general relationship between fictional theory and practice, we
can expect still less from his confreres. Richardsonians flat-
tered their master's opinion of his originality by assuring him
that his work was sui generis, with its own laws. "New and extraordinary," Smollett called it, and shunned it, for he himself
conceived of his novels, from *Roderick Random* on, in terms of a
quite different procedure. Fielding too tended to isolate his
work as "a species new and yet undefined," as did others, so
that "Dr. John Hill asserted that [Fielding] was the inventor of
a new form, and Warburton and Coventry said much the
same."[2] Confronted with such diversity, critics can easily be
pardoned their failure to arrive at "principles," even if they
closed their eyes—Ogilvie courageously did not—to the
pranks of Sterne.

Two centuries later, "principles" in Ogilvie's sense seem
distant and futile. A row of *oughts* cannot bring to order such a
willful garden as the experimental and unprogrammatic fiction of the eighteenth century. This book of mine, therefore, is
more modest. My thesis, at its most limited, is simple: that
radical similarities of method inform five major works of later
eighteenth-century fiction, works that appear, and are, markedly different. In all five novels, form—pattern, design,

2. T. C. Duncan Eaves and Ben D. Kimpel, *Samuel Richardson: A Biography*
(Oxford: Clarendon Press, 1971). p. 292, paraphrase Sarah Fielding's com-
ments on *Clarissa*'s originality, for which the author may make his own laws.
See also pp. 241-42; and Ronald Paulson and Thomas Lockwood, eds., *Henry
Fielding: The Critical Heritage* (London: Routledge & Kegan Paul, 1969), p. 24, n.
32. Smollett's comment comes from his *History of England from the Revolution to
the Death of George the Second*, 5 vols. (London, 1807), 5: 382 (Book III, chap. 14).
For Fielding, see Paulson and Lockwood, p. 14.

order—is keyed to a concern with epistemological inquiry that is as broad and as narrow as is suggested by Pope's "The proper study of Mankind is Man." Moreover, the formal procedures cohere as a system; so do the epistemological ones; hence my terms "system of order" and "system of inquiry." Finally, the systems of the five novels closely resemble each other.

This thesis, with the idea of system, returns us perhaps to history. Many individual procedures, like the use of analogy or a central intelligence or literary burlesque, are common to great bodies of fiction from all periods. A certain mode of inter-action among procedures, however, in terms of intention, of relative strength, and of characteristic use, may be peculiar to a given period within the continuum of historical change. If—and this "if" is a further hypothesis—a system found in a group of eighteenth-century novels coincides with a system peculiar to the eighteenth century, literary history can devel-op a powerful means of historical definition. Such definitions lead to critical inferences. They can help critics evaluate the functional limits of certain forms and the formal adaptations needed for certain functions, as morphology lets biologists examine the historical (evolutionary) and adaptive forms and functions of living beings. The thesis about five novels be-comes most fruitful in the degree that it points to this historical hypothesis. My book can hardly verify such a hypothesis, but it tries to set up the terms in which the hypothesis might be put and more conclusively tested.

My thesis is founded upon analyses of *Rasselas, Tristram Shandy, Humphry Clinker, Amelia,* and *Caleb Williams,* in that order.[3] These five analyses do not document but give rise to

3. I have used the word "novel" for *Rasselas* in accord with eighteenth-century usage. For example, William Rider (?) calls it "a Novel in the oriental Way" in *An Historical and Critical Account of the Lives and Writings of the Authors of Great-Britain* (London, 1762), p. 9, reprinted with introd. by O M Brack, Jr., Augustan Reprints 163 (Los Angeles: William Andrews Clark Library, 1974); the *Annual Register for 1759* also uses "novel" (6th ed., London, 1777), p. 477.

the thesis. Each of them tries above all to take into account the relevant facts, convenient or inconvenient, rather than to select what neatly suits the demands of my argument. Obviously the novels are too long and time is too short for the analyses to be complete, but ideally each analysis offers an operative model to answer any question of the type "Why, given the basic assumptions of this novel, are elements x, y, and z plausible in it?" or of the type "Why is it plausible that elements x, y, and z appear in the order in which this novel presents them?" Implicit in this ideal is the conscious assumption that models can be offered, that the five books are neither simplistic nor negligent, that their richness and control in their own terms is as great as that of any English fiction. If my analyses hold water, they stand ready to help launder away what may still remain of the image of the coarsely charming, helter-skelter, convention-cribbed novelistic toiler. More important, they can help divide what is central from what is casual or cursory in the novelists' formal strategies.

So as to avoid a "proof" by preselection, I have let popular consensus choose my five novels. Those chosen must surely now be among the most widely read works of fiction published in the later eighteenth century. Their possible rivals in popularity, aside from *A Sentimental Journey* (omitted so as not to have two novels by one man), are artistically inferior to them: *The Vicar of Wakefield, The Castle of Otranto*, and perhaps *Evelina*. Two novels in no way inferior to my five, both published just before mid-century, have been left out for technical reasons, I must confess, as well as because it seemed sensible to start after the formal innovations of these two monumental books,

---

This usage is not meant to vie with the different generic terminology advocated by Sheldon Sacks, *Fiction and the Shape of Belief* (Berkeley and Los Angeles: University of California Press, 1964); I am sympathetic with Sacks's distinctions, and have borrowed his term "apologue" for *Rasselas* when I thought those distinctions germane to my argument. (I might add that I am indebted to Sacks for other terms, like "paragon," and for several methodological assumptions.)

Clarissa and *Tom Jones,* had brought eighteenth-century fiction triumphantly into its own. Richardson's alterations of *Clarissa* made me wary of trying to handle it, as I had originally hoped, until a critical edition became available. The planned essay on it has therefore been postponed, to my regret, for *Clarissa* fits in beautifully with my thesis. As to *Tom Jones,* so much has been written about it that I thought my reader's time and mine might be better spent on *Amelia,* as profoundly conceived if not so superbly done. In any case, the five books chosen are certainly familiar enough to guarantee that they do not appear here through any wheedlings of my secret biases. I hope that they are familiar enough, too, that I have been safe in keeping plot summary to a minimum: the chapters are already too long—and the books so enticing to reread—that I have preferred to risk bemusing the casual reader at times rather than tax the good will and patience of everyone.

The continuing popularity of these novels from the time they were published makes me doubt that in relying on a modern consensus I am canonizing specifically modern values and interests. Works that stay familiar, moreover, are likely to be good, and if good, they can tell us more than mediocre works. I largely agree with Edgar Wind, that it is "a lesson of history that the commonplace may be understood as a reduction of the exceptional. . . . Both logically and causally the exceptional is crucial, because it introduces (however strange it may sound) the more comprehensive category."[4] The superior coherence and elaborate order of our five books illustrate options open to all within the aesthetic of the time. There is a way, however, in which Wind's "lesson" does not apply. The exceptional, because there is so little of it, only imperfectly comprehends the range and variety of a genre or style; its success keeps it from illuminating the pitfalls to which a genre

4. Edgar Wind, *Pagan Mysteries in the Renaissance* (Harmondsworth, Middlesex: Penguin Books, 1967), p. 238.

or style is subject. For this double reason, I cannot claim that my thesis must hold for the great bulk of later eighteenth-century fiction. Nor can I claim that the system I describe was dominant for the full half century. (I doubt that it was: *Caleb Williams* is, I think, a bit of a throwback.) None the less, historical inferences are encouraged by the fact that the five works include so many of the styles and types most successful in eighteenth-century England. "Writing to the moment" shows up in Sterne and Godwin; the epistolary form, in Smollett; sensibility, in Fielding, Smollett, and Sterne; the Gothic, in Godwin; topical social satire, in everyone but Johnson; doctrine and didacticism, in everyone, particularly Johnson and Godwin; the procedures of the novel of education, in everyone but Sterne; and so forth, through the picaresque, the melange of "humorists" and "originals," and varieties of the self-conscious narrator. Because our five writers used the idioms of fiction common in their time, the technical problems they faced stand a good chance of being those to which so many happy, tepid, or fatal solutions were proposed during the course of fifty years. And the habit(s) of mind which guided their handling of those problems must almost surely have been shared with scores of their humbler contemporaries.

Most of the terms I use to explore the habit or habits of mind need no prior explanation. Every scholar, I suppose, banks on a small fund of pet words, if only for the sake of clarity; I do too. But I have tried to keep to common use, and when I could not, to be sure that the words would gather operational definitions quickly. Terms like "perspective" and "rhythm," for instance, should not be found too slippery to support the structures my discussions make them bear. Three notions, however, are too central to be let pass so easily. One, "modification," *is* my own jargon. The other two, "analogy" and "system," are used broadly enough to require justification. Without that, I might seem to be unwittingly herding different beasts into one flimsy verbal fold. Because the force of "system," "analogy," and the idea of modification (if not the word) is historical, eighteenth-century thought has been my source of unity for each.

A glance at the *Oxford English Dictionary* will show that in the eighteenth century, as now, "system" had a wide range of meanings. I have already used it, in "system of order" and "system of inquiry," to refer to a body of procedures whose interdependence results from some sort of conceptual principle, perhaps conscious, perhaps not. In this sense one may also talk about the "system" of the novels, which results from the interdependence of the systems of order and inquiry, again in terms of conceptual principle. My thesis depends on the depth and intricacy of the system the five novels share, on how thoroughly they speak the same structural language and how thoroughly responsive that language is. Within this definition of "system," certain discriminations must be made. "System of order" can only refer to artifacts. Novelistic order, for example, is constitutive of the presentation of experience, but only indirectly interpretive of that experience. A system of inquiry can also apply to a novel as artifact, when one tries to assess and predict events through rules of economy, idiom, coherence and verisimilitude, or probable intention. These rules apply to the presentation of experience, but only some, altered, to experience itself. When systems of inquiry are applied to experience, they are always inadequate. "Of arts," as Hobbes wrote, "some are demonstrable, others indemonstrable; and demonstrable are those the construction of the subject whereof is in the power of the artist himself. . . . Civil philosophy is demonstrable, because we make the commonwealth ourselves. But because of natural bodies we know not the construction, but seek it from the effects, there lies no demonstration of what the causes be we seek for, but only of what they may be."[5] Systems of order can be adequate;

5. "Epistle Dedicatory" to *Six Lessons to the Professors of Mathematics* (1656),

systems of inquiry, when applied to novels, less so, because
novels present an image of nature, where no system of inquiry
works well.

The best we can manage with nature is to hew systematically
to the values inherent in the system of the novels: observation,
inductive order, analysis, and willingness to accept an equilibrium rather than a resolution. Our results will often be
fragile, but some progress can be made. The protagonists of
the five novels, faced with a quicksand of conjecture, begin in
the worst possible way. Each of them tries to be led by a system
in a new sense, a governing hypothesis taken as true. Their
systems are a priori tyrants of the mind, by which experience is
reduced as though it were an artifact, even an extension of the
ego. Thus Rasselas asks only one kind of question, whether
each mode of life he sees can give him the same thing with
which the Happy Valley has tantalized him, a static "choice of
life" in which he can confidently repose. Toby Shandy, aching
from and for war, interprets life as should an ideal soldier, and
soldier in idea. The invalid Matthew Bramble makes nosology
an absolute.

Interpretive, deductive systems of this sort occur in our
novels only when characters employ them. They are not useless for the characters, who benefit from them psychologically
and even epistemologically, to an extent. For us, they may be
amusing, help organize the novel we are reading, almost
certainly offer insights into the springs of human action, and
give us a (negative) exemplum of human behavior. Neither for
the characters nor for us, however, can the formal and
cognitive patterns of such systems be of more than limited
utility. To live by them leaves one restless and foolish, often

---

in *English Works*, ed. Sir William Molesworth, 11 vols. (London, 1839-45), 7: 184.
As R. G. Collingwood points out, the same assumption is made by Vico: "The
condition of being able to know anything truly, to understand it as opposed to
merely perceiving it, is that the knower himself should have made it." *The Idea
of History* (New York: Oxford University Press, Galaxy Books, 1956), p. 64.

embittered; to read by any single perspective, at least in these novels, has the same results. The most visible attempts to rationalize experience, those that treat life as an artifact with a preset idiom, turn out to be insufficient and harmful. A central theme in all five novels is the foolish willingness of those with most at stake, protagonists who have little margin for error in decisions to be made on little information, to risk what Pope called "the high Priori Road."

Because the interplay of different kinds of "system," with different kinds of validity for readers and characters, dominates this book, one should recall that the subject also dominates discussions of method in England and on the continent in the eighteenth century. As Ernst Cassirer says, "The whole theory of knowledge of the eighteenth century strives to confirm this distinction" between the inductive and rational "esprit systématique" and the deductive, rationalistic "esprit de système." Georges Gusdorf is equally absolute on this point: "Toute recherche de la vérité au siècle des Lumières comporte, comme un rite initiatique, quelques imprécations contre l'esprit de système," while the inductive system of Newton, with its epistemological monism, "est admis comme le prototype de toute connaissance parvenue à son état d'achèvement definitif." Thus Hartley can speak of his "System," which (he says) uses Newtonian induction, but can insist that despite his being "complete and systematical," he "cannot be called a System-maker, since I did not first form a System, and then suit the Facts to it."[6] Although in practice this ideal often got causal treatment, the conceptual framework was ubiquitous; our five authors acted predictably in drawing upon it.

6. Cassirer, *The Philosophy of the Enlightenment*, tr. Fritz C. A. Koelin and James P. Pettegrove (Boston: Beacon Press, 1955), p. 8. Gusdorf, *Les Principes de la pensée au siècle des Lumières* (Paris: Payot, 1971), pp. 265, 180. David Hartley, *Observations on Man, His Frame, His Duty, and His Expectations*, 2 vols. (London, 1749), I: vi (and cf. I: 6).

This is particularly true inasmuch as formal models for characters governed by an "esprit de système" were so ready to
hand. The logic of ethos (in Aristotle's sense) or "conservation
of character" (in Fielding's) had often led to characters' nour-
ishing their own systems by twisting facts, or less exorbitantly,
to characters' maintaining different but personally valid points
of view. The use of personae in late seventeenth- and early
eighteenth-century fiction provides still another precedent.
An assumption in philosophical argument about personal
identity, moreover, may be worth mentioning as a means by
which the authors' attention might have been called to the
relationship of empiricism and personal systems. I am thinking of the redefinition of personal identity as a system or
associative group of perceptions, past as well as present. The
mode of argument originates in the phenomenalism practiced
not only by Locke but also by many of his adversaries. For
instance, Henry Lee, attacking Locke in 1702, declares, "No
Body believes that the real Essence of any Individual is any
thing more than its Properties."[7] Lee's "no Body" overstates
the case, but Locke (*Essay* II.xxvii.9) certainly defines the conscious self, which is what we are interested in, in terms of its
perceptual properties alone: "For, since consciousness always
accompanies thinking, and it is that which makes every one to
be what he calls self, and thereby distinguishes himself from
all other thinking beings, in this alone consists personal
identity, i.e. the sameness of a rational being: and as far as this
consciousness can be extended backwards to any past action
or thought, so far reaches the identity of that person."
    This argument was tempered by Butler, extended by Hume;
but for our purposes what is important is the attention it
focuses on grouping properties into coherent and continuous
systems, for such the "self" is.[8] "Substance" and "individual"

7. Henry Lee, *Anti-Scepticism: or, Notes upon Each Chapter of Mr. Lock's
Essay* . . . (London, 1702), p. 232.
8. Joseph Butler, "Of Personal Identity," appended to *The Analogy of*

are conveniences for denoting properties perceived as a system extended in space and perhaps in time; "identity" designates not a thing but a process, "that connected succession of perceptions, which we call *self*."[9] Every object we see or conceive becomes a means of organization, of individuating and interrelating groups of "ideas" (in the Lockean sense). The structural consequences of such a view are clear, at least in logic. The small units of which our five books are mosaics, and which lend themselves to associative groupings, make up (in our minds) the object "book"; and the object "character" is the whole inferred from a multiplicity of overt or implicit acts of consciousness ascribed to a Booth or a Bramble. For us as readers, our order of perception translates itself into operational definitions of the characters—none of the five novels gives its protagonists, I might note, enough physical description to risk forming rival centers of identity—and any inconsistency in their behavior runs the risk, accordingly, of destroying them by damaging our definitions of them. "Conservation of character" becomes, in this light, not only a good idea but a pressing necessity. The self-generated system, as a crystallization of the self, is natural in such a context of Lockean thought.

The most important formal procedures in the novels (although less important in the characters' imposed systems) are modification and analogy. These are the best ways of appeasing the critics' cry for unity (or uniformity) and variety, as for instance, in James Harris: "It seems true in *every Species of Composition*, that, as far as *Perplexity* and *Confusion* may be avoided, and the *Wholeness* of the Piece may be preserved *clear and intelligible*; the more ample the *Magnitude*, and the greater the *Variety*, the greater also, in proportion, the *Beauty* and *Per-*

Religion Natural and Revealed, to the Constitution and Course of Nature (1736) (5th ed., London, 1765); David Hume, *A Treatise of Human Nature* (1739-40), ed. L. A. Selby-Bigge (Oxford: Clarendon Press, 1896), I.iv.6.

9. Hume, *Treatise*, II.i.2 (p. 277).

fection."[10] Analogy gives clarity and a sense of the whole, for "the moment we perceive that the parts of any object are analogous to one another, and find, or are informed, what that analogy is, the sight of a part, without any farther investigation, suggests the idea of the whole."[11] Retrospectively, the partial resemblances of analogy make coherent what one has read by giving a complex unity to a variety of phenomena, a unity of intermeshing grids or nets. As to events to come, reasoning by analogy must be the main guide of one's expectations. It serves the ends of inquiry as it serves those of order.

So, in fact, does modification, which I might define as the principle and demonstration that any state, any formulation in the novel is merely partial or provisional. Modification acts as a drive toward completeness, toward the "Magnitude" and "Variety" that Harris requires. It also gives impetus to inquiry by reminding man that he must act in a "state of mediocrity and probationership," in which, "by every day's experience . . . made sensible of our short-sightedness and liableness to error," our inferences deserve no more than "degrees of assent" (Locke, *Essay* IV.xiv.2, xvi.1). These inferences hang on probability, and so, in turn, demand the use of analogy, for "in things which sense cannot discover, analogy is the great rule of probability" (*Essay* IV.xvi.12, marginal heading). In systems of order, analogy gives unity so as to allow magnitude and variety through modification; modification sets up a dialectic toward completeness, a dialectic whose movements analogy controls. In systems of inquiry, modification encour-

10. *Three Treatises* (2nd ed., London, 1765), p. 64 n. (g). At about the same time as the first edition of the *Three Treatises*, 1744, an anonymous contemporary of Harris's across the Channel was writing about history painting, "On doit chercher toujours à l'augmenter [i.e., one's historical subject], comme on doit aussi chercher à répandre de la variété dans la composition, si cela se peut sans rompre son unité, ou détruire la vraisemblance." *Observations sur les arts* (Leyden, 1748), p. 73.

11. Joseph Priestley, *A Course of Lectures on Oratory and Criticism* (London, 1777), p. 164. The lectures were composed in 1762 on Hartleyan principles.

ages doubts that force us to analogy for probable inferences, which force us in turn to realize how tenuous they are, how dependent on further testing in modified perspectives.

Analogy and modification, as drives acting upon the basic situation of a novel, can make one feel that events are being generated naturally, without contrivance. The bounds of discourse are set by the initial situation (for instance, a disillusioned but affectionate young man seeks the calm of true friendship) or the initial matrix (for instance, a travelling party of a half dozen quite different people, with different perspectives on what they see). The adventure that forms the first exposition of the situation or matrix also forms the basis for analogy and contrast, a component and limiting form of analogy. A fawning man will be followed by a bluff one who is equally treacherous, a poor one whose seeming obsequiousness springs from true gratitude, a cringing politician; and they in turn by their moral, social, and psychological kinsmen and foils. The appearance of the testy, learned, paternal, and benevolent clergyman who is to be a main character is prepared for by the creation of an analogical context for his traits, so that he can be precisely appraised. Although the boisterous, engaging squire of dubious moral character escapes his just deserts, our sense of justice is calmed vicariously when we see a close analogue of his, a brawling ruffian, blunder into a near-fatal duel; and because the ruffian is far more unrelievedly nasty than the squire, our distaste for the squire is lessened by the comparison, and our pleasure in his charm increased, so that we are content to see him chastised merely by mild pain or embarrassment. By analogy, the ruffian becomes a surrogate for the squire. When the wandering hero finds his father unexpectedly, the episode echoes two or three other such discoveries, which have been increasingly close to the center of the plot, increasingly complicated in their use of repeated motifs; this augmentation of episodes and motifs is incremental repetition, also an effect of analogy. In our hypothetical novel, analogy generates content (or the options for content) and encourages such procedures as the use of surrogacy and incremental repetition. Analogy also transforms the novel as temporal experience into a pattern, a pattern increasingly enlarged because no single analogy or group of analogies can be final or formally stable as long as the principle of modification is in effect.

My hypothetical novel, of course, is no more than a sketch of a skeleton. Still, one can see in it how analogy and modification at once create natural-seeming structures of order and inquiry, how the appraisal and inferential force of characters and events may be developed along with aesthetically satisfying forms. The cognitive and formal fields are broad and yet controlled by the principle of unity in variety without which analogy cannot exist. By no means is analogy the only way in which an author can achieve these ends, nor, as I have said, is analogy at all unique to the eighteenth century. There are, however, reasons to suspect that eighteenth-century authors in particular found it an appealing way to achieve these ends. I should like to discuss two of these reasons, briefly, here. One has to do with systems of order. Contemporary associationist philosophy taught that analogy was constitutive not only of artifacts like novels, but also of the external reality that mimetic art renders. This is not surprising. If we can know the external world only as phenomena, through the mediation of a mind that works by association (that is, by a constant process of comparing and matching data), the world is very likely to be informed by analogy. The second reason for the appeal of analogy in the eighteenth century has to do with systems of inquiry: scientific probabilism made analogy the key to inferential knowledge.

The constitutive role of analogy in associationism can be exemplified in Hartley. He saw analogies—transfers of knowledge about A to apply to B—"present[ing] themselves to us every-where in natural and artificial Things":

The more anyone looks into the external natural World, the more Analogies, general or particular, perfect or imperfect, will he find every-where. . . . Earthquakes, Storms, Battles, Tumults, Fermentation of Liquors, Law-suits, Games, &c. Families, Bodies Politic lesser and greater, their Laws, Natural Religion, Revealed Religion, &c. &c. afford endless instances of Analogies natural and artificial. For the Mind being once initiated into the Method of discovering Analogies, and expressing them, does by Association persevere in this Method, and even force things into its System by concealing Disparities, magnifying Resemblances, and accommodating Language thereto.[12]

Hartley's statement makes internal the sort of conventional sense of an analogical universe which Renaissance scholars have presented as an "Elizabethan world picture" and which glimmers in the *Essay on Man*; he permits the old correspondences to be used by empiricists and the epistemologically cautious. If analogies exist or, to be more exact, are seen everywhere in nature, then works that imitate nature might well imitate her analogies too. More important, I think, is Hartley's assumption that the discovery and even creation of analogies occupy "the Mind . . . once initiated into the Method." If readers, not to mention authors, think analogically, and unconsciously desire analogies to such an extent that they will even warp reality to create them, analogies ought to be central in fictions designed to entertain and insinuate themselves into the minds of such men. Language and phenomenal reality, which meet in imitative literature, both point toward that way of proceeding.[13]

If reality itself, reality as we can know it, has the sort of structure Hartley assigns it, then analogy ought also to be

12. Hartley, *Observations*, 1: 293, 295, 296-97. Cf. Jean-Paul Marat's blanket "the mind, in its progress, always proceeds by analogy." *A Philosophical Essay on Man*, 2 vols. (London, 1773), 1: 210.

13. On this whole subject, see Earl Wasserman's synoptic "Nature Moralized: The Divine Analogy in the Eighteenth Century," *ELH* 20 (1953): 39-76.

valuable in systems of inquiry. The modern scholar, unless he has a specific interest in the history of science, is perhaps most likely to associate this idea with Bishop Butler. For man, as a limited being, says Butler, "Probability is the very Guide of Life," and therefore we may be "unquestionably" assured that "Analogy is of Weight, in various Degrees, towards determining our Judgment, and our Practice." "The Rule and Measure of our Hopes and Fears concerning the Success of our Pursuits; our Expectations that Others will act so and so in such Circumstances; and our Judgment that such Actions proceed from such Principles; all These rely upon our having observed the like to what we hope, fear, expect, judge; I say upon our having observed the like, either with respect to Others or Ourselves."[14] Butler's own attempt to give theology an empirical ground must be based on analogy, as it is, because all empirical reasoning is analogical.

This line of argument is clearly important to a branch of literature so empirical in texture as fiction. It had long been used by critics to support verisimilitude, a device that makes readers find the concerns of a book analogous to their own. More important for my argument is analogy within a book, by which readers assess what has happened and what may happen next. The judgment of what characters are likely to do, of their value, of the way situations are likely to be resolved, is very much what Butler calls "Hopes and Fears," "Expectations," and causal "Judgment." A fuller argument can be inferred from Hume, for one, who points out that "abstract or demonstrative reasoning . . . never influences any of our actions, but only as it directs our judgment concerning causes

14. Butler, *Analogy*, pp. iv, v-vi, ii-iii. Cf. Paul Vernière's statement that, for Diderot, "l'analogie est . . . plus qu'un jeu: c'est l'intuition d'un ordre," and again, "Le raisonnement analogique pour Diderot est non seulement l'élément essentiel du mécanisme intellectuel, mais la seule voie de la découverte philosophique." Denis Diderot, *Oeuvres philosophiques*, ed. Paul Vernière (Paris: Garnier, 1964), pp. xxi, 280 n. 1. Jérôme Richard wrote that "tous nos raisonnements concernant les choses de fait" are founded on causal analogy. *La Théorie des songes* (Paris, 1766), p. 26.

and effects," and thus persuades the passions. Causal reasoning in turn is promoted by analogy, to a greater or less degree as the analogy is "more or less firm and certain." A double flexibility inheres in Hume's position: the causal strength of analogy varies, and the effect of causal decisions also varies through the need to convince the passions, which are subject to the "variations of temper" common to us all.[15] As will become clear, this kind of flexibility lies behind the authors' testing of characters' systems and behind what I have called "modification," the provisory nature of one's formulations.

Let me be a bit less abstract and, before passing to the analyses themselves, call attention to one formal and cognitive effect of an interest in and bias toward analogy in the arts. The ideal of discriminated variety, to which eighteenth-century readers were peculiarly alert, shows how analogy calls on the combined faculties of "wit" (seeing resemblances) and "judgment" (seeing differences). To explain what I mean, I will yield the floor to Parson Adams as he describes Homer's treatment of "Manners" to a stunned Mr. Wilson and company. "I am at a loss," says Adams,

whether I should rather admire the Exactness of his Judgment in the nice Distinction, or the Immensity of his Imagination in their Variety. For, as to the former of these, how accurately is the sedate, injured Resentment of *Achilles* distinguished from the hot insulting Passion of *Agamemnon*? How widely doth the brutal Courage of *Ajax* differ from the amiable Bravery of *Diomedes*; and the Wisdom of *Nestor*, which is the Result of long Reflection and Experience, from the Cunning of *Ulysses*, the Effect of Art and Subtilty only? If we consider their Variety, we may cry out with *Aristotle* . . . that no Part of this divine Poem is destitute of Manners. Indeed I might affirm, that there is scarce a Character in human Nature untouched in some part or other.[16]

---

15. Hume, *Treatise*, II.iii.3, I.iii.12 (pp. 414, 142, 418).
16. Henry Fielding, *Joseph Andrews* (1742), ed. Martin C. Battestin (Oxford: Clarendon Press, 1967), p. 198.

The good parson was not, this time, singular. His praise for this mixture of variety and precision is a commonplace. The Chevalier Ramsey, for example, in his "Discours de la poésie épique" prefaced to Fénelon's *Télémaque* and repeatedly reprinted in French and English throughout the century, also exclaims over the discriminated variety of characters in Homer: "Le courage d'Achille & celui d'Hector; la valeur de Dioméde, & celle d'Ajax; la prudence de Nestor, & celle d'Ulysse; l'amour d'Héléne, & celui de Briséïs; la fidélité d'Andromaque, & celle de Pénélope, ne se ressemblent point. On trouve un jugement & une finesse admirables dans les Caracteres du Poëte Grec." Addison had made similar comments about Homer and Milton, Dennis had praised Virgil in the same way, and others had followed suit.[17]

What was sauce for the epic, not to mention history painting and the theatre, was sauce for the novel, as the two most influential and most imitated novelists openly testified.[18] Fielding surely is speaking through Adams in the passage quoted above, occurring as it does in a book that he relates to the epic in his preface. Arthur Murphy commends him along these lines. "Still observing the grand essential rule of unity in

17. Ramsey (1717), in *Les Aventures de Télémaque* (Amsterdam and Rotterdam, 1734), p. ix. Addison, in *Spectator* 273. Dennis, in *Remarks on a Book Entituled, Prince Arthur* (1696), *The Critical Works*, ed. Edward Niles Hooker, 2 vols. (Baltimore: Johns Hopkins Press, 1939, 1943), 1: 109-23. See also Thomas Blackwell, *An Enquiry into the Life and Writings of Homer* (London, 1735): "Both Achilles and Ajax, Diomedes and Hector, Ulysses and Merion, are all *brave*; but it is in a different manner" (p. 304), on which he elaborates. John Newbery (?) makes similar comments on Homer in *The Art of Poetry on a New Plan*, 2 vols. (London, 1762), 2: 184; so does James Beattie, who extends the idea to Milton, in *Essays on Poetry and Music . . .* (3rd ed., London, 1779), pp. 84-86. Also see, for Homer, Henry Pemberton, *Observations on Poetry* (London, 1738), p. 46; for Homer and Ossian, Hugh Blair's *Critical Dissertation on the Poems of Ossian* (2nd ed., London, 1765), p. 51; for Ovid, Christian Ludwig von Hagedom, *Réflexions sur la peinture* (1762), tr. Huber, 2 vols. (Leipzig, 1775), 1:34.

18. History painting and the theatre are, along with the epic, the specific prestigious sources on which the novel drew; hence their critical importance. I

the design," wrote Murphy in 1762, "I believe, no author has introduced a greater diversity of characters, or displayed them more fully, or in more various attitudes. . . . Every thing has *Manners*; and the very manners which belong to it in human life." Richardson, who said that *Clarissa* contained "the whole compass of human nature, as far as *Capacity would allow*, or the *Story admit*," also strove for what Parson Adams calls "Exactness of Judgment" as well as "Immensity of Imagination": he wrote Lady Bradshaigh that he had been "complimented wth: giving a Stile to each of my various Characters, yt: distinguishes *whose* from *whose*, ye Moment they are entred upon." Perhaps the compliment came from Stinstra, who praised Richardson's "profusion of characters," each of whom "preserves his own personality consistently, and each is completely the image of himself."[19]

---

will limit my documentation to the most prestigious painter and playwright, Raphael and Shakespeare. Raphael's Cartoons embodied for Englishmen the art of giving each participant his own expression with justice and delicacy. See Jery Melford's letter of June 11; Steele, *Spectator* 226; Jonathan Richardson, *The Theory of Painting* (1715), in *Works* (London, 1792), pp. 42-44; George Turnbull, *A Treatise on Ancient Painting* (London, 1740), p. 149; Daniel Webb, *An Inquiry into the Beauties of Painting* . . . (London, 1760), pp. 179, 188. On what Nicholas Rowe called Shakespeare's "well-distinguished Variety" see comments by Rowe (1709), Dennis (1712), Pope (1725), and Theobald (1740: "What Variety of Originals, and how differing each from the other!") in *Eighteenth Century Essays on Shakespeare*, ed. D. Nichol Smith (2nd ed., Oxford: Clarendon Press, 1963), pp. 10, 24, 45, 60. Also see William Belsham, *Essays, Philosophical, Historical, and Literary* (London, 1789), p. 21. J. G. Sulzer discusses discriminated variety more generally in his *Nouvelle théorie des plaisirs* (n.p., 1767), pp. 80-81; and Jacques Lacombe, *Le Spectacle des beaux arts* (Paris, 1763), p. 14, declares it one of the surest sources of pleasure in the arts, "le premier caractère des bons ouvrages en tout genre."

19. For Murphy's comments, see Paulson and Lockwood, pp. 430, 426-27; and cf. Fielding's own comments, not overtly applied to himself, in the first chapter of *Tom Jones*, Bk. X. Richardson is quoted by Eaves and Kimpel, pp. 312, 246. For Stinstra, *The Richardson-Stinstra Correspondence, and Stinstra's Prefaces to "Clarissa,"* ed. William C. Slattery (Carbondale and Edwardsville: Southern Illinois University Press, 1969), p. 117.

The ideal of discriminated variety is thus associated with the particularization of characters, with an interest in motives and in personal psychology, and with an ideal of decorum, that of "conservation of character," as Fielding calls it in *Tom Jones* (VIII, 1). It is also directly connected with analogy, as Parson Adams's and the Chevalier Ramsay's lists suggest: comparison is the means by which the precision of "manners" is appreciated. For this reason, we find eighteenth-century fiction full of characters conceived in binary relationships. In the novels we are to consider, one only has to think of the romantic naiveté shared by Lydia Melford and Winifred Jenkins, the combination of sense and passionate insensibility in the Shandy brothers, or the virtue of Amelia and Atkinson to see how novelists cultivated a delicacy of discrimination through pairings. In each case, similar "ruling passions" produce dissimilar results as they percolate through the constant "manners" of each character. This context helps explain Fielding's interpolation of the Old Man of the Hill into *Tom Jones*, where similar forces have worked in the lives of the Old Man and Tom both, but where they manifest themselves in opposite attitudes. Fielding enlarges the scope of his narrative, but also deepens his characterization of Tom through greater definition. Similarly, analogy within a group defines Clarissa's siblings or Lovelace's party of rakes. We shall see it at work in each of our five novels.

The preliminary evidence I have offered about my use of "system," "analogy," and "modification" should make the terms clear and justify paying them special attention, at least for the moment. The ultimate reasons for using them, of course, must emerge from the analyses. I propose, therefore, not to spend more time here discussing road signs. Let us set out; and if the course is not even, I hope that we will not careen too much, for I have tried to keep in mind (as much as a modern critic can) Pope's wise reprimand:

In vain the Sage, with retrospective eye,
Would from th'apparent What conclude the Why,
Infer the Motive from the Deed, and show,
That what we chanc'd was what we meant to do.

(*Epistle to Cobham*, lines 51-54)

A NOTE ON TEXTS

Most, if not all, the works I discuss may well appear in standard editions soon, though none has yet. Therefore, the only references I have given are parenthetical chapter numbers for *Rasselas*, letter dates and authors for *Humphry Clinker*, and volume and chapter numbers for the rest. Some experiments have convinced me that this method will not cause much inconvenience and will result in a more agreeable reading text, uncluttered with page references now useless to the reader who does not have at hand a given nonstandard edition, and soon useless to everyone when the standard editions supersede what we have at present. For quotations, I have tried to find modern texts with the greatest authority. Since there is none for *Amelia*, I have used Fielding's revised text in vol. 4 of his *Works*, 4 vols., (London, 1762), with accidentals (but not chapter numbering) from the first edition. All other texts used derive from first editions, corrected only for errors in accidentals (*Tristram Shandy*, *Humphry Clinker*) or for substantive authorial variants as well. They are as follows: *Rasselas*, ed. Geoffrey Tillotson and Brian Jenkins (London: Oxford University Press, 1971); *Tristram Shandy*, ed. James Aiken Work (New York: Odyssey Press, 1940); *Humphry Clinker*, ed. Lewis M. Knapp (London: Oxford University Press, 1966); *Caleb Williams*, ed. David McCracken (London: Oxford University Press, 1970).

All translations, unless otherwise specified, are mine. I have transcribed in Roman type those passages entirely italicized in the original text.

Abbreviations for scholarly journals are those listed in the front matter of the annual *PMLA International Bibliography,* vol. I.

Rasselas

What book looks simpler than *Rasselas*, with its unforced, unpolemic, but irresistible gravity? Only on second thought does one realize that such simplicity is likely to be an illusion in a book with two contradictory purposes, to promote and to confute human wisdom, and with a successful argument for what so few people really believe, the vanity of human wishes. The texture of *Rasselas* in fact is richer than it seems, and its look of simplicity is kept up by Dr. Johnson's having an almost absolute control: how else does one achieve simplicity? Perhaps we might most conveniently start to examine Johnson's control and his book's richness by choosing one unit of the book, most sensibly the first, the chapters about the Happy Valley. We will find it shaped by the two procedures singled out in the Introduction, modification and analogy. As I have said, neither of these procedures is merely an operation, like transposition in music or braising in cookery; both derive from certain habits of mind and give the work a distinctive intellectual shape as well as a measure of formal coherence.

It is easy to see some of the reasons why Johnson might want to use modification, apart from his being by temperament a great scrubber of cant from others' minds. The vanitas vanitatum of *Rasselas* was, after all, so conventional that it might be lightly accepted or crustily scorned—both dangerous extremes—unless it was plainly the result of thought and experience. A certain measure of skepticism had to precede belief. Johnson therefore cultivates in us, through modification, a zest for probing and debunking, although without malice. We discover, for example, that the prince's original discontent draws him "to feel some complacence in his own perspicacity, and to receive some solace of the miseries of life, from consciousness of the delicacy with which he felt, and the eloquence with which he bewailed them" (2). The old sage, uneasy at the backfiring of his counsel, will not be uneasy long, for "in the decline of life shame and grief are of short duration"(4). The mind is happily weak, collapsing under attack into specious comfort. By the same token, every improvement in consciousness also improves one's sense of his own misery. Yet in no case is the character left in unmitigated evil, so that we, spared the melodrama of feelings, can continue in our critical spirit with pleasure.

Modification, then, gives Johnson a way of at once affirming and denying certain kinds of progress and of making that paradox enticing to us. Clearly enough, these forward and retrograde motions coincide with Johnson's two Solomonic purposes of promoting and confuting human wisdom. I say Solomonic because Solomon's three books of the Bible, the Song of Songs, Proverbs, and Ecclesiastes, are oddly complementary. Taken together, they offer a balance, like Johnson's, between earthly pleasures and wisdom, and the vanity of those pleasures and wisdom. It is not for nothing that Rasselas himself is a descendent of their royal author, as Father Lobo, in Johnson's translation, announced: "The Kings of *Æthiopia* draw their boasted pedigree from *Minilech* the Son of this Queen [of Sheba] and *Solomon*."[1]

1. *A Voyage to Abyssinia*, tr. Samuel Johnson (London, 1735), p. 45. The most authoritative statement is that of Thomas R. Preston, "The Biblical

Johnson, as expected, refuses to infer from this "boasted pedigree" its least ambivalent title: Rasselas never grows very wise. Nevertheless, Solomon's secular, stained Eden of Ecclesiastes 2:4-11 does provide a putative model for the Happy Valley of Abyssinia. This, like the heritage of Rasselas, is a received idea for Johnson. Kolb has pointed out that the royal retreat in Abyssinia had been compared to the terrestrial paradise; and even writers like Lobo and Job Ludolphus, who impugn the princes' retreat, connect the country with a paradise: "In Abyssinia they enjoy a perpetual Spring," the Nile has Edenic connections, the Ethiopians "extol their own Country for Paradise: For you must understand, that many of the Fathers of the Church were of the same opinion."[2] Johnson's modification does not deny the received idea but calls it as witness for the prosecution, partly because Rasselas is unhappy in his ersatz Paradise, and partly because Johnson can keep to biblical expectations and geography in having the prince and his party flee to Egypt, the type of the land of bondage. At first his irony is subversively simple: the fallen world yields a freedom and a promise that the makeshift Eden excludes. That simple reversal then is modified. Man in his present state enjoys so little freedom or promise that Eden and Egypt are in essence the same.

Johnson's authority for this virtual equation is good. Although some historians and more poets had kept alive a Happy Valley as lush as the one in Rasselas, more reputable sources did not. Lobo writes of it as miserable and barren, and Job Ludolphus agrees: "The reports concerning the Pleasant-

Context of Johnson's Rasselas," PMLA 84 (1969): 274-81, which discusses biblical commentaries on Ecclesiastes. He is inclined to trace the double message of Rasselas to Ecclesiastes alone; my broader use of the Solomonic books requires a somewhat less specific exegetical tradition to make clear its lines of force.

2. Gwin J. Kolb, "The Structure of Rasselas," PMLA 66 (1951): 698-717. Lobo, Voyage to Abyssinia, p. 48. Job Ludolphus, A New History of Ethiopia, tr. J. P. (London, 1682), pp. 34-35.

ness of those Rocks, and the splendid attendance upon those
Royal Exiles, are all ridiculous Falsities." "Formerly," he says,
"those miserable *Ethiopic* Princes were here cag'd up in wild
places" and "themselves were harshly us'd."[3] Johnson keeps,
but modifies, both the amiable and the grim versions of the
Valley, by accepting its physical delights but translating its
confinement and sterility into psychological terms. Two kinds
of history jostle into a synthesis which is both and neither.
The more we know of outside accounts of the Valley, the more
we understand Rasselas's restlessness, for in the paradoxes
that come from the clash of received ideas—the paradise that is
also an Egypt, the retreat that is both splendid and empty—lie
the allusory symbols of the prince's inner discontent. Once
more, I must insist on the essentially fluid, even equivocal
results of Johnson's reworking received ideas. In some ways,
life in the Valley is patently better than "cages" and "wild
places" would be; in some ways, given Rasselas's experience,
it is patently equivalent; perhaps in some ways, if one is a
stricter Christian moralist than Johnson's role permits him to
be in this book, it is even worse. Through modification
Johnson achieves precise equilibrium: each element of what he
is saying here is a complex realization built from the reinterpreted forms of public knowledge.

Johnson treats moral lectures and aphorisms, which are in a
sense the personal form of received ideas, with the same kind
of modification. Rasselas, for instance, declares that the flyer (6) ought to impart his soon-to-be-tested skill in aero-
dynamics to all men. Since each person has a debt of gratitude
to his fellows, "all skill ought to be exerted for universal
good." The flyer replies at length that he dare not do as the
prince says, for fear of encouraging aerial invasions from the
wicked. We are led to three simultaneous conclusions from

3. Ludolphus, p. 197. See Gwin J. Kolb, "The 'Paradise' in Abyssinia and
the 'Happy Valley' in *Rasselas*," *MP* 56 (1958): 10-16.

this moral exchange. First, that the flyer is right in his quiet rebuke of the prince's abstraction. What Rasselas says may be "true," but it is too unempirical to be germane to much of anything. His aphorism is not refuted but qualified as of limited utility, since the skill of moral reason, in the service of "universal good," denies mankind the skill of flying. Second, modification operates in that the good of flying has its evils, the evil of being earthbound its benefits. We can and should accept both these points without losing sight of a third, that the flyer's earnest expostulations are silly, since they are a lengthy and judicious preface to a short shocking drop into the lake.[4] The fall does to the flyer's moral comments what his comments do to Rasselas's: contexts of validity are set. Our own reaction to this scene itself has two external frames. One, the obvious comic version of the adventure of Icarus, strikes at our faith in human pretensions. The other, our just having seen a prince learn from a clumsy maid (4), encourages us by analogy to think that two chapters later one may also learn from a fallible engineer. Wisdom is thus affirmed and debunked, and we find ourselves not with a credo but with an equilibrium among logical incompatibles.

We readers, who have seen moral lectures and received ideas modified, can hardly help being gun-shy about the lessons pronounced by Imlac. When the flyer's carefully imitated bird's wings become water-wings instead, we learn enough to wince at Imlac's later "the master of mechanicks laughs at [physical] strength," or his praise of borrowing "many arts from the instinct of animals"(13). Fittingly, Johnson has the success of the tunnelling depend not on mechanics, not on

---

4. On the flyer, see Gwin J. Kolb, "Johnson's 'Dissertation on Flying'," in *New Light on Dr. Johnson: Essays on the Occasion of His 250th Birthday*, ed. Frederick W. Hilles (New Haven: Yale University Press, 1959), pp. 91-106; and Louis A. Landa, "Johnson's Feathered Man: 'A Dissertation on the Art of Flying' Considered," *Eighteenth-Century Studies in Honor of Donald F. Hyde*, ed. W. H. Bond (New York: The Grolier Club, 1970), pp. 161-78.

animal instinct, but on pure chance, a fissure that happens to
be in the rock. No doubt, as Imlac tells Rasselas, "great works"
may be "performed, not by strength, but perseverence," but
the fissure makes this great work easy, and Imlac's maxim
irrelevant. A bit earlier, Imlac's lofty but absolutely conventional ideals for the poet have been qualified, in our eyes and in
the prince's, by their impracticability and by the egoism that
leads him to "aggrandize his own profession"(11). His sensible
skepticism about pilgrimages is balanced by what we
Europeans know to be exaggerated reverence, based only on
hearsay, for European power and knowledge. If he appears to
redeem himself with an a fortiori argument for the much to be
endured and the little to be enjoyed everywhere in human life,
we may recall his having learned that truth too late to keep him
from the prison of the Valley.[5]

These doubts about Imlac mean simply that he is a fallible
guide, often misleading or of limited use. He rises easily
enough above the competition, such as the brisk imperious
Rasselas, who much of the time spouts cant. It is Rasselas who
envies the Europeans the physical "facility with which separated friends interchange their thoughts" (11), a convenience
he himself can never have needed in the Happy Valley except
to feed his romantic fancies; we soon learn (14) that he has
never "interchanged thoughts" with his favorite sister and
daily companion, Nekayah. It is Rasselas who scoffs at "specious" European refinements (12), which he respected while

5. Among those who have doubted the universal wisdom of Imlac are
Alvin Whitley, "The Comedy of *Rasselas*," *ELH* 23 (1956): 48-70; Clarence F.
Tracy, "'Democritus, Arise!' A Study of Dr. Johnson's Humor," *Yale Review*
39 (1949): 294-310; and in scholarly detail, Howard D. Weinbrot, "The
Reader, the General, and the Particular," *ECS* 5 (1971): 80-96, especially
pages 80-86. W. K. Wimsatt remarks that Imlac replies with maxims to
Rasselas in Chapter 13 "almost like a wound-up automaton, a speaking toy-
philosopher"—"In Praise of *Rasselas*: Four Notes (Converging)," in *Imagined
Worlds: Essays . . . in Honour of John Butt*, ed. Maynard Mack and Ian Gregor
(London: Methuen, 1968), p. 127.

he thought that they guaranteed happiness. In moving thus from one extreme to the other, he not only misses Imlac's point but also dangerously undervalues such "refinements" as freedom from disease, ease of communication, and security of possession; for as he is to find out from a quick succession of personal experiences (18-20), disease can drive a Stoic from his philosophy, lack of communication leaves peasants brutish, and an insecure station keps a prosperous man in constant fear. Rasselas's vaporous idealism and his jumping to conclusions make us take a comparative measure of Imlac and realize that he has enough dignity for Boswell to have been able to call Johnson himself "our illustrious Imlac."[6] Imlac's failures modify this dominant image but do not nullify it or leave it hollow.

Modification, finally, applies not only to states, ideas, actions, and the evaluation of characters, but also to pervasive imagery. I do not mean the author's metaphors, where order is not inquiry, but the sense impressions on which empiricism puts special weight. That category includes reflexive impressions, the mind looking at itself and interpreting what it feels, sometimes through metaphors born from external experience. Thus, when Rasselas tells himself that his "hopes and wishes have flown beyond" the mountain, and Johnson adds in the next chapter (5) that he was "impatient as an eagle in a grate," the metaphors take on meaning only as part of a perceptual sequence, in this case the consistent comparisons between man and the animals (2-5) leading to the flyer's essay at being a bird in Chapter 6. The style, that is, remains as self-effacing as ever, steadily maintaining its grave richness throughout so as to launch events effectively without calling attention to itself. Visual information, like the imagery we have just been discussing, does have independent strength, and is tied directly to the action portrayed in the narrative. One can easily see why

6. To Mrs. Thrale, July 9, 1782; *Letters of James Boswell*, ed. Chauncey Brewster Tinker, 2 vols. (Oxford: Clarendon Press, 1924), 2: 313.

it might or must be subject to modification, like other elements in the depicted world.

For example, Johnson uses water in terms of its manifestations in the prince's experience. The flyer himself makes his fate clear through the "engines" he has previously contrived, a water pump, artificial showers, and fans and musical instruments played by water power. With air and water so mixed in his past triumphs, no wonder he confuses the elements, conceives flying and swimming as versions of each other, and finds, ironically, that the wings designed for the subtler fluid suit only the grosser. The water which saves his life and kills his hopes (6) becomes the flood of Chapter 7, which seems to cut off Rasselas's escape and does cut him off from the beasts who take to the hills. It thus carries out its previous two functions of separating man from freedom and from the animals (whom the flyer would have imitated). In doing so, however, it brings Rasselas to Imlac. Eventually, it even brings him to freedom (13 by leading him to imitate the coneys driven by the rain from their burrows; appropriately enough, the first thing the prince sees when he breaks through to the top of the mountain (14) is "the Nile, yet a narrow current, wandering beneath them." Yet this symbol of liberty has its dark side: Imlac's dash to an illusory freedom (8) had also begun when he cast his eye "on the expanse of waters," and the image he chooses for the pains of the world (12) is that of the tempestuous and boiling sea. There is an obvious logic in Johnson's development of this emblem, for such it becomes as it gains incremental force; but just as obviously, it is as multivalent as is the flyer's sententiousness. Through it, we get variations on the theme of liberty or power, all of which are important elements in this section of the book, and all of which must be held in equilibrium.

My discussion of our reaction to Imlac and imagery assumes, of course, a certain control of our responses by the second of our two procedures, analogy. We find Rasselas's history, for instance, echoed in Imlac's, down to their school-masters who deserve no reverence, their fathers' subterranean treasure vaults, their pained consciousness of passing time and aging, and their youthful longing for escape from the material pleasures that a rich father provides, escape over the water into the world of men and observation. Any reader of fiction, of Fielding for example, would see the parallel rapidly enough. An interpolated story told by an older man who bore analogies to the hero was common. What is interesting about this analogy of Johnson's is its use in developing a complex, modified situation. Mr. Wilson's or the Old Man of the Hill's story is admonitory: it preserves Joseph Andrews or Tom Jones—actually or under a rubric of surrogacy—from certain experiences, certain choices of life. Imlac's story is premoni-tory: it preserves Rasselas from nothing, but foretells the essence of his travels, as the first paragraph of the book, with its whispers of fancy and phantoms of hope, leads us to guess. Whereas, like Fielding, Johnson uses analogy for its inferential value, he takes the results of inference to a near paradox. Nature is so uniform that all actions essentially copy familiar patterns of history. In gross, vicarious experience is accurate; it is also unbelieved, properly so, in detail. Rasselas's refusal to infer his own failure from Imlac's is wrong as to outcome but right as to skeptical procedure. His rights and wrongs are further modified if one notes that he acts not out of the sort of intellectual suspicion that Johnson's modifications have been making us nurse, but out of his own desires. Tempted but untutored by an elder self whom he refuses to accept as such, Rasselas asserts his autonomy as the result of psychological compulsion and makes the choice that he would have made anyhow had he been able to act rationally.

A dialectic movement in the book exploits analogy to ratify Rasselas's choice. Since Eden and Egypt are in essence the same, the Happy Valley and Imlac's described world should also in essence be the same. That is why Imlac's poems, instruction, and history repeat, in a new and pointed way, the entertainments of the Valley. His work and the entertainments alike convert human time, lived time, into other forms which have special relevance to the conditions of life in the Valley. The Valley makes institutional this conversion of time. Its relics of the past—the iron gates, the cemented palace, the policy of sequestering the royal family—are too old to have a place in time, and they provide no knowledge to inform or guide the line of uninitiated princes who are to deal someday with the evils outside. In a spurious version of paradisal time-lessness, time in the Valley loses its progressive nature, its bond with aspiration, hope, and fear, and thus with empirical knowledge. Time for the royal children is only cyclic, marked by the emperor's annual visits and "the soft vicissitudes of pleasure and repose" (2), in which the products of art and ima-gination are served them. The flux of entertainments to which the princes' tranquillity is subject represents within the Valley a tawdry analogue to the flux of events, the time and chance, of the excluded world. Imlac, who is poet, historian, and sage, combines in himself the variety of performers gathered for the princes' benefit. For him, however, time and thought are per-sonal, not institutional: time is progressive for him, knowl-edge empirical. It is in following the direction marked by the movement from one analogue to the other, from the prear-ranged *partis pris* and artifices of the Happy Valley to Imlac's greater empiricism, that Rasselas must search the world for himself.

Perhaps a more exact statement would be that Rasselas moves through a succession of analogues, a dialectic of his own consciousness, from his rejection of the dogma and pas-sivity of the Happy Valley to his rejection of the vicarious suffi-ciency of Imlac's experience. In broad terms, we may say that chapters 2 and 5 deal with observation, 3 and 6 with practical reason, 4 and 7 with imagination. We have, that is, a rhythm of discovery in 2-3-4 repeated by analogy in 5-6-7, with qualitative change. In Chapter 2, we find Rasselas watching animals to discover how he differs from them; in Chapter 5, exploring the valley to discover a natural way of escape, and incidentally amusing himself with "the various instincts of animals and properties of plants." His observations are directed, not passive—especially in Chapter 5—and lead to thought. The qualitative progression from 2 to 5 marks his growing distance from his siblings, just as his sharpening of the difference between himself and the nonreflective, atemporal animals marks his distance from the sensual ethos of the Happy Valley, with its factitious unity of the natural world. Since empirical observation leads to thought, Johnson logically follows each of these two chapters with one devoted to applied speculation. Chapter 3 concentrates on the dogma of the sage, who proves by sorites that Rasselas cannot feel unhappy; the aviator in Chapter 6 similarly proves that men can fly. Here Johnson uses two common butts of satire, the rationalist and the projector, to localize the failures of a partial empiricism. Once more, a qualitative progression from mere statement (3) to the actual testing of hypotheses (6) marks Rasselas's growing distance from the formulaic life of the Happy Valley. Each of the speculative failures drives the prince to refuge in "visionary bustle" (4), first trying to make for himself "that world which he had never seen," and then, through Imlac's guidance and verses, projecting the self with augmented means. The qualitative progression from 4 to 7 completes the two analogous rhythms of discovery, which supply Johnson his yardstick of development.

The next five chapters have a different rhythm because they have a different purpose, that of tying Imlac's adventures to the themes already broached. Chapters 8 and 9 therefore offer Imlac's story, making clear the analogies between him and the prince; 10 and 11 cap Imlac's voyage by adding to the empirical observation of 8 and 9 the other two themes of imagination (10) and practical reason (11) carried over from the first seven chapters. Here are universals for earlier particulars: not only may ideal poetry (10) and (as Imlac describes it) European skill (11) stand for the highest reaches of imagination and practical reason, but ideal pilgrimage (11) repeats another theme, directed movement in space and time. The frail world of *Rasselas* will not of course permit any of these three ambitious reshapings of nature—corresponding to the traditional divisions of humane letters, practical science, and metaphysics—to be more than an aspiration, perhaps a chimera. They enjoy a certain unity in tradition, in that the poet (typically liable, like Imlac, to "the enthusiastic fit") stands in between *scientia* and *sapientia* (the respective goals of science and pilgrimage). In *Rasselas*, however, their deepest unity is to point to Imlac's universal, "Human life is every where a state in which much is to be endured, and little to be enjoyed." Here in Chapter 12 we have not only the conclusion and potential transfiguration of Imlac's voyage of 8 and 9, but also a personal response to the universals of 10 and 11. If Rasselas's chapters, 2-7, embody a rhythm and a dialectic leading to openness and hope, Imlac's modify them with a movement, also through thematic repetition, that is more philosophical and final.

No final resolution, no matter how philosophical, suffices in this book. In chapters 13 and 14, Johnson reinterprets poetry, science, and pilgrimage: poetry spurs the prince to leave the Valley in fact, science ("diligence and skill") gets him and his party out, and pilgrimage, or directed movement in time and space, becomes the matter for the rest of the story. Now the practical failure of the flyer in the next-to-last of the first group of chapters (6) is balanced by the practical success of the escape in the next-to-last of this group (13), although, with a Johnsonian touch, success comes from imitating not an eagle but a coney.[7] A narrowing of space earlier brought Rasselas to

7. On the coney, see Proverbs 30:24, 26.

Imlac, to vast spaces and broad experience through discourse; now, entering a crevice brings Rasselas to real prospects and real experience. Or so he thinks. When another kindred spirit, Nekayah, joins him, life in the Valley ends, as theatre buffs say, on the upbeat, once again to be modified.

Our sense of an upbeat that we know will be questioned, in fact our whole climate of expectations for *Rasselas*, has to do with system, analogy, and modification. As yet, Rasselas has no conscious system of inquiry, but his natural process of inquiry sets the order of events in these chapters. Analogy has little inferential, "Butlerian" weight because nature is too uniform to require inferences. In the system of order, however, "Hartleyan" analogy marshals rhythms, gives Imlac his place (as poet, as moralist, as older Rasselas), and helps develop the emblem of water. The system of inquiry involves modification, to deal with Rasselas's initial probings of his discontent, and also with the ways in which our preconceptions impinge on our reading of the book. We have some notion of what to expect from sages in oriental tales, Abyssinians and their paradise, moral lectures, interpolated stories, and emblematic consistency. Johnson tunes our minds by modifying those prior notions, each into a discordia concors. Rasselas's discontent itself modifies the posture of bliss in the Valley, and the psychological value of truth (when told second hand), so as to keep enlarging the empirical scope of the book. Working alone or together, analogy and modification are the most central, though not the sole, means by which the systems of order and inquiry define the stuff of the novel. Understanding them leads one to understand the details of inclusion and sequence, so that partial answers can be given to such questions as why a flood occurs in Chapter 7 or why Imlac is a poet. With a knowledge of them and of Rasselas's planned system of inquiry, we can pass with more speed through a sort of blueprint for the novel to consider the resolution of the matters that these early chapters broach.

II: THE BLUEPRINT OF *RASSELAS*

The portion of the book before the party sets off for Egypt, chapters 1-14, holds together as a unit but also breaks in half, so that chapters 1-7 have their own rhythm and 8-14 theirs. Can one extend these seven-chapter groups further? Perhaps so: the book has forty-nine chapters, and *Rasselas* breaks down quite naturally into seven groups.[8] Two of these groups are lengthened by set pieces, chapters 22 and 44, "The Happiness of a Life Led According to Nature" and "The Dangerous Prevalence of Imagination"; these complementary discourses cap the first three and the second three groups so as to leave the last group only five chapters long.

We have seen that the first seven chapters bring us through Rasselas's longings for freedom and up to his confinement by flood with Imlac, and that the second seven present Imlac's story and the little troupe's escape. The third seven take us through a trial of modes of personal life in city and country, ending with an eighth chapter about man within nature. The fourth group of seven is devoted to a long discussion between the prince and his sister about the modes of governmental and familial life. By way of change, the fifth and sixth groups, each

---

8. It is tempting to suppose that Johnson made himself a schedule, the first and last resort of the indolent, so that he could write the book in a week, as Boswell says he did. *Life of Johnson*, ed. George Birkbeck Hill, rev. L. F. Powell, 6 vols. (Oxford: Clarendon Press, 1934-50), 1: 341; and cf. Mrs. Piozzi's "week or ten days' time," in *Johnsonian Miscellanies*, ed. George Birkbeck Hill, 2 vols. (Oxford: Clarendon Press, 1897), 1: 285. Even if Johnson did take many notes for his descriptions of Ethiopia and Egypt—and I am unconvinced that he did—he might well have had them at hand, as Arthur J. Weitzman points out: "Brought out of his usual lethargy by the demands of paying for his mother's funeral, Johnson may have turned to these notes and written *Rasselas* in the evenings of a week as Boswell asserts." "More Light on *Rasselas*: The Background of the Egyptian Episodes," *PQ* 48 (1969): 58. The case for the notes is made by Weitzman, pp. 42-58, and by Donald M. Lockhart, "'The Fourth Son of the Mighty Emperor': The Ethiopian Background of Johnson's *Rasselas*," *PMLA* 78 (1963): 516–28.

self-contained, are split, the fifth between the travellers' view of the pyramid and Pekuah's abduction, the sixth between Pekuah's tale and the case of the astronomer. (In other words, Johnson gave Pekuah seven chapters, and seven to the egocentric delusions of the Pharaoh and astronomer, which surround her adventures.) Group VI, like Group III, has an eighth terminal chapter about the dangers of what one might call the celibacy of the mind. This chapter serves not only as a summary but also as a bridge to Group VII and the inconclusive conclusion to *Rasselas*. In tabular form, we get

Group	Chapters	Group	Chapters
I	1-7	V	30-36
II	8-14	VI	37-44
III	15-22	VII	45-49[9]
IV	23-29		

The two main purposes of these groups have been touched on in the discussion of the Happy Valley. The first is to give the text a sense of dialectic in terms of the prince's growth. This is difficult, since he has no psyche, and since the book is necessarily too brief for Johnson, whatever his desires, to show us with subtlety and consistency a growth in wisdom. One

---

9. Anyone who divides *Rasselas* into groups nowadays is joining in a numbers game: other critics have suggested two, three, four, and six. I would be more hesitant about my seven if my scheme did not work out in precise detail, using divisions that also come up in others' schemes. All partitioners agree that the book has a rhythmic pulse. See Frederick W. Hilles, "*Rasselas*, An 'Uninstructive Tale'," pp. 111-21 in *Johnson, Boswell, and Their Circle: Essays Presented to Lawrence Fitzroy Powell . . .* (Oxford: Clarendon Press, 1965); Emrys Jones, "The Artistic Form of *Rasselas*," *RES* n.s. 18 (1967): 387-401; D. J. Greene, *Samuel Johnson* (New York: Twayne Publishers, 1970), pp. 133-39; Mary Lascelles, "*Rasselas*: A Rejoinder," *RES* n.s. 21 (1970): 49-56; and Wimsatt, "In Praise." Johnson can make use of such a pulse because the book is short enough to be read naturally at one sitting, as Boswell did and Johnson hoped he would. *Boswell in Extremes, 1776-1778*, ed. Charles McC. Weis and Frederick A. Pottle (New York: McGraw-Hill, 1970), pp. 139, 152.

means of making believers of us is to imply artistically that the
events speak for themselves, that to grow, Rasselas need only
look at what he is shown. To this end, the groups and their
inner shaping are of utmost importance. We participate in the
forms of thesis, development, and then resolution that itself
becomes a thesis to be developed and resolved. No doubt a
"realistic" Rasselas would not participate in these forms. He
would move steadily through situations of whose complexity
he would be able to perceive progressively more. But the only
Rasselas we have is not realistic; his life is limited to this book;
and therefore the logic of events seems to be his logic too. We
are quite ready to accept an artistic structure as at least a correlative to his learning, and to assume about him on the
grounds of form what we could never bring ourselves to
assume on the grounds of narrative or of empathy. At the
same time, by presenting facts independently of the prince,
Johnson makes sure that his own solemn argument cannot be
compromised by subjectivity.

The second purpose of the groups is that of giving *Rasselas* a
rhythm, a pulse, a sense of cumulative elements. In managing
this, Johnson had to make sure we would feel the waves of evidence one after the other cresting over us, without our becoming bored or impatient. Thus he uses groups of about the same
length, but varies their inner structure so that we should feel
both insistent order and empirical diversity. In Group III
(chaps. 15-22), for example, Johnson divides Egyptian modes
of life into the rural and the urban, but gives the group its distinctive beat by moving through these modes of life one by
one, making them as swift and simple as they must seem to the
travellers. In Group IV (chaps. 23-29), he again offers a division of attention, now between high and low life, but the beat
of the group is set by having the two halves of the division
occur at the same time, in Rasselas's and Nekayah's two
viewpoints and subjects during five chapters of conversation.
The characters' wrangling interdependence, echoing that of

the people they have observed, differs in pulse from the swift simplicity of Group III and the four blocks of narrative—the pyramids, Pekuah's abduction, her tale, the astronomer—that compose V and VI. These different structures are compounded by a difference of narrative modes, sometimes first-person, sometimes third-person, sometimes philosophical discourse.

None the less, so that our sense of cumulative evidence cannot flag, Johnson repeats a pattern: experience to discourse to resolution in experience. Rasselas's frustrations (Group I) lead to Imlac's discourse (most of Group II), and then to a resolution, escape, that promises a personal test of Imlac's discourse. The test, in systematic form, begins in Group III; it turns into discourse in Group IV, where Rasselas and Nekayah look at greatness and family life; that then becomes the subject of the experience of Group V, about the Pharaoh's monument to his own greatness (the pyramid) and the loss of Nekayah from the "family" of the travellers. Finally, the mixture of experience and discourse in Group VI, on the mind without prey in the harem and with itself for prey in the astronomer, leads to Imlac's great speech on the imagination, the unifying theme for the sequence of events that end and resolve the book as far as modification allows. The "choice of life" turns out to be delusive, the quest is inverted, and the travellers earn that oscillation between hopes and fears for now and hereafter which is the closest human beings are likely to come to real resolution and repose.

Johnson does not abandon his more detailed procedures with the Happy Valley. In Group III, modes of life—Epicureans, Stoics, shepherds, squire, hermit, natural philosopher—are tightly arranged, to move from man alone (the first two) to man within nature, and from the more physical to the more mental within each of the subgroups. This order also sets up antitheses, quite naturally so, since each failure urges a new beginning elsewhere; but antitheses in which the second term needs correction by the first as well as vice versa. The Sto-

ic (18), for instance, seems to promise what the Epicureans lack
(17), but alternatively, if only the Stoic lived more for the
present, like the Epicureans, his bereavement over his daughter would hurt less. If the shepherds were, like the Stoic, philosophers; if the squire were lowly like the shepherds; if the
hermit lived, like the squire, among friends—if each had
something the man before him had, he would not suffer as he
does. By modification, each time a style of life is corrected, a
shield it lent is surrendered. This discovery is not pursued
logically—what kind of life would a lowly squire have?—but
the logic of emotion, here as elsewhere in *Rasselas*, is more
important than the logic of reason. Johnson, by selecting all his
examples from classical formulas for happiness, sows received
ideas like dragon's teeth, effective for mutual destruction.
Their very mutuality gives us the sense of a closed, exhaustive
set in our empirical progress.

The illusion that Group III is a closed set also gains from its
having a defined beginning and end. The royal travellers enter
Egypt like the naive foreign observers made familiar by
Montesquieu, ingenuous and distracted by novelty. This
typical gambit (15-16) is balanced by a typical end, a comprehensive summary. The unmitigated blaze of cant from the
natural philosopher (22) recapitulates the group, its thought-
lessness and blind rationality, passivity and choice, self-
sufficiency within nature and absolute dependence. What
comes in between beginning and end seems still more complete from Johnson's retrospective analogies. Every one of the
episodes in this new Egyptian setting—voluptuaries, sage,
men in rural retreat, and the rest—looks back to the Happy
Valley, as one might reasonably expect if Eden is Egypt. The
effect of repeating experience under new circumstances is to
make us feel that we have arrived at universals of behavior
such as Rasselas has sought. Through using the order fixed by
a system of inquiry, and analogy and modification to complete
a set, Johnson transfers the statements of the Happy Valley

into the real world of space and (in the light of the classical formulas) cultural history, such as was only broached in Imlac's tale.

Groups IV–VI build on the base of III by adding a new technique, that of incremental repetition. Repeated elements, that is, not only confirm an inferential value of an analogy but also enlarge the inference; the method is a variant of the "discriminated variety" mentioned in the Introduction. For example, the Bassa's fall (24) repeats the message of Imlac's father (8) and of the squire (20), that greatness bears within it the conditions of its instability. Yet in the repetition, Johnson makes us aware of a new kind of vulnerability, for the Bassa must depend on his inferiors, the servants and janissaries, within his extended family. The man whom the squire has feared suffers, not inflicts, a downfall, and from below, not (as in the squire's fears) from above. This incremental analogy stresses a sense of mutual menace that Nekayah properly applies to the tanglings of familial relations. Meanwhile, Johnson uses the *de casibus* analogies among merchant, squire, Bassa, and Sultan (24) to build a strong line of inference, which he qualifies by further analogy, based on the motif of transience. The Squire and the Bassa suffer from external temporal forces, on which one might blame their plight if public transiency were not matched by internal atemporality, as with the prattling girls (25), in whose minds "every thing floated . . . unconnected with the past or future"; and the two kinds of transiency merge at the end of the chapter with the social hypocrites, who support themselves forever "by temporary expedients, [while] every day is lost in contriving for the morrow." The procedures of the group, then, involve a forward movement through the inferences of the narrative and the speakers, and a modifying reductive movement in which all states of life are levelled.

An emotional increment develops in the analogies, too, as Rasselas and Nekayah become more active observers, committed in argument.[10] The Stoic in Group III loses a daughter and is left "a lonely being disunited from society" (18). He appears above all a stranger who unwittingly proposes and fails a test.[11] When Nekayah loses her friend Pekuah, solitude and grief afflict a member of the party, and pain, not theory, generates Johnson's subject. Similarly, Pekuah sees in the seraglio the pettiness, superficiality, and idleness that Nekayah found among the girls in Cairo; but she does not see them in the manner of Nekayah, as a passing inspector with a report to make. Pekuah speaks as a captive suffering the trivialities of the seraglio with no prospect of escape or friend with whom to share her feelings. Imagery of transitory floating and inoffensive animals, shared by the princess (25) and her favorite (39), marks the analogy and thereby the difference in the degree to which the events have repercussions within personal time. The Bassa's inefficiency in catching Pekuah's kidnappers (34) likewise recalls earlier, less acutely felt instances of political mismanagement, so that official as well as social and individual events are transposed from abstraction into personal experience. They do not become darker, since we are not really involved with the characters, but they do become more trenchant because their new emotional implications make them more nearly complete as replicas of real life. As a result, the terms of the frustrated, frustrating search for "the choice of life" grow more and more strained, so that its inversion and alternative, "the choice of eternity," has a logic of pent desire behind it. An examination in detail of groups V and VI will make clearer what I mean.

10. As Hilles says, p. 113, "the observers become participants."

11. Johnson's treatment of the Stoic is very well analyzed by Sheldon Sacks, *Fiction and the Shape of Belief* (Berkeley and Los Angeles: University of California Press, 1964), pp. 57-59, in the context of a perceptive discussion of *Rasselas*, pp. 49-60. Our sense that the Stoic is a man who fails a test is increased because the test was conventional, as Kolb points out in "The Use of Stoical Doctrines in *Rasselas*, Chapter XVIII," *MLN* 68 (1953): 439-47. Johnson might well have renewed his knowledge of Epictetus, in whose *Enchiridion* death poses a test to Stoical principles, through the translation which his friend Mrs. Carter had seen through the press ten months before.

III: THE JOURNEY TO THEODICY

The pyramid, that "monument of the insufficiency of human enjoyments," as Imlac calls it, dominates these two groups. First it is a topic of discussion, a source of moral lessons; then it sprouts analogies. Imlac's lecture on its architect, the bored materialistic Pharaoh (32), takes place at the very moment that the Pharaoh's modern counterpart, the sheik, is carrying off Pekuah (33). Then Nekayah imitates in her mind the memorial pomp which the pyramid symbolizes and enshrines (35, 36). Group VI begins with the return of Pekuah, whose fear of the pyramid's ghosts had led her to be seized by a real pharaoh's-ghost of sorts, and as we now learn, to be locked in his fortress, as she had feared being shut in the "dreadful vaults" of the pyramid. Furthermore, from the sheik she has learned to make "celestial observations," which, although Imlac for obvious argumentative reasons does not mention it, also has to do with the pyramids. At least from the time of Proclus, scholars had claimed that the pyramids in various ways reflected the Egyptians' knowledge of astronomy, and in Johnson's development of groups V and VI that common connotation is useful.[12] Pekuah can now deal with the mad astronomer as an extension of her dealings with the sheik: the one man, in his mental loneliness and his illusions of heavenly control, follows logically from the other, in his more mundane loneliness and his illusions of earthly control.

Analogy binds together groups V and VI, giving the pyramid a place of special importance. There is also room to con-

---

12. See Giovanni Piero Valeriano, *Hieroglyphica, sive De sacris Aegyptiorum aliarumque gentium literis commentariorum libri* . . . (Frankfurt, 1614), p. 754; Noël-Antoine Pluche, *Histoire du ciel* (1739), 2 vols. (Paris, 1778), 1: 34; Jean-Sylvestre Bailly, *Histoire de l'astronomie ancienne depuis son origine jusqu'à l'établissement de l'école d'Alexandrie* (Paris, 1775), pp. 176-80: "Les pyramides, ce monument de la puissance & de la vanité des rois d'Egypte, sont aussi un monument de leur astronomie"; William Guthrie et al., *A General History of the World* . . ., 12 vols. (London, 1764-67), 1: 61-62.

jecture that, in his treatment of the pyramid, Johnson is modifying a received idea more or less as he has modified the
poetically glowing version of the Happy Valley and classically
recommended modes of life. There were, as with the Happy
Valley, two traditions about pyramids on which Johnson could
have drawn. One is the tradition on which he does draw
openly. The other was quite different in tone and meaning,
although iconographically compatible with it. George Sandys,
for example, captures both. After calling the pyramids "barbarous monuments of prodigality and vaine-glory," he goes on
to say: "By such the ancient[s] did express the originall of all
things, and that formlesse forme-taking substance. For as a
Pyramis beginning at a point, & the principall height by little
and little dilateth into all parts: so Nature proceeding from one
undevideable fountaine (even God the soveraigne Essence)
receiveth diversitie of formes; effused into severall kinds and
multitudes of figures: uniting all in the supreme head, from
whence al excellencies issue."[13] The symbolic pyramid, along
with the vainglorious pyramid, was current from before
Sandys's time to well after Johnson's. The Great Seal of the
United States has a pyramid which terminates in a luminous
triangle filled with a numinous eye; the Virgilian mottoes
above and below it refer us to a prayer in the first Georgic and
to the Messianic Eclogue. In Mozart's *Zauberflöte*, Masonic
pyramids appear, because the Masons knew that the Egyptians used pyramids "to allegorize the soul, or the principle of
immortality." Sculptors like Rysbrack employed the pyramid,
which "symbolizing eternity, had long been in use as a decora-
tive feature on monuments." Encyclopaedias, like Croker's
Complete Dictionary of Arts and Sciences (1765), mention a
symbolic function for the pyramid; and, of course, so do emblem books, like Valeriano's *Hieroglyphica* and Ripa's *Icono-*

13. *A Relation of a Journey Begun An: Dom: 1610* (3rd ed., London, 1632), p.
127.

logia. Some of these works have more metaphysical explications, like Sandys's and some start from the physical stability of the pyramid, as Johnson himself does. But all of them treat the pyramid—not the historical object but the idea—positively, with reference to immortality or eternity.[14]

Johnson's insistence in *Rasselas* that the imagination must work from the object itself rather than from traditional or subjective notions may take on added emphasis because he is shouldering aside such a widespread understanding of the pyramid. But his shouldering aside is less rejection than reinterpretation. As Johnson's use of both traditions of the Happy Valley lets him include in his paradise Lobo's land of physical pain, here reinterpreted as psychological and moral pain, so he insinuates the psychological truth of the apparently rejected tradition about the pyramid, which points to God precisely because it is the epitome of proof for the vanity of human wishes. It is, in its various forms throughout groups V and VI, the end of the dialectic; and its humblest form, the vain tomb of the catacombs in Chapter 48, becomes the symbolic agent for the pilgrims' last and deepest lesson. They have grown ready

14. On Masonic use, see George Oliver, *Signs and Symbols Illustrated and Explained, in a Course of Twelve Lectures on Free-Masonry* (Grimsby, 1826), p. 11. On sculptors' use, see M. I. Webb, *Michael Rysbrack, Sculptor* (London: Country Life, 1954), p. 83. Also see the following emblem books: Valeriano, *Hieroglyphica*, p. 754; Cesare Ripa, *Iconologia*, tr. P. Tempest (London, 1709), fig. 141; *La Science des hieroglyphes . . .* (The Hague, 1736), plate 14 and its explication, p. 16; Johann Michael Van der Ketten, *Apelles symbolicus* (Amsterdam, 1699), pp. 207-14; Nicolas Verrien, *Recueil d'emblèmes* (Paris, 1724), pp. 42, 62; *Emblems, for the Entertainment and Improvement of Youth* (London, [1750]), plates 34, 36, 60, 62. In order to indicate the currency of positive connotations for the pyramid, without any claims implied about Johnson's knowledge of the books I cite, I have limited myself to emblem books roughly contemporary with him, except for Valeriano, which he owned. Johnson himself, of course, uses pyramids positively in his "Drury-Lane Prologue" (1747), in speaking of Ben Jonson: "A mortal born he met the general doom,/But left, like Egypt's kings, a lasting tomb." *Poems*, ed. E. L. McAdam, Jr., with George Milne, The Yale Edition of the Works, 6 (New Haven: Yale University Press, 1964): 88.

to learn in the burrows of death what the mountains of death might have taught them. Such a lesson, by which the pyramid can point to God, requires two things from Johnson, both of which he provides: a heightened sense of time and eternity, and the knowledge that privations can be goods. The first is a function of analogy or its simpler form, repetition, and the latter gives modification an additional, profitable twist.

From the moment we enter Group V, Johnson heightens our sense of time with Imlac's oration praising history (30); the group is to show us the imperium of the Pharaoh, of the sheik, and of the astronomer, the "control" of the past, present, and future.[15] He symbolizes this repetitive pattern with the pyramid, "a fabrick intended to co-extend its duration with that of the world"(31), and gives three historical relationships to the Pharaoh, its builder. To the Pharaoh's own society, as he solaces ennui by driving porters and masons to useless work, he is a tyrant. For the travellers, he points a moral and adorns a tale among lesser bored and deluded men, like the sheik. Finally, he has a cosmic function, for he has parodied eternity in physical terms as the game preserve of the Happy Valley parodies prelapsarian concord. To these temporal relationships in history, whose weight in *Rasselas* is new here, Johnson adds cyclical and continuing patterns of time, made emblematic in the sidereal time, with its perfection of order, over which the astronomer watches.

The cyclical and continuing patterns of time in groups V and VI replace the largely spatial experience of the travellers. We have the rhythm of the stages of Pekuah's abduction and recovery, the daily ritual of Nekayah's sorrow (36), patterns of destructive and regenerative time in the heavens and on the land (38), Pekuah's nightly return to astronomy (39), and the regulatory "powers" of the astronomer, involving his watch

15. This subject is treated in Geoffrey Tillotson's "Time in *Rasselas*," in Magdi Wahba, ed., *Bicentenary Essays on Rasselas* (Cairo: S.O.P. Press, 1959), pp. 97-103.

overstellar and seasonal progressions. From this watch he discovers the most important fact in *Rasselas*, that the world we
live in cannot really be improved upon. No doubt he means
only the weather when he says, "I have found it impossible to
make a disposition by which the world may be advan-
taged" (43), but he sums up what we have seen in the smaller
but equally repetitive movements of human psychology. The
astronomer, that is, offers us his own version of modification:
each seeming evil, Monday's storm over Cairo or Tuesday's
drought near the upper Nile, is a real evil within a whole that
cannot be bettered. If we extend this discovery by analogy, we
come close to the central contention of theodicy, that the
world, however little there is to be said for it, is as close to
being perfect as it can be. *Rasselas*, from that knowledge, tells
us to examine the world for its hidden utility, for what is positive in its repeated negatives, and to cherish no "choice of
life." That is precisely the advice the travellers try to take in the
catacombs.

If the pyramid is to point to God, Johnson must make us feel
what is implicit in the astronomer's discovery, that privations
can be goods (or relative goods). We come to this knowledge
most directly through Johnson's deepening of the personal in
groups V and VI. In this context, the historical reassessment of
the past, introduced by Imlac's lectures on the pyramid,
returns in the personal form of Nekayah's brooding on
Pekuah, which we observe historically in its effects upon her
over a period of months. It returns in the personal form of the
sheik's use of his own history, his pedigree from Ishmael, as a
licence for theft (38). Finally, it returns in the personal form of
the astronomer's inferences—all induction requires history—
from the cycles of the skies. Each of these three reassessments
of the past brings us to a different kind of evil, moral error, for
each historical act—Nekayah's, the sheik's, the astronomer's—depends on a false relationship between the individual, taken as a constant, and the temporal environment.

Nekayah's "accidia" makes her try, and fail, to pursue romantic grief by withdrawing from time and then by using nature as
a clock for the unnatural "duty of periodical affliction." The
sheik's avarice makes him a "natural and hereditary" gatherer
of tribute who ironically pays tribute (to gold, in the person of
the ransomable Pekuah). Despite his civilized mind, his real
historical place is among those barbarians on whose work he
reflects to Pekuah (38), those who despoil palaces and temples
for "stables of granate, and cottages of porphyry": he has used
his birth and merit merely to deck out his unambitious avarice.
The astronomer's vainglory has the greatest temporal sweep
and the least plausibility of the three. It is a gross historical
blunder, and, unlike the vast majority of episodes in *Rasselas*,
has a historical, biographical genesis.

Evil suffered, as evils are throughout *Rasselas*, is obviously a
form of privation. What is crucial here is that Johnson turns
moral error—"evil" done—into privation too. The moral labels
I have used—"accidia," avarice, vainglory—are technically
right, but in this book tonally wrong. In this connection, one
should recall that Imlac recommends virtue to Nekayah (34)
for prudential rather than moral reasons. The imprudence of
moral error also comes to the surface with the sheik, who
suffers not from the law or his conscience, but from the wished
consequences of his choices. He wanders in the freedom of
ennui. Nekayah's fortunate backsliding from a life of grief
empties her memorial acts of their intended meaning. As to
the astronomer, his sense of ultimate command forces him to a
sense of his ultimate powerlessness. What might have been
treated as a Satanic challenge becomes, like the disposition of
the weather itself, simply a public proof and a private embarrassment. Johnson's and Imlac's procedure is not of course
amoral. Any Christian's scorn for sin may remove or make
irrelevant his moral inclination to loathe and blame the sinner.
Since the limited development of character in *Rasselas* would
keep Johnson from asking us to loathe anybody in the book,

his focus on the folly and sadness of sin makes good sense. The firmly exemplary nature of events is maintained by his extraordinarily compact kind of poetic justice.

But upon this reasonable point the whole of *Rasselas* swivels. We learn during the course of the book to accept certain privations as our agents. These are of two sorts: the privations that we have been discussing, which replace rancor and external punishments as the means of dealing with moral error; and some of the privations that fit in with what we have been calling modification. In this second category falls, for instance, the solace that age affords the sage in the Happy Valley, in making "shame and grief . . . of short duration" for him. Given the frailty of men as Johnson in all orthodoxy portrays them, we are too good-natured, if not self-aware, to wish a better memory on the sage or a more steadfast melancholy on Nekayah, any more than the astronomer, given the system of the heavens, can wish to redispose the weather. If the nature of human life makes us, as benevolent observers, desire that certain human limitations remain, we are part of the way to a theodicy. The astronomer's discovery, I think, is the point at which we realize that what had seemed pathetic, people's need for their own weaknesses, may point to a world order that is far from pathetic.

With this understanding, we can more easily understand the climactic scene in the catacombs, in which Johnson implicitly puts forth the use of unjust and unmerciful privations, the privations that we cannot desire for ourselves or others until we see that they teach us to look to the choice of eternity, as the speaker does at the end of *The Vanity of Human Wishes*. We may also see, retrospectively, that Johnson has given us an empirical version of the speculative "principle of plenitude," from which writers like Pope and Jenyns inferred the necessity of "metaphysical evil." By hypostasizing the stations of life in his exhaustive review of various human conditions, Johnson has defined, and therefore delimited, each choice of life a man can

make. By definition, that is, the shepherds cannot have what
the squire has, and vice versa, so that each remains prey to
evils from which the other is shielded; an obvious argumentative analogy appears in Pope's note to his *Essay on Man*
(I, 182): "It is a certain Axiom in the Anatomy of Creatures, that
in proportion as they are form'd for Strength, their Swiftness
is lessen'd; or as they are form'd for Swiftness, their Strength
is abated." Johnson is too down-to-earth to debate from
axioms or build systems. Still, each of his characters must forego the goods proper to other men's conditions, so that each
individual suffers from his own specific privations as well as
from those privations that afflict humans as a species.

When I liken *Rasselas* to theodicies, I am not suggesting that,
for example, Johnson is contriving another response to
Jenyns's *Free Inquiry*, which he had reviewed with acerbity two
years before. I am saying that *Rasselas* shares with them a
double perspective, seeing human wisdom and morality as at
once important and vain—a perspective that one finds neither
in *The Vanity of Human Wishes* nor in the tale of Seged (*Ramblers*
204 and 205). *Rasselas* shares with them the problem of recon-
ciling a faith in an ordered world with everyone's continuing
experience of chaos and pain; and shares Jenyns's pragma-
tism: "Happiness is the only thing of real value in existence;
neither riches, nor power, nor wisdom, nor learning, nor
strength, nor beauty, nor virtue, nor religion, nor even life
itself, being of any importance but as they contribute to its
production. All these are in themselves neither Good nor Evil;
Happiness alone is their great end, and they desirable only as
they tend to promote it."[16] Johnson's kinship with these theodicies does not, of course, extend to their tone and mode of

16. *A Free Inquiry into the Nature and Origin of Evil . . .*, in *Works*, 4 vols.
(London, 1790), 3: 56-57 (Letter III: "On Natural Evils"). Paul K. Alkon notes
that Johnson was sometimes capable himself of adopting a homiletic tone in
his sermons, and to a lesser degree in his periodicals, which bears a family
resemblance to Jenyns's more ethical, less metaphysical arguments in the *Free*

argument. Pope and Jenyns, in Johnson's opinion, tried to sweep evils under the rug of cosmic good and offered the appalled homeowners nothing better than dark glasses. Johnson affirms evil in experience and provides at least some experiential reasons why one might think of it as part of a pattern, sometimes giving error its due, sometimes urging man to turn from the world to its Creator. His special achievement in groups V and VI is to join an acute awareness (through analogy) of what pain means personally with an awareness (through modification) that it may have its own profits. That complexity, which abstract theodicies failed to seize, comes about only when fictional form and fictional logic re-create the conditions of life.

Why, in an eighteenth-century work, the conditions of life in an astronomer? For two reasons. One is that astronomy was a very common science from which physico-theological tracts, like William Derham's repeatedly reprinted *Astro-Theology* (1715), could draw the argument from design. The well-known piety of men like Newton (cf. *Life of Johnson* 1:455), Flamsteed, Whiston, and Keill only made the argument seem more natural. Where theorists led, poets followed suit. Much of Night 9 in *Night Thoughts* involves a rove through the heavens, with such physico-theological assurance that Young can exclaim (lines 722-73): "Devotion! daughter of Astronomy!/An undevout astronomer is mad." The orderly mind will make the order of the skies a cosmic axiom. Johnson disrupts the order of his astronomer's mind so that this cliché becomes distinctive and credible to those who distrust adages:

Inquiry: Samuel Johnson and Moral Discipline (Evanston: Northwestern University Press, 1967), pp. 195-201. Other perspectives on Johnson's antagonism to Jenyns and Pope can be found in Richard B. Schwartz, *Samuel Johnson and the Problem of Evil* (Madison: University of Wisconsin Press, 1975); much of what Schwartz says, particularly about "Johnson's psychological orientation with regard to the problem of evil" (p. 79), is germane to my reading of *Rasselas*, although Schwartz does not actually discuss *Rasselas* as a version of theodicy. Nicholas Joost does, in "Whispers of Fancy; or, The Meaning of *Rasselas*," *Modern Age* 1 (1957): 166-73.

although madness is self-centered and the axiom of control-
ling divinity is not preached in Egypt, the astronomer comes to
the brink of truth.[17] He cannot go further until he is cured,
because his empirical discovery about the weather has no context, no meaning save that the most powerful man in the
world, he who can wield the heavens, has no real power. He
can do nothing, that is, which does not violate the inner moral
order that he still retains; and even if that were to be put aside,
he could make no self-interested use of his power except to
exalt himself to one of the worldly positions that have already
been exposed to us and to the travellers as vain and perilous.
In short, the astronomer is at the same ebb as are the rich, free,
unsatisfied members of the royal party. He therefore stands in
a special analogical relation to them; it is no accident that he
remains with them after his cure, apart from his dubious
romance with Pekuah.

This special relation suggests Johnson's second reason for
using an astronomer. He needed an empirical scientist, as a
man who requires all three faculties, observation, practical
reason, and imagination, which the voyagers, on their own
scientific expedition, require. To Johnson, born less than
twenty-five years after Newton's *Principia*, an astronomer
would fit the bill par excellence. The three faculties themselves
give shape, as we saw, to Group I, and the order of increasing
complexity thereafter has given Rasselas and Nekayah a good
deal of practice in observation and practical reason. Groups V
and VI, as they become more personal, dwell more on the third
faculty, imagination. We see its disorder in the Pharaoh,
Nekayah, perhaps the sheik, and obviously the astronomer.

17. If Johnson had Young more or less in mind—and I have no reason to
suppose he did—lines 1644-54 of Night 9 (1745) add an ironic note. There,
Young's Lorenzo is a "fond astronomer" of sublunary beauties, and his
preference for carnal over celestial pleasures makes him "run mad, / Darken
his intellect, corrupt his heart." Johnson reverses the moral cliché by
showing Pekuah's sublunary beauty curing a mad astronomer.

The logic of the book makes us and the travellers ready for Imlac's beautiful discourse on the dangerous prevalence of the imagination, which completes the experience we have had and leads us into the final section of *Rasselas*. This experience, I should note, has nothing to do with an abstract hierarchy of the faculties. The sage of Chapter 3 and the flyer of Chapter 6 show how the faculty of reason can itself become an idle part of the subjective imagination; and in totally different ways, the astronomer's heuristic delusion and the fictional mode chosen by Johnson for *Rasselas* both show how imaginative experience can give sinew to reason. What Johnson requires, what the form of the book and the astronomer as man and scientist require, is what the weather possesses, an equilibrium.

The danger of the prevalent imagination is that its simulacra of nature deny each experience a proper context and thus an inferential meaning. In life, as in an apologue so full of analogy and incremental repetition, an experience makes sense only in relation to other experiences, from which the prevalent imagination isolates it. Imlac has already explained how the imagination can function properly in the poet's reflection of nature. When fancy wanders from nature, even toward the ideal forms of innocence and virtue of which the travellers have daydreamed (44), it corrupts itself. One starts daydreaming in solitude, and the act of the daydream then forces one into epistemological solitude. At this culminating point in Rasselas's search, he, like the astronomer, faces the solipsistic negation of searches and learning. Therefore, through the astronomer, Johnson lets us glimpse the near neighbor and distant opposite of negation, the knowledge of Providence before which we are at once weak and strong. None of the party can come to it without submitting to nature instead of making imaginative impositions upon her. At this stage in *Rasselas*, then, with the ideological energies and paradoxes of the book brought tautly together, Imlac's three fellow travellers must do what he has implicitly done, purge their own madness—as they do by confession—to make themselves ready for the learning to which reason and past observation entitle them, the learning of the catacombs.

Confession and self-realization cannot go unmodified. Our friends have a relapse as soon as they meet the logical embodiment of Imlac's discourse, the old man (45). He has no illusions. He has studied "the qualities and the causes of all that [he] behold[s], the laws by which the river flows, the periods in which the planets perform their revolutions." Having passed through social experience and temporal nature, he can evaluate them. He uses them negatively, to make their failure turn his heart toward "a better state," and also positively, to rescue from failure "that happiness which here I could not find, and that virtue which here I have not attained." The young travellers no sooner hear this paragon then they reject his mood and question his motives, very much as Rasselas had rejected Nekayah's discoveries in Group IV. Such a contravention of the spirit of Chapter 44, Imlac's discourse, leads to simpler lessons being extended them in the rest of Group VII. The group itself contains four discrete solutions to "the choice of life," arranged logically: man alone (the old man), man active in society (the cured astronomer), man contemplative in society (the monks), and man using reason and imagination to comprehend metaphysics (the catacombs)—this is roughly like the arrangement of Group III, the earlier look at modes of life. Within this structure, the astronomer and monks present once more the secular and pious attitudes rejected with the old man (45), but which the royal party must accept.

Like the old man, the astronomer (46) cannot buoy his solitude with learning or virtue, and he too looks back on a life of lost chances, but the travellers have learned the reason for his judgment in such a way that they do not challenge *his* melancholy or quiet hopes, but pass with him to increasing frankness and generosity. Chapter 47 similarly explains the monks' ability to live in cheerful anticipation of eternity. By accepting them as well as the astronomer, the travellers have repaired, at least for formal purposes, their willful doubts about the old man; and the lesson, through analysis and repetition, seems to have had some effect. When the old man spoke of "endeavour[ing] to abstract my thoughts from hopes and cares, which, though reason knows them to be vain, still try to keep their old possession of the heart," Nekayah thought him querulous; now she is silent when Imlac warns that otherwise harmless pleasure "may become mischievous, by endearing to us a state which we know to be transient and probatory." The chapter ends with the party going to stare at the mummies, uncorrupted in a material facsimile of that eternal life which death brings.

The catacombs, the tourist's version of the Valley of the Shadow of Death, may remind us of the Valley from which we began, with its "timelessness." Johnson himself reminds us of the eternal pyramid: Nekayah mentions Pekuah's fear of entering it (47); in both burial places the party talks about physical and spiritual presence (ghosts, the soul); Imlac gratuitously uses the idea of a pyramid in proving that substance does not imply extension. Needless to say, Johnson's insistence on the contexts and inferential force of particulars makes us and the travellers look at these old experiences in new ways. There are revelations through analogy, a growth of intensity, a dialectic. The mummies seem a more poignant, more personal parody of immortality than does the pyramid, since they are a quintessential memento mori. Our party has moved from the most material of spiritual beings, the spectres of Group V, to the "impassive and indiscerptible" soul; from the fleeting phenomena of the imagination, on which groups V and VI dwelled, to the present consideration of the soul as noumenon. Johnson has grimly compressed Nekayah's grief and the sheik's avarice into Imlac's remarks on the rows of carcasses, embalmed (as Pekuah was to have been in memory) "from tenderness to the remains of relations or friends," and kept "secure" (as the fortressed sheik was to be) because they had been "rich or honorable." Now security and the pomp of grief are given their final definition in eternity. Imlac also somberly defines the astronomer's delusion of power in remarking that the Egyptians thought they could preserve the soul by embalming the body, not knowing that the soul "receives from a superiour nature its power of duration": like the astronomer, the embalmers achieve their results despite the paradox of their actual impotence.

These incremental repetitions and redefinitions, which seem to scoop together so much of groups V and VI, build the rhetoric of the chapter to a head. By its end, Johnson has driven home the realization that the travellers have been getting the wrong answers because they have been asking the wrong question. Each privation and demonstration of worldly vanity should have been as painful or more painful than it has been; but it also should have been, not a counsel of despair or a chance for self-delusion, but a small signpost pointing toward providential eternity.[18] The choice of life must be turned inside out, so that individual, cyclic, perpetual, and historical time can be referred to their source in eternity. This is what happens in Chapter 48, which leaves the assembly silent and collected, and then sententious. But as one might expect, the transfiguration of time into eternity can only be transient in this life. Modification pecks at the finest maxims, and thus in Chapter 49 the girls return to their dreams of virtue and learning, Rasselas to his of justice, and nothing is concluded. We end with another flooding of the Nile, like that with which our voyagers began; another use of water and navigation imagery ("be driven along

18. Like many others, I agree with Boswell that "Johnson meant, by shewing the unsatisfactory nature of things temporal, to direct the hopes of man to things eternal" (*Life* 1: 342). His intentions to this end are questioned by John M. Aden, "'Rasselas' and 'The Vanity of Human Wishes'," *Criticism* 3 (1961): 295-303; and his success in achieving it by Patrick O'Flaherty, "Dr. Johnson as Equivocator: The Meaning of *Rasselas*," *MLQ* 31 (1970): 195-208.

the stream of life without directing their course to any particular port"); and a return to Abyssinia, although, one must suppose, not to the Happy Valley, which has become an
irrelevancy.

We should not pass by Group VII, finally, without noting
Johnson's technical brilliance in making us take the prospect of
eternity as he intended. Johnson's biography and other writings would prove, if such proof were needed, that he meant it
to be taken seriously, but we might expect him to have trouble
keeping the reader from doubts. The form of *Rasselas* is so
fiercely efficient that eternity too, as men conceive it, might
seem the last and most pathetic delusion of the book. Perhaps
with an audience of at least habitual Christians, Johnson did
not have trouble. All modifications aside, *Rasselas* encouraged
familiar belief with a familiar pattern—the proof that life is a
vale of tears, and the advice to turn one's eyes and hopes
upward—couched in solemn words. But Johnson also went
beyond these conventional means, in leading us by steps to his
conclusion. Rasselas and his party leave the barren stasis of the
Happy Valley to look systematically for its fruitful counterpart,
a single condition of happiness, in the rest of the world. They
discover that the world, like the Happy Valley, involves the
movement of time and thus the ruin of single conditions. In
Group VII, however, after Imlac's discourse (44), Johnson
changes tack. The old man of Chapter 45 has himself emerged,
even if imperfectly, from a series of conditions. He is in
between life and death, where he is not really imitable, and he
has an awareness and sureness of purpose modified only by
his own self-criticisms and the travellers' anodyne doubts.

From the change in tone that this chapter represents,
Johnson can pass to the cure of the astronomer, the first hopeful episode in the book. Again, the sanity of the astronomer is
not a single condition in the way that being a shepherd or a
sheik is, nor is it imitable as a solution to "the choice of life." It
depends, like the old man's state, on retrospection: "I am

always tempted to think," says the astronomer, "that my
enquiries have ended in errour, and that I have suffered much,
and suffered it in vain." He now can work toward inner peace
and acquiescence. The monks of St. Anthony (47) cap this
ascending triad.[19] They are at peace in this world because they
have sureness of purpose and an occupation while they wait
for eternity. Still more hopeful than the episode of the astronomer's cure, this chapter finally presents a state of life, theoretically imitable, in which men can be happy. Rasselas makes a
direct comparison between the monks and the princes in the
Happy Valley, which has become metonymous for the world,
so that Johnson can focus on the inner meaning of a life lived
for "the choice of eternity." The praise of the monks is qualified, as is that of the old man and astronomer, but the path to
the revelation in the catacombs is clearly marked. Johnson
then lifts some stress from that revelation by making it satisfy
the travellers only in part, as their return to daydreams in the
last chapter proves. So prepared for by structure, and so
protected from having to bear a heavier burden than a skeptical book might allow, the promise of eternity can withstand
doubt, as Johnson meant it to.

IV: POSTSCRIPT

My introductory comments about system, analogy, and modification set forth a context of intention, either a beacon or an
ignis fatuus, depending on the analyses. Therefore, a review of
the context might be of help now that the first analysis can be
judged against Johnson's book. The principle of unity and
variety is self-evident in a novel that explores a world of possibilities with a single question in mind. Analogy, often in the
form of incremental repetition, supplies conceptual unity

19. The age of the monastery, which is the oldest in Christendom, and the
associations of St. Anthony with the temptations of the world make this setting perfect for Johnson's purposes.

because the answer to the question is the same in such various but overlapping ways. Modification, since the answer is never what Rasselas wants, leads to empirical breadth. Analogy is constitutive, "Hartleyan," of this closed world of wrong answers; and of course the inferential value of each episode comes from the "Butlerian" principle that nature is uniform enough to support judgments of probability, especially when one knows causes, as the characters in *Rasselas* typically do. Johnson's skepticism as well as Rasselas's discontent make modification a rule of thumb. Everyone is questioned, everything down to Imlac's truisms is open to challenge as half true or partly irrelevant. Allusions to the world outside the book, be they to pyramids, an Abyssinian paradise, classical advice for happiness, "projectors," categories of sin and madness, even the monks whose earthly "silent convent" represents both an ideal and an abdication of will by the "weak and timorous"—on each of these Johnson's modifications give us at least double perspectives. That is one of the reasons why *Rasselas* is not subject to the accusation its author made against the *Essay on Man*: "Surely a man of no very comprehensive search may venture to say that he has heard all this before."[20] It is also why our system of inquiry allows for multiple questions and partial acceptances, while Rasselas's allows for only one question and glum rejection.

Our system of inquiry and his are both based on one principle, that of skeptical empiricism. His systematic procedure produces a system of order, the only visible order in *Rasselas*. Johnson does give us additional order covertly, through extending to literature the spatial principle of rhythm. Painters had long recognized rhythmic procedures quite openly. In 1670, at the height of French "classicism," Henry Testelin, "peintre du roy," summarized deliberations of the Académie

20. *Lives of the Poets*, ed. George Birkbeck Hill, 3 vols. (Oxford: Clarendon Press, 1905), 3: 244.

des Beaux Arts for the great Ministre d'État, Colbert. The composition he advocates is precisely what I have ascribed to
Rasselas, with its analogies, its groups, and its rhythms that
develop their own massed power. "Le Peintre," writes
Testelin, "doit . . . concevoir de grandes parties comme de
puissantes masses, soit dans les groupes, soit dans les ombres,
soit dans les couleurs, parce que c'est ce qui donne de la
beauté & de la noblesse a l'Ouvrage."[21] Testelin thus breaks
down the visual phenomenon into such components as spatial
relationships, light, and colors; and from phenomena with
analogous components are created, conceptually, "powerful
masses." These masses, as anyone who has seen work by
Poussin or Le Brun knows, do not destroy the individuality of
figures, but offer a way of seeing, a way of "reading" relationships. The same is true in music; in literature, where these
rhythmic methods were given much less critical attention, one
can look for parallels—if the shade of Johnson will forgive
me—in the great Pindaric odes of Gray, published two years
before *Rasselas*. *The Progress of Poesy*, for example, gives us sets
of three stanzas that work by contrast and analogy. The first
ternary presents forward motion with water imagery, power
in stasis with aerial imagery, and cyclic movement with earthly
imagery; the second presents the cycle from night to day, the
simultaneity (temporal stasis) of savage benightedness and
poetic glory, and the forward motion of poetry from Greece to
England following liberty; the third (from Shakespeare, to
Milton and Dryden, to Gray) repeats versions of the same
imagery in new order. Gray's methods (or Bach's, whose fugal
themes are augmented, diminished, inverted, and juxtaposed), if not Testelin's, are analogy and modification. Johnson's covert system of order, in accord with practice of his
time, follows the same methods in its use of rhythm as does his

21. Henry Testelin, *Sentimens des plus habiles peintres sur la pratique de la
peinture et sculpture* (Paris, 1696), p. 27.

open system of order, that which results from the prince's natural inquiries.

We now have reason to believe that the theory outlined in the Introduction carries over into some artistic practice. Systems lead to a highly ordered book with emotional logic, a scientifically cautious book which contradictions keep in precarious equilibrium. The formal implications for *Rasselas* follow from what has been said, and I submit that they hold for all five novels we are to examine. [22]

22. Some comparisons between the modes of *Rasselas* and *Tristram Shandy* are to be found in Jones, "Artistic Form," (n. 9 above).

Tristram Shandy

Everyone knows that the author of *Rasselas* remarked, "Nothing odd will do long. *Tristram Shandy* did not last."[1] Johnson was, as usual, more right than wrong: if oddity had been the main source of *Tristram*'s success, Sterne would have gone the way of those imitators who "made themselves ridiculous by dull imitation of [his] sudden sallies of fancy and unconnected breaks of sentiment."[2] The readers of the 1760s knew how to enjoy *Tristram* because its formal idiom was in some degree familiar, not to say orthodox. A self-conscious narrator who writes breathlessly "to the moment"—even if it is a moment of mental behavior—is the son of Fielding and Richardson.[3] More to the immediate point, *Tristram* has systematic affinities

---

1. As reported by Boswell. *Boswell's Life of Johnson*, ed. George Birkbeck Hill, rev. L. F. Powell, 6 vols. (Oxford: Clarendon Press, 1934-50), 2: 514 (March 20, 1776).

2. James Boswell, *The Hypochondriack* 35 (August, 1780), in *Boswell's Column*, ed. Margery Bailey (London: William Kimber, 1951), p. 192.

3. This becomes evident from Wayne Booth's discussion of narrative techniques in "The Self-Conscious Narrator in Comic Fiction before *Tristram Shandy*," *PMLA* 67 (1952): 163-85. I am inclined to play down what many other critics have played up, Sterne's interest in parodying the established

with *Rasselas*. As we have seen, the initial situation in *Rasselas* provides a matrix of themes in which the contents of the whole book are virtually present. The contents become actually present as parts generate parts, working toward completeness in large measure through analogy and modification. The same holds true for *Tristram*, except that behind the matrix of themes is a matrix of three characters, the Shandy men, conceived in two binary relationships. One is between the brothers, Walter and Toby; the other between Tristram and his elders. From these two relationships, and from themes implicit in them (systems/authorship and brotherhood/family are the most important), the contents of the novel emerge. The two familial relationships are developed early in the book, and in the first chapter the themes have appeared, typified by a begetting botched by its authors because of a familial system. Analogy and modification take over from there.

If one understands the relationship between Tristram and his elders, one understands the strange kinship of Walter and Toby, which is a simpler version of the same type. Tristram, as narrator, creates his family for us: in the order and the rhetoric he chooses, he tells us all we know of them. As a man, however, he is their joint creation; his personality develops no possibility that they do not offer. Given that the book of Tristram's life and opinions mostly concerns not him but his father and uncle, logic suggests that the bases for his life and opinions are to be found in them. Fact confirms logic, for there is, as we shall see, the fullest sort of familial sharing and reciprocity. The reader discovers this family resemblance slowly,

---

novel: his techniques of parody, if such it is, have so many precedents, as Booth points out, that their primary functions are unlikely to be satiric of the Richardsons and Fieldings. For Fielding's suspicion of set forms and systems, see Leo Braudy's discussion of him in *Narrative Form in History and Fiction: Hume, Fielding, and Gibbon* (Princeton: Princeton University Press, 1970)—the aims of the two men resembled each other in this regard far more than they differed.

because narrators are privileged characters. They seem human because they speak to real humans, and to enjoy free will—at least as a normal state—because readers think they themselves do. At the other extreme, Walter and Toby start from the simplicity of humours, or hobbyhorses. Yet the novel brings Shandy fathers and son closer. Tristram's free whimsy hardens into fixed personality as we start to know him better and begin to sense an ultimate point of convergence between Life and Opinions, between the time-bound and family-bound child of the 1720s and the author of the sixties.[4] We welcome this procedure: Walter and Toby have meanwhile become sympathetic and complex enough that Tristram's dwindling into a mere character tends to his advantage. His failures as an author are redeemed, in a different context, by his being so perfectly a Shandy, tested by the affectionate criteria we apply to his father and his uncle. Let us look in more detail at the correlatives to this loss of privilege.

The alignment of the three men as Shandys gives the analogies among them full play. Each, obviously, has his hobbyhorse, a system of reference that interprets facts and defines priorities in his mental world. The hobbyhorse of each becomes public through a form of authorship, Walter's philosophy through verbal discourse, Toby's military history through mimetic reenactment, and Tristram's book through

---

4. Howard Anderson, "Associationism and Wit in *Tristram Shandy*," *PQ* 48 (1969): 27-41, discusses the deductive way in which we begin to aproach Tristram's family and the inductive way in which we approach Tristram himself. Cf. Ronald Paulson's remark that Sterne "makes us see his characters and situations first as the old satiric ones and then as the new recipients of comic-sympathetic laughter. The thesis is as much a part of the effect as the antithesis, and the transition becomes for Sterne a basic theme." *Satire and the Novel in Eighteenth-Century England* (New Haven: Yale University Press, 1967), p. 249. The background for Paulson's analysis is provided by Stuart M. Tave, *The Amiable Humorist: A Study in the Comic Theory and Criticism of the Eighteenth and Early Nineteenth Centuries* (Chicago: University of Chicago Press, 1960).

the verbal and mimetic both. The two brothers are traditional complements, the contemplative and active men, Walter devoted to logic and analogy, Toby to chronology; Tristram takes his thematic and rhetorical sequence (and the subject matter "opinions") from his father, and the sequential order of his recollections (and the subject matter "life") from his uncle. His trains of mental experience are the private version of Walter's public trains of logical ideas, and his fascination with sex the private version of Toby's public gallantry, if I may use that equivocal word to suggest Sterne's equation between the bowling green battles and the amorous siege of the Widow Wadman. This equation is important enough to lie behind the disaster of Tristram's following in the traces of his unhappy Cornish original, a wounded hero frustrated in love, and thus confirming Walter Shandy's theory of Christian names.[5] The hobbyhorse of all three men, finally—hobbyhorse, with that word's implications of self-propulsion and naiveté—serves as a symbol for the whole of the mind. Philosophy, soldiership,

---

5. A. R. Towers, "Sterne's Cock and Bull Story," *ELH* 24 (1957): 12-29, discusses the way in which Toby's "fortifications are regularly feminized and sexualized," pp. 21-24. I do not know where Sterne read about Tristram's "Cornish original." Possibly he simply took the name from Ephraim Tristram Bates, the eponymous hero of a novel (1756) to which he was patently in debt. See Helen Sard Hughes, "A Precursor of *Tristram Shandy*," *JEGP* 17 (1918): 227-51. This seems to me highly unlikely, because the traditional story of Tristram, even to the madness in at least one version, suits Sterne so well; and because the Trismegistus-Tristram conflict, in this novel with its theory of Christian names, requires that "Tristram" equal "Trismegistus" in connotative strength. The irrational, passionate, wounded warrior of the epic, acted upon from without (through the potion), contrasts beautifully with the self-controlled philosophical rationality of Trismegistus, "most fully imbued with every kind of learning." (The quotation is from Lactantius, in Frances A. Yates, *Giordano Bruno and the Hermetic Tradition* [New York: Random House, 1969], p. 7.) There are reasons to speculate, in any case, that Sterne may have used Malory's version, where, within the first few paragraphs of the story, he would have found that Sir Tristram's mother was Elizabeth and that "Tristram" was so named for his sorrowful birth; Tristram Shandy's mother is Elizabeth and his birth is certainly difficult (III, 13).

and memoirs alike are what only memoirs admit to being,
autobiography.

The Shandys also share techniques. They all digress at the
drop of a suggestive word. They all battle: Walter, we are told,
entrenches and fortifies his ideas "with as many circumvalla-
tions and breast-works, as my uncle *Toby* would a citadel"
(III, 34). When he embarks on the profession that is to be his
son's, he is pleased to agree with Giovanni della Casa that the
life of a writer is "a state of *warfare*; and his probation in it,
precisely that of any man militant upon earth" (V, 16). In their
skirmishes, the three Shandy men make use of what matériel
they can. Walter, who inhabits a world of hieroglyphics, tries
to turn names, noses, children, brothers, and breastworks into
ideas. Toby's "wit" (in Locke's sense) lets him furnish a
battlefield from Shandy Hall, the order of mind "revealing" to
him that jack boots are really mortars in disguise (III, 22). Some
of Tristram's double entendres and most of his typographical
makeshift—black and marbled pages, Gothic type, juggling of
chapter numbers—fit into the same class.[6] The objects shed
their civilian clothes, their normal, hereditary meanings (or
relative meaninglessness) for the sake of a system within
which, and only within which, they can truly conquer the
understanding. A fourth family habit is the urge to be thorough, in research and in publication. Walter, sitting down to
learn about noses, reads Bruscambille, then Prignitz, "*Scrod-
erus, Andrea Paraeus, Bouchet*'s Evening Conferences, and
above all, the great and learned *Hafen Slawkenbergius*" (III, 35).
Toby's library contains maps of all the fortified towns of Italy
and Flanders, and the works of over a dozen named and
perhaps a hundred unnamed books of "military architecture"

6. Conceivably the marbled paper, with its mystic meanings, is a reply to
Noël-Antoine Pluche, who used it as an example of meaningless color
unconnected to objects. *Le Spectacle de la nature*, 9 vols. (Paris, 1732-42), 7: 68;
Sterne's copy of volume 7 (Paris, 1746) is item 2202 in *A Facsimile Reproduction
of a Unique Catalogue of Laurence Sterne's Library* (London: James Tregaskis &
Son, 1930).

and ballistics (II, 3). From them both comes Tristram's delight in the apparatus of pedantry, and his dismay when he sees that his compulsion to tell all, which is the other side of pedantry, will lead him into an impossible situation: "as at this rate I should just live 364 times faster than I should write—It must follow, an' please your worships, that the more I write, the more I shall have to write" (IV, 13). His difficulties come from his pursuing Toby's plan of rendering each day in full detail, or alternatively from using his father's method in writing the *Tristrapaedia*, a "most painful diligence, proceeding step by step in every line, with . . . caution and circumspection" (V, 16), so that the object of its counsels grows up too fast for the book to be used.

To understand these family resemblances is to understand how Tristram writes his book. His choice of form has public and private bases. The public basis follows logically from his being an interested historian: he develops that form of history—memoirs—best suited to merge objective and subjective points of view. Memoirs give events a due judicious distance, at which they can be seen as fragments of chronicle; such a chronicle in turn keeps confounding itself with personal judgment, sometimes with idiosyncrasy, so as to give readers the flavor of personality which they relish. Style and form can then express the self at the core of recollected history. As Marmontel pointed out: "A l'égard des *mémoires*, où, sans attention pour ces convenances de moeurs, l'auteur n'aura voulu qu'obéir à son propre génie, le ton, le style, la couleur, tout doit s'y ressentir et de son caractère, et de la situation où étaient son esprit et son âme."[7] *The Life and Opinions of Tristram Shandy*, a novel whose forms Laurence Sterne has subverted,

---

7. *Elémens de littérature*, s.n. "mémoires," in Jean-François Marmontel, *Oeuvres complètes*, 18 vols. (Paris, 1819), 14: 213. Marmontel's comments, published in the *Encyclopédie* in 1765-66, are contemporary with *Tristram*. Critics have insufficiently stressed *Tristram*'s relations to history (which, after all, it claims to be), where similar "self-consciousness" is found. See William J. Farrell, "Fielding's Familiar Style," *ELH* 34 (1967): 65-77.

is also what the title suggests it is, Tristram's memoirs written precisely in tune with the decorum of the genre. The historical value of such a work depends on the reader's seeing events and minds as the memoirist sees them, or saw them; and so Tristram has every right to ask us to learn to think in his patterns, so that at least moment by moment we reaffirm his way of seeing things by sharing it with him.[8] Hence his confidential tone, and his casting his book in the form of gossip, where he sets the order of events but makes that order plain to us. Rarely are the connections between one sentence and the next, one scene and the next, left foggy. If we must on occasion wait to find out how to track Tristram's errant mind, we remain assured that in time we will find out.[9] In any case, he could hardly give us much more help without concealing the workings of his mind and thus falsifying his memoirs. His ingenuousness is a pledge of his good faith and a precondition of our trust.

The private basis of the memoirs is familial. Tristram, for reasons of familial inheritance and perhaps (one cannot tell) familial piety, must reorder the methods of his father and uncle so as to give them a new context, in which they may be free from childishness and futility. His memoirs can then assert the public value of Walter's classifications and Toby's imitative structures in modified form. Walter's philosophy remains useless because it cannot adapt to the essence of specific events, which it interprets as symbolic action. At the other extreme, Toby's history is totally adaptable to events, never ascending beyond them.[10] Both therefore are time's vic-

8. Cf. Marmontel's discussion; and John Ogilvie, *Philosophical and Critical Observations on the Nature, Characters, and Various Species of Composition*, 2 vols. (London, 1774), 1: 69.

9. Arthur Cash has untangled Tristram's train of ideas from the irrational associationism so often charged to him: "The Lockean Psychology of *Tristram Shandy*," *ELH* 22 (1955): 125-35.

10. "After all, [Toby's] imagination turns out to have been essentially inert and uncreative. He has been slavishly dependent on events and, in the end,

tims, proved not wrong but irrelevant. The succession of events at Shandy Hall bypasses Walter's theories, phenomenon by phenomenon; and day by day, the succession of events in Marlborough's campaigns bypasses Toby's mummery. Tristram's memoirs try to dedeem history and philosophy by correcting the excesses of servitude to, and abstraction from, particulars. First, he revalues Toby's and Walter's work by making it say something about them instead of their ostensible subjects. Then he himself takes over their crafts, joining history and philosophy in his memoirs of life and opinions.

His medial position between the particular and the abstraction, history and philosophy, is the place that classical criticism assigns to literature.[11] Tristram, therefore, does his best to offer us memoirs *ab ovo* that are epic in sweep, in the morality of precept and plot, and in patriotic devotion. From the world of history come a wide range of characters from many classes and countries, with a central trio representing thought, action, and (taking Tristram as an author) creative force. War, love, birth and death, adventures in foreign lands (Trim and Tristram), comparisons with heroes (Cyrus, Hamlet, and Tristram's namesake), romantic passion (Slawkenbergius's Diego, Tristram, Toby), spiritual fervor (Ernulphus, and, in a different sense, Phutatorius)—all these replace the ephemera of Toby's green. Nor is our hero less at home with ideas. Dr. Slop's advances in medical science, Stevinus's in military science, Phutatorius's in moral science, and the Sorbonneans' in baptismal casuistry join the wisdom of Walter

---

is just as much at their mercy as ever he was. Hence our mixed feelings about him." John Preston, *The Created Self: The Reader's Role in Eighteenth-Century Fiction* (London: Heinemann, 1970), p. 174.

11. As in Aristotle, *Poetics* 1451b, and Horace's second Epistle of the First Book, lines 3-4. Sterne's contemporary Robert Lowth endorses this view in his first lecture, "De poeticae fine et utilitate" (delivered 1741) in *De sacra poesi Hebraeorum* (1753) (2nd ed., Oxford, 1763), especially pp. 6-11.

Shandy, John Locke, Tristram himself, and many other famous men too numerous to mention. If the private memoirs of a Shandy could succeed in such serious designs, Tristram would gain the laurels for which his father and uncle, professionally considered, might strive.

From his vantage point as litterateur, Tristram can rework not only his father's ideas and his uncle's chronology, but also such subsidiary Shandeisms as his father's theory of names. The theory, worthless in real life, fits a literary work perfectly. That is where one expects charactonyms. Under the guise of literary convention, we find a Walterian world, where nonsense comes from a Slawkenbergius and a book on concubines from a Phutatorius, where defilement by the uncircumcised (a coachman) stains the history of a Dinah (I, 21), bridges are demolished by the sexual exploits of a Bridget (III, 24), a Yorick jests and perishes, and the bevy of Shandys are what their name implies.[12] Toby's methods too are made literary. Does

12. Overton Philip James, *The Relation of "Tristram Shandy" to the Life of Sterne* (The Hague: Mouton, 1966), discusses "Dinah," pp. 46-47. Joseph Wright, *The English Dialect Dictionary*, 6 vols. (London, 1898-1905), defines "shandy" as, among other things, "wild, romping, boisterous, merry." Cf. the "wild and shandy" nature of Venus in James Robertson's "Jove's Charge to Venus," in *Poems* (2nd ed. revised, London, 1780), p. 232; and the definition "wild" in Francis Grose, *A Provincial Glossary* (London, 1787), sig. G8ᵛ. The "crack-brained" offered in *The Winged Skull: Papers from the Laurence Sterne Bicentenary Conference*, ed. Arthur H. Cash and John M. Stedmond (London: Methuen, 1971), p. 280, is therefore extreme. I might add to the discussion of names, that Tristram has his Locke from a most unlikely source, his mother, whose maiden name was Mollineux: the distinguished philosopher William Molyneux (1656-1698) was the correspondent of Locke's who posed the celebrated problem about the blind man, the cube, and the sphere. Contemporary readers would have been likely to catch the allusion, for Molyneux's correspondence with Locke was often reprinted, and his problem was of "decisive systematic significance" in eighteenth-century philosophy—the judgment is Ernst Cassirer's, in *The Philosophy of the Enlightenment*, tr. Fritz C. A. Koelin and James P. Pettegrove (Boston: Beacon Press, 1955), p. 109. By the 1750s, Molyneux's biography had appeared in Birch's expanded Bayle, the *Biographia Britannica*, and Chaufepié's *Dictionnaire*.

Toby follow Marlborough "step by step," measuring fortifications to the inch (VI, 22)? Such finicking is foolish in a toy,
but exactitude is a great virtue in memoirs. Tristram gives us
exact detail about scenes (e.g., III, 29, Walter's pose on the
bed), the process of reading a letter to oneself (V, 2) or a
sermon to others (II, 17), the documents involved in his
parents' marriage and infant baptism (I, 15, 20), and even,
drawing on all the devices of authorial ingenuity, Le Fever's
spasms of breath and pulse, marked by dashes with or without
commas, trochees ("fluttered") and spondees ("went on"),
single syllables and cretics (VI, 10).

The ultimate refinement of Tristram's reworking of his
elders' methods comes in his discovery, within the conventions
of literature, of a replacement for his father's uncomprehend-
ing audience, too small-minded and mundane for philosophical discourse, and for his uncle's bowling green, too small and
domestic for scenes of martial glory. The replacement, of
course, is us. He goes out of his way to persuade us of, and
make us create, his system. Each docile "Sir" and "Madam" of
us becomes complicitous with him, particularly in the search
for double entendres.[13] Tristram's final claim to the laurels for
which Walter and Toby might strive is that we, unlike their
media for their systems, become active mills for Tristram's
grist, creating his system from the experience we share with
him. That is success for a systematic author of any sort, and the
sweetest of triumphs for the son of the Shandys.

Tristram can rework Walter's and Toby's methods by analogy, and by modification of their contexts, can claim for the
reworkings a genuine validity that the originals lacked. He

13. The most interesting of the many discussions of this complicity is
Robert Alter's "*Tristram Shandy* and the Game of Love," *American Scholar* 37
(1968): 316-23, which unfortunately damages its argument by conflating
Sterne and Tristram. Also see Towers, "Sterne's Cock and Bull Story," and
Frank Brady, "*Tristram Shandy:* Sexuality, Morality, and Sensibility," *ECS* 4
(1970): 41-56.

also performs another act of salvage. He makes us feel that the analogies between the two frustrated systematics show them as true brothers, who produce their seemingly opposed forms from the same impulses. Our amused scorn for their professional activities turns to generous indulgence when those activities become autobiography and proof of familial bonds. This sort of redemption costs Walter and Toby as much as the reworking of their methods. Tristram by analogy portrays them as he does himself, in social undress at the table or hearthside. Although the normative image of a man speaking to men, however, suits memoirs perfectly, it makes rational, Hermetic philosophy look emptily grandiose, and military monomania look unworthy. The generic form of memoirs, too, lets Tristram's Shandeian obsessions be consonant with his professional requirements, but his father and uncle, as unwitting autobiographers, have no professional way of justifying their quirks. His analogical method, in short, transplants Walter and Toby into a mode in which he alone consciously works, and which is alien to their intentions. They gain our good feelings and lose our respect. Yet Tristram leaves us no more flattering alternative idiom within which we can imagine them. If they are not simply to be obscure failures, he implicitly argues, they must be pulled out of time and absorbed into his exegetical, redemptive system. There and there only, like marbled pages or buttered buns, do they take on their fullest and best-of-all-possible meanings.[14]

14. Walter and Toby become atemporal, with no capacity for change, fit for the pictorial vignettes which, as William V. Holtz notes, are static elements. *Image and Immortality: A Study of "Tristram Shandy"* (Providence: Brown University Press, 1970), pp. 106-15. I am unsympathetic with Benjamin H. Lehman's eloquent "Tristram understands [the Shandys] all, and the power of imagination that makes that possible dissolves the loneliness in him." "Of Time, Personality, and the Author," reprinted in *Laurence Sterne: A Collection of Critical Essays*, ed. John Traugott (Englewood Cliffs, N.J.: Prentice-Hall, 1968), p. 28. The statement is a tautology: Tristram understands them because he cannot tell us anything about them that he does not understand. The logical extensions of what he shows us form the limit of Walter's and Toby's implied being.

As though in return for his family's easy submission to him, Tristram orchestrates his handling of them and gives them (and himself) more comparative dignity by mauling the socially reverenced: Walter and Toby are lifted above Locke, whose theories turn out to be irredeemably reductive.[15] Tristram picks no serious quarrel with what Locke says, but shows it to be irrelevant in the face of historical fact such as his memoirs provide, and pretentiously somber if one sees life in its absurd particularity, as his memoirs try to do (II, 2; II, 8). Nor can Locke's categories even cover what they claim to, as Tristram proves in "THE AUTHOR's PREFACE" (III, 20), when he pretends to discuss wit and judgment. He arrives at his supposed thesis about these two faculties after some twenty paragraphs of scudding through false authorities, petty scatology, mechanistic metaphors, fits of rapture, geographical excursions (leading to more mechanistic metaphors), a "dialectic induction" about the confusion of systems, and a quotation from Rabelais about the "laudable desire for knowledge." The quotation comes from a section in which Rabelais is talking not about learning but about prophesy, so that Tristram's authority for his mundane allusion, to a chair, really implies that he is about to draw occult meaning from it.[16] Nothing could be less Lockean and thus so perfect a point for Tristram to tell the reader about Lockean distinctions. He does so with a metaphor: wit and judgment are complementary like

15. Sterne's favorable attitude toward Locke is documented by Wilbur L. Cross, *The Life and Times of Laurence Sterne* (New York: Macmillan, 1909), p. 282, and discussed by Ernest Tuveson, "Locke and Sterne," in *Reason and the Imagination: Studies in the History of Ideas, 1600-1800*, ed. J. A. Mazzeo (New York: Columbia University Press, 1962), pp. 255-77. The parodic use of Locke in *Tristram Shandy* is discussed at length by John Traugott, *Tristram Shandy's World: Sterne's Philosophical Rhetoric* (Berkeley and Los Angeles: University of California Press, 1954), pp. 3-75.

16. The passage that Tristram quotes, from Chapter 16 of Rabelais' third book, comes in a discussion between Pantagruel and Epistemon about consulting a woman who may be a sibyl or a witch.

the knobs on the back of a chair, which have "sense and symmetry" only in tandem. Therefore, he ends, "your graver gentry" (including "the great *Locke*") should never have hailed judgment and "halloo'd . . . boisterously" at wit. The reader may be too giddy at this point to pick holes in Tristram's outrageously specious analogy. Knobs are "the highest and most ornamental parts" of a chair in terms of location and utility; wit and judgment, of a human in terms of dignity. This play on words, which makes hierarchy no more than physical, follows all too well from other mechanistic metaphors in the earlier parts of the chapter, reducing even them from serious causal explanations (the climatic influence on mind) to non-sense through carrying mechanical imagery to deliberate absurdity. The chair metaphor, although witty in the Lockean sense, argues for complementarity of wit and judgment only by abandoning judgment—the discrimination of ideas—completely. The chapter as a whole, worse yet, demonstrates neither wit nor judgement. It works much less by any appeal to the faculties of the mind than by tone—a dizzy élan in the prose, trumped-up pedantry that throws guilt by association on Locke, a breaking of convention in placing the "Preface" so as to warn the reader that nothing closely reasoned is on its way. The argument about Locke's categories is in fact a mock argument by which his categories are bypassed, placing him lower in Tristram's hierarchy than Walter and Toby, whose methods can be revamped.

Tristram's own system, which one might (overphilosophically) label "sensationalistic egoism," is expressed in the memoirs. If this expression of it is adequate to experience, Tristram has mastered his heritage by trapping his world in an iron web of analogy. We prefer, however, to consider him a third familial fly as well as the mechanician spider. We are not eager to be bound to such complicity as Tristram's "egoism" demands, which is as much greater than the complicity asked by Robinson Crusoe, say, or the narrator of *Tom Jones*, as

Tristram is more eccentric and addled than they. It is also as much harder to maintain as the alternatives to the narrator's point of view in *Tristram Shandy* are more appealing and overt. Our alignment of Tristram and his family involves our assuming that Sterne's novel treats Tristram as he has treated his elders: the novel is a redemptive, exegetical structure within which he and his memoirs are redefined. Failures in one genre become autobiography in another; wrongheaded individual exclusiveness takes on value as one point of view within a complementarity.

Our preferences for this kind of reading are reinforced in two ways. One is that Tristram's adequacy is enveloped in a cloud of doubt through analogy and pattern. He himself makes us so sensitive to innuendo, he himself so often teases us into taking hints for truths, that he cannot escape the effects of these doubts. Analogy, for example, calls his disinterest into question, by implying that his system responds to a temperamental legacy from the Shandys rather than to objective experience. His confessed and self-evident "thousand weaknesses both of body and mind" (I, 2) strengthen the analogy and blight his credibility. We see, besides, that all his ills of body and mind—his prenatally shattered sense of time, his squashed nose and ominous name, and his impromptu circumcision—record the evils of Shandy systems. Are his memoirs likely to be different? Even the truth as he perceives it seems to be too various and unwieldy for his memoirs (e.g., III, 23), which leaves every reason to wonder if his methods do not reduce or cripple reality as his father's and uncle's have reduced and crippled him. Our direct response to these analogies reverberates against Tristram's continual satire of systems other than his own—Locke's, the critics' (I, 9; III, 12), guidebooks' (VII, 5, 9), and theologians' (I, 20; IV, 26-9). The only way he could expect to be spared from the momentum of such satire is if we had to accept his system in order to enjoy the satire; we do not, and his is not spared.

Our preference for evaluating Tristram as we do his family is reinforced in a second way: his "sensationalism" diverts us from the simplicity of feeling in which, as Toby's various relationships (with Le Fever, with Trim, with Walter, with the fly) show us, true humanity abides. Because all ideas must have external correlates, Tristram likes to reduce all matters to sensibilia. Wit and judgment become knobs on a chair (III, 20), the mind resembles red wax (II, 2), memoirs are machines with "digressive and progressive movements" (I, 22), the Shandy family turns into a sort of "*Dutch* silk-mill" (V, 6), and poor Walter, after the baby has been misnamed, is spoken of in terms of "a rotation of the same ascending and descending movements," involved in a distress which is a "disorderly transport of the humours" because of events with "dark sides" and "crannies" (IV, 17).

It is no wonder, then, that the celebrated pathos of his book must be put in terms of mechanics. The incident of Toby and the fly (II, 12) begins with chemistry ("a peaceful, placid nature,—no jarring element in it,—all was mixed up so kindly within him") and ends with Hartleyan music (an "action . . . in unison to my nerves . . ., which instantly set my whole frame into one vibration of most pleasurable sensation"). Tristram begins his pathetic meeting with Maria in a flurry of mechanics (IX, 24): "[I] felt the kindliest harmony vibrating within me, with every oscillation of the chaise alike; . . . every thing I saw, or had to do with, touch'd upon some secret spring either of sentiment or rapture." In a fit of enthusiasm at a tender cadence, he springs from his chaise to help her, and returns to it "with broken and irregular steps" in sympathetic rhythm, one is led to assume, with the tune she plays on her pipe. Tristram's colloquy with the ass (VII, 33) warns against substituting mechanism for feeling: "My heart smites me, that there was more of pleasantry in the conceit, of seeing *how* an ass would eat a macaroon—than of benevolence in giving him one, which presided in the act." Even so, in the next paragraph but one, the combined force of a physiological pun on "ass," of a sympathetic pain in that part of the body when the muleteer strikes "the poor devil's crupper," and an equivocation on Tristram's shocked "Out upon it!" leads inevitably, by associative mechanics, to our being diverted from humane pathos to jokes about Tristram's torn breeches. Tristram is either the helpless prey of his own "vibrations" or is trying cynically to manipulate ours. He, the exhibitionist homme-machine, on one side; the simple candor of Toby, Maria, and the "pensive," "patient" ass on the other: the contrast resembles that in a fourth famous (or notorious) bit of pathos, where Toby's intensity of feeling is lavished on the dying Le Fever, and Tristram's on the ingenious machinery of punctuation and rhythm with which the death agony is mimicked (VI, 10). The scenes involving Toby and the fly, and Maria and her pipe, distract one from act to mechanism by the intrusion of unverifiable and therefore uninformative causes; the scene with the ass and the death of Le Fever, by the author's virtuosity in playing on us in the same rhythmic and vibratory fashion.[17]

When bungling, gaudy, pert, lip-licking Tristram irks us, we have additional impetus to take his author's privileges from him and read the book as Sterne's novel rather than as Tristram's memoirs. This is an aesthetically satisfying option when, intermittently, we feel uneasy, claustrophobic within the insistent egoism of the memoirs. To read *Tristram* as Sterne's novel is to read a controlled book. It sets itself no

17. I read the death of Le Fever as a typically Sternean play on the clash between letter and spirit, and would apply to it Gilpin's formula: "If . . . in literary . . . composition you endeavour to draw the reader, or the spectator from the *subject* to the *mode of executing it,* your affectation disgusts." William Gilpin, *Three Essays* (1792) (3rd ed., London, 1808), p. 18. For contrary readings of this passage, see Ian Watt, "The Comic Syntax of *Tristram Shandy,*" in *Studies in Criticism and Aesthetics, 1660-1800,* ed. Howard Anderson and John S. Shea (Minneapolis: University of Minnesota Press, 1967), pp. 315-31; and Melvyn New, *Laurence Sterne as Satirist: A Reading of "Tristram Shandy"* (Gainesville: University of Florida Press, 1969), pp. 150-52.

extravagant tasks but portrays the portrayable, Tristram's attempts to write memoirs, in terms of linear chronology. Sterne's novel has no conflicts between mimesis and rhetorical demands. It follows through on its analogies, reinterpreting Tristram exactly as he has reinterpreted Walter and Toby. Its unseen author has no ulterior motive in trying to make us see things his way, no a priori schemes or family legacies that we can detect. He permits us simple feeling, often in the form of annoyance at Tristram. He does not compel us to adopt a system; in fact, he shows us reasons not to adopt any except the systems of order and inquiry through which Tristram's chosen genre undergoes modification by analogy with his elders' chosen genres.[18]

When the mangled memoirs become a successful novel, the Shandys, as satiric agents, temper each other. Tristram's hierarchy is modified because Sterne, unlike Tristram, denies the adequacy of any one point of view. Two of the three Shandy men, however, have privileged positions. Toby, because his system takes in the smallest area of experience, most often eludes system and can exercise spontaneous feeling. Tristram, because he can recognize his elders' follies, can reach a level of skepticism denied them. As a result, each of these two men, as we shall see, has a limited positive potency in the real world. Toby can launch the obscure, painful, but heroic career of young Le Fever as a military complement to his otherwise ephemeral hobbyhorse. Tristram's memoirs, alone of the three men's hobbyhorses, find a public and actual success in doing some of what Tristram wants to do. No such presents come to Walter, although within the group of Shandys his energy and efficiency—it is he, we cannot forget, who owns, finances, and directs Shandy Hall—give him enough

---

18. Melvyn New documents fully and shrewdly the Shandys' deficiencies, Tristram's included; I disagree with the thesis for which he does this, that all the Shandys are principally satiric butts, but find a great many of his analyses acute.

personal force to keep an analogical equilibrium with his brother and son. Outside the group of the Shandys, in the real world represented by the subsidiary characters, however, he lacks their strengths.

Minor characters emerge from the matrix of the Shandy men. Each of the men is associated with a woman (Walter with two, in his two roles as head of the family and master of the Hall) who shows us his futility in dealing with the world. Images of war emblazon the Widow Wadman so that she forces Toby's retreat from both of the soldier's traditional fields of conquest, sex and battle. Mrs. Shandy and Susannah have a hand in the collapse of every one of Walter's schemes for his son, from the moment of Tristram's begetting to his being put in breeches. As to Tristram's own "dear, dear" Jenny, we hardly know what to say about her, a faithful wraith, save that she appears in connection with ideas of deprivation, poverty (I, 18), offending the world (IV, 32), "eternal squabbles" (V, 24), sexual frustration (VIII, 11; perhaps VII, 13), or the ravages of age (IX, 8).

The subsidiary men, on the other hand, extend the actions of the Shandy men to the next level of efficacy in the real world. Tristram, of course, has no male companion, but his counterpart is Yorick, who sustains as a character the role that Tristram takes as author: the dying, misunderstood, harried, but jaunty moral jester. Hence Tristram cultivates Yorick's history early in Volume I (10-12), where it is used to introduce a tone and values, and later lets it lie fallow, once his own character is firmly set. When on occasion Tristram needs a spokesman within the action of the book, Yorick reappears. A much more obvious version of this relationship appears in Toby and Trim, captain and corporal, *caput* and *corpus* of the military endeavor. If the variously crippled Toby keeps being trapped when translating letter (Walter's or the Widow's) into spirit, or spirit (patriotic fervor) into letter, Trim provides a model of interpretive action. His understanding of the green, his stick (IX, 4) and hat (V, 7), the borrowed sermon (II, 17), and the formulaic catechism (V, 32) prove his potency to clear up his master's muddles. Trim shows us the implications of Tobyism unfettered from Toby, Yorick the implications of active Tristramism as Tristram would like us to conceive it.

Walter has Obadiah to act for him as he has Susannah to thwart him, but Obadiah is worth attention only as an example of the theory of Christian names: his means "servant of the Lord." Far more complex is Dr. Slop, who extends Walter's ideas into action by serving as a cathode around which Tristram's vigorous anti-Catholic satire encrusts itself. The eventual referent of this satire, both attacked and shielded by it, as we shall see, is Walter himself. Slop comes into Shandy Hall because Walter, who has "peremptorily insisted" on invoking a clause in his marriage contract (I, 15), needs a "scientifick operator" to deliver, according to system, a child misbegotten by system. The "scientifick operator" appears with "instruments of salvation and deliverance" (II, 11), the mechanical means akin to Walter's political and familial theories: they are a baptismal "squirt" for salvation, an embryotomy hook for deliverance, a *"tire tête"* for dragging out a dead fetus (by the noblest portion of its anatomy), and of course the famous forceps that crush Toby's knuckles to a jelly (III, 16) and squash Tristram's nose.[19] As Walter has insisted on the binding contract and, shortly thereafter, on "the monarchical system of domestick government established in the first creation of things by God" (I, 18), so the Catholic Slop brings with him constraint and absolutism, in the forceps, his own squat and distorted figure, and his apology for the Inquisition with its "racks and instruments of torment" (II, 17) like those

19. When Slop reappears (VI, 3) he makes a weapon of another instrument of healing, the cataplasm for Tristram's impromptu circumcision, by throwing it in Susannah's face. Arthur H. Cash has discussed in detail the tools Slop carries, in "The Birth of Tristram Shandy: Sterne and Dr. Burton," in *Studies in the Eighteenth Century*, ed. R. F. Brissenden (Canberra: Australian National University Press, 1968), pp. 133-54.

in his knotted baize bag. Walter's peevish retaliation on his wife, which leads to his invoking the clause in the contract and thus to maiming his son, has its grotesque echo in that immense engine for destructive passion, the curse of Ernulphus (III, 11), in which a physician invokes a litany of spiritual and physical disease, "non sit in eo sanitas."

Yorick, the sane Quixote, proclaims Tristram's personality free from Shandeism, within the novel; loyal and affectionate Trim allows Toby to shine forth disencumbered; the normative force of a Yorick or a Trim makes clearer, by analogy, his counterpart's shortcomings and virtues. Walter, as I have said, has no privileged position like his brother's and son's, and can have no normative extension like Trim or Yorick. Therefore, Slop, a vitriolic absolutist, must clarify Walter's subacid authoritarianism by showing us how evil the potential of Walter's attitudes is, and also how mild is their actuality. The job of these three subsidiary men has to be done early, and is essentially done by the end of Volume II, Sterne's first installment in December 1759. In these two volumes, and the next two, Tristram wants not only to etch the characters of his elders and himself, but also to set up contrasts between them. Yorick, Trim, and Slop help him do this through his satire on Catholicism. At the end of the sermon on conscience, Yorick, a Protestant commentator, joins the religious and civic duties of the individual in a political metaphor: conscience is "like a *British* judge in this land of liberty and good sense, who makes no new law, but faithfully declares that law which he knows already written" (II, 17). Tristram, writing during war against popish France, loyally dedicates his book to Pitt. What else could be expected from a descendant of great-uncle Hammond Shandy, a soldier in Monmouth's anti-Catholic rebellion (III, 10)? What else from a man born on November 5, which, as the standard services on that day reminded everyone, commemorates both the Gunpowder Plot and William of Orange's landing at Torbay? Mechanical logic, if nothing else, would make Tristram an enemy of the religious and political authoritarianism that French popery stood for. His uncle Toby has fought Protestant battles in the field under William III and on the bowling green under Marlborough. "Lillabullero," Toby's favorite whistling tune, comes from the Revolution of 1688 against the Catholic James: he whistles it as loudly as he can through the Catholic oath of Ernulphus. Toby's agent, his batman Trim, is really James Butler, a loyal version of James Butler that Duke of Ormonde who took a principal part in the Protestant wars, who was wounded like Trim at Landen (II, 5), and who, despite his later defection to the Pretender, remained proof against all lures to abandon the Protestant religion.

Walter has no direct regard for Catholicism either (II, 17), but he thinks England in little danger "of losing our liberties by *French* politicks or *French* invasions" (I, 18) and is "hugely tickled" (IV, 31)—unlike Toby—by the Catholic sophistries at the Anglican visitation dinner (IV, 29). He is linked with Slop in the way we have seen, and Slop's deformities are those of Catholicism. The "squirt" of this accoucheur, as he likes to Frenchify his profession (II, 12), is the device praised by the Sorbonneans Le Moyne, De Romigny, and De Marcilly, who pronounce on prenatal baptism by a parody of sexual intercourse, *"par le moyen d'une* petite canulle" (I, 20). Slop's fondness for the Inquisition and his use of Ernulphus come naturally to a man who prides himself on his church's demands for unquestioning reverence: "If, in our communion, Sir, a man was to insult an Apostle,—a saint,—or even the paring of a saint's nail,—he would have his eyes scratched out" (II, 17). Even without Slop, the logic-chopping of the Sorbonne and the imaginary grandeur of dogma would come too close to Walter for comfort. Through Slop, Catholicism grafts Walter's activities into the real world, where they have real consequences. In contrast, not until VI, 32, and then in extremely different terms, does Tristram bring Toby to face the real world of patriotism and valor amid blood and shrapnel.

One gains insight into Sterne's procedures by turning from the first three volumes, which contain most of the matters we have been discussing, to the last three volumes of the book. In those volumes, we find the same materials given order by the same matrix of Shandy men, but for a different inquiry: Toby's romance with the Widow, introduced near the end of Volume VI, becomes the principal topic for analogy and modification. Slop has disappeared, and so has the kind of anti-Catholic charges associated with him; new ones must be developed, fit for the specific job of commenting on Toby's genuine purity and the Widow's frank lust. We can see how that is done by looking first at the Shandy matrix. Toby's purity, in these volumes, is set against Walter's sardonic misogyny, Tristram the author's sardonic prurience, and Tristram the character's romantic wistfulness about grisettes and peasants, the unattainable and the picturesque. Of the two possibilities open to Toby with the Widow, Walter reflects the pain of commitment, Tristram the pain of privation. Through narrative, Trim exposes to Toby both the entrapment Walter fears and the futile longing Tristram suffers; his modified personal versions use the idea of repression, associated with Catholicism through the Slop section and the tale of Slawkenbergius. The more innocent version of captive desire is that of the fair beguine (VIII, 20, 22), who caritably massages Trim's leg with ever-lengthening strokes till he comes to aposiopesis.[20] The more malign is that of Trim's brother Tom, locked in the Inquisition's dungeons for his frank ecumenical concord with a Jew's widow over satisfying natural appetites (IX, 4-7).

20. For the shady reputation of the German beguines, see Louis Ellies du Pin, *A New History of Ecclesiastical Writers* . . ., 3 vols. (3rd ed., Dublin, 1732-34), 2: 555; and Collier's Moréry, *The Great Historical . . . Dictionary*, 2 vols. (2nd ed., London, 1701), s.n. "beguards, and beguines." Although those in seventeenth-century Flanders had no long-standing charges levelled against them, Sterne may have counted on dubious connotations still clouding the name of the order.

These stories, with their force as analogues to Toby's
options, spring in turn from a pair of Tristram's stories that
closely precede them. We have a saint's chastening her body
with hot spikes (VIII, 17)—shades of the kicked-out corking
pin used for warmth by Widow Wadman (VIII, 9)!—called
"pricks which enter'd the flesh of St. *Radagunda* in the desert,
which in your road from FESSE to CLUNY, the nuns of that name
will shew you for love" (VIII, 17). "Fesse" is French and
"clunis" Latin for "buttock," so that this spiritual voyage
becomes a shifting of hams with "pricks" *in media re*. Since the
tale has to do with the lustful Widow's having snared Toby in
his sentry box, the physical entrapment of the cloistered nuns
and immured saint, for such she was, answers to Walter's
fears. Trim's beguine, who appears three chapters later, confirms the innuendos about the nuns' "love." The other story of
Tristram's, a book earlier, also has to do with nuns and
confinement, false chastity, and double entendres. The abbess
of Andoüillets (VII, 20-25) goes off to cure her stiff leg or
"white swelling" (literally, a watery tumor; in slang, a pregnancy).[21] She has tried to cure it with the thigh-bone of an
impotent man, through a kind of dry intercourse by proxy
with someone who could not have a "stiff leg" of the sexual
sort. Now she takes as a companion not a sciatical invalid but
a novice "who had been troubled with a whitloe in her middle
finger, by sticking it constantly into the abbess's cast poultices,
&c." These floating bits of smut—for they are not really
charges—eventually settle on target. Fearful of being ravished
when the balky mules strand them, the nuns urge on the
beasts by crying out the muleteer's imprecations, "foutre"
and "bougre," syllable by syllable so as not to say anything
improper; but aside from their verbal casuistry, they are pretty
plainly bawling out invitations to the acts, fore and aft, that

21. Francis Grose, *A Classical Dictionary of the Vulgar Tongue* (3rd ed., 1796),
ed. Eric Partridge (London: Routledge & Kegan Paul, 1963), s.n. "white
swelling."

they only claim to fear (cf. VII, 43).[22] If they were not, surely the stiff abbess or the supple novice would have walked back half a hill to collect the errant driver instead of chanting obscenities in the manner of "our complines." These stories show us how natural, how universal, and in its candor how healthily desirable, is the Widow's lustful campaign to capture Toby; and by the same principle of discriminated variety we see the genuine purity (and lamentable barrenness) of Toby the shamefast celibate.

Before closing this discussion, perhaps it would be in place to note how Sterne frees these elements of I-III for their new ends in VII-IX. He uses structural analogy to alter the two principal thematic groupings connected with Slop, absolutism/law and the association of physical mishap with Catholicism/France. The first of these groupings, absolutism/law, is expressed through four documents framed to control any contingencies: the marriage contract, the Sorbonne deliberation, the sermon on conscience, and the curse (I, 15, 20; II, 17; III, 11), on matrimony by rule, salvation and damnation through ritual, and the court of conscience. Each is connected with Slop, who comes because of the contract, comments sourly on the sermon, speaks the curse, and carries the squirt of salvation. Sterne discharges this group by adding to it the tale of Slawkenbergius, formally continuous with the others in its attack on Catholicism and its bilingualism, like the Sorbonne deliberation and the curse (and even the contract, with its legal jargon); but absolutism/law, far more tangential although still present in the university debates, touches Protestants, the Lutheran Antinosarians, as well as Catholics. Shortly thereafter, Walter suffers from the Anglican curate who bindingly misnames the child Tristram after himself, and from Anglican

22. As Wilbur Cross hints, p. 336, these obscenities had been used, or, rather, referred to by their first letters, in Gresset's "Ver-Vert" (1734): Diderot amuses himself with them in his imitation of Sterne, *Jacques le Fataliste*. (*Oeuvres romanesques*, ed. Henri Bénac [Paris: Garnier, 1962], pp. 701-02, 714-15).

hagglers whose love of Catholic decretals and concubines makes them much like their popish brethren (IV, 14, 27-29). The old association, based on Walter's willfulness, a strict division between Catholics and Protestants, and the coordinating figure of Slop, now dissolves.

Similarly, Sterne discharges the second thematic grouping, the connection of physical mishap with Catholicism/France. The grouping depends on Dr. Slop and on the wounding of Toby and Trim in Protestant wars abroad, as well as the Sorbonneans, Inquisitors, and Ernulphus's curse. Sterne removes Catholicism from the grouping in the next analogue, Bobby Shandy's death just before his prospective Grand Tour (IV, 31-V, 14), and keeps it tangential though present in Volume VI, with young Le Fever's sickness at Marseille, the death of his mother at Breda, and of his father on the way to Flanders. Catholicism once more is not in question during the first half of Volume VII, when Tristram runs from death in France, bitterly contrasting travel guides, the textbook "culture" of a Grand Tour, with whatever is human rather than national across the Channel. Here the new associative structure, although it relies on the old, supports cosmopolitanism instead of the old opposite value, patriotism. Thus Tristram regains health and joy in Provence, pricking his horse toward "the ring of pleasure" (VII, 43), and our minds turn toward sex, as fits Toby's romance, not death. France is redeemed, Catholicism given the new turn we have already remarked.

Our discussion of *Tristram* has not yet taken us far enough to see if it shares the sequential procedures of *Rasselas*, such as the use of masses and rhythms, associationist transitions, or a fulcrum corresponding to a dramatic peripeteia. We have, however, seen how fully Sterne employs analogy to constitute his world of Shandys and to allow inferences about it. The portrayal of the family, the use of surrogate characters like Yorick and Slop, and the deployment of associative groupings like that around Toby and the Widow, all need analogy and discriminated variety. Tristram's reinterpretation of Walter's and Toby's hobbyhorses, and ours of Tristram's memoirs, need analogy and modification. The multiple perspectives of the Shandys, complemented by Slop, Yorick, Trim, and the Widow, also involve modifications; so much, in fact, is modified that *Tristram*, like *Rasselas*, can offer no more than an equilibrium without resolution, a tale of (depleted) cock and bull in which *doing* is foolish but necessary, *being* is valuable but nearly sterile. Every assessment we can make of the Shandys is provisional; and as with homilies in *Rasselas*, received ideas in *Tristram*, be they Locke's or travel books', tend to be irrelevant even when true.

As in *Rasselas*, the central character's systematic reading of the world creates the logic of the book, while the author keeps hands off. Tristram's system and reading are not, of course, like Rasselas's. For him in recollection, analogy can have no predictive force, although it has for us, who know that it is constitutive of his system. Nonetheless, Tristram does move forward in time, unlike the impersonal makers of systems, such as Locke and de Piles, and his elders, whose systems, as we have seen, are timeless (Walter's) or temporally fragmented (Toby's). Tristram seeks to squeeze his mental life, a temporal continuum, into the form of a book, sometimes adapting mind to conventional book form, sometimes vice versa, always reducing reality to a flow of sensibilia assessed from a single perspective. His systematic reduction through time gives us several points of similarity to Rasselas. Both heroes come from all-expenses-paid utopias on which reality rudely intrudes. Both fall into systems that derive from what the utopia tries, but fails, to provide. Both engage, with mixed success, in observation and appraisal so as to make subjective perceptions tally with objective norms of truth: a relationship and procedures that I take to be the core of any epistemology. Both, in different ways, insist that truth must be felt as well as abstractly known. That is why Rasselas cannot accept Imlac's word, and why the incremental repetitions bring events closer to the travellers. That is also why Tristram can absorb the personal systems of Walter and Toby, neither of which involves empirical appraisal, and can modify them so that they do, when they become autobiographical. Conversely, the systems of a Locke or a de Piles, which compete with Tristram's as systems of empirical appraisal, are discarded as irrelevant because they have no roots in individual human life and feeling.

II: EPISODES AND VOLUMES

Rasselas has groups made up of chapters; *Tristram* has chapters, episodes or narrative chunks (the episode of Tristram and the ass, of the abbess of Andoüillets, of the courtship of Tom Butler and the Jew's widow), and volumes. For associative transitions we may look principally to the chapters and episodes, connected by the mental processes of continuity and resemblance. For rhythms and fulcrums, we may look principally to the volumes. The most important chief procedures remain analogy and modification, so that each unit in the book—character, event, episode—keeps its own use and integrity, but as part of a larger discordia concors or equilibrium that itself is open to modification. For an example, we may look at the loose episode of eight chapters that lead to the Widow Wadman's siege of Toby. From the moment that we turn from "matter copulative and introductory" to the Widow herself, her thoughts bursting from her bedroom and into Toby's as she kicks out the corking pin that seals her in her night-shift (VIII, 9), we enter upon a crowd of puns in which, through words, objects and ideas constantly change place. The eleven years of European war, which distract Toby and insure peace between him and the Widow, are to him a paradoxical "armistice," but to her, with different equipment in mind, a "vacancy" (VIII, 10). Tristram explains the verbal discrepancy by fixing happily, but occultly, upon anatomy, discussing *"cock'd old hat"* and "wide difference" in this chapter, "infernal nitch," "centre of the milky-way," "all that is hirsute and gashly," and "a finger in the pye" in the next.[23] Meanwhile, the roles of the Widow and Toby shift to Jenny and Tristram (VIII, 11) with a change in point of view from the woman's to the man's, and a change in tone from the objective and comic to the subjective and tragicomic. The metaphoric "old hat" of Chapter 10 turns into Tristram's actual "furr'd cap" of Chapter 11, a pudendal cap twisted on his finger and pressed about his head; the nonmetaphorical heat of the Widow, implied in her kicking out the corking pin that kept "shivering and tempestuous nights" from under her shift, leads to Tristram's "infernal nitch" in *"Terra del Fuogo,"* and so on to the "devil," whose "inflammatory dishes" heat Tristram's—at the least (and perhaps the most)—"imagination." A little later, heat and head (both phallic and imaginative) recur in the image of the man who "may be set on fire [by love] like a candle, at either end—provided there is a sufficient wick standing out." Wicks, of course, bring us back to engines of war (an image revived in Chapter 14), and Chapter 16 presents the widow's attempt to light Toby, "like a prodigal's candle, . . . at both ends at once" in his sentry box. She tries to make his passions "catch fire" by returning to literalism and commandeering his hot "tobacco-pipe." Finally, Tristram returns to the corking pin with which he began. Calling forth the documentary gravity of an author, he tells us about the holes pricked in the map that bears witness to, and has been made a map of, the sentry-box skirmish in which Toby is "sore

23. James Work, in his edition of *Tristram* (New York: Odyssey Press, 1940), glosses "old hat," p. 549. See Eric Partridge, *A Dictionary of Slang and Unconventional English* (5th ed., New York: Macmillan, 1961), s.n. "old hat," "milk." In their lengthy entry under "monosyllable," John S. Farmer and W. E. Henley give "old hat," some five variants on "centre," three on "milk," and two on "niche." *Slang and its Analogues, Past and Present*, 7 vols. (n.p., 1890-1904).

push'd on both his wings." It is these pin holes that remind
Tristram of the "pricks which enter'd the flesh of St. *Radagunda*," an image that we may now see suits with the notion of
the devil as the father of appetites (VIII, 11), invoked euphe-
mistically by the "sore-push'd" soldier when he finds "his
centre [in] disorder": "—The duce take it! said my uncle *Toby*"
(VIII, 16).

This sequence of chapters shuttles between objects and
words in terms of several points of view: Mrs. Wadman's, two
of Tristram's (as objective narrator and as Jenny's companion),
Toby's, even Walter's (philosophical in Chapter 13, witty in
Chapter 15), and perhaps by innuendo St. Radagunda's. To
understand what is happening, that is, we must know something of the mental habits of each of these characters, whether
he is someone being analyzed (like Widow Wadman), being
used as an example (St. Radagunda), or merely filling a
neglected post (Walter, after Tristram has so committed himself to personal reflections about Jenny and himself that he
must temporarily vacate the role of the detached commentator).

This technique of elaborating analogies from multiple points
of view is not the one Tristram always prefers. He is just as
happy modifying a set of analogies through rhetorical means
which are free of points of view. For example, just before the
falling sash circumcises Baby Tristram, we see Walter slowly
composing the useless *Tristrapaedia* (V, 16), and being "hugely
pleased" with the theory that "the life of a writer, whatever he
might fancy to the contrary, was not so much a state of *composition*, as a state of *warfare*; and his probation in it, precisely
that of any other man militant upon earth." The analogies
implicit in this theory are then shrunk. First of all to suffer are
Walter's pretensions to be a warrior, and the similar pretensions that his allusion to the *Cyropaedia* forces upon his son.
Tristram's accident puts an end to both claims: Walter's
"probation" ends in failure, and Tristram himself becomes a

war victim, given that the circumcision is due to Trim's having taken the sash-weights to make demi-culverins for Toby's campaign. As a warrior, poor Tristram's martial models are incapacitated, his namesake and his uncle; as a warrior's victim, he is later to write a genuine, but also mutilated, *Tristrapaedia* of sorts, called *Tristram Shandy*. His maimed talents parallel those of the only authorial warriors, the Shandys, who take part in his *paideia*. Tristram therefore keeps up the imitation by adopting, at the end of the chapter, the "parabolical" and "allegorical" mode his father has just been admiring. Even if he had not been circumcised, he says, time would have crippled Walter, whose written precepts keep lagging behind his son's growth. Walter would have been left "drawing a sun-dial, for no better purpose than to be buried under ground." If Tristram's growth would have led to the burial of a sundial (or son-dial, after the manner, I suppose, of the *Diall of Princes*), Tristram's curtailment leads to the dial's being worthless through the burial of its other requisite, Tristram's gnomon.[24]

24. Tristram may have hit on this metaphor because the name Cyrus means "sun," as Moréry says. *Le Grand Dictionaire historique . . .*, 4 vols. (nlle. ed., Paris, 1707), 2: 457, s.n. "Cyrus." Sterne might have known this from biblical commentaries: Matthew Henry, for instance, says in his discussion of the first chapter of Ezra that "Cyrus," " some say in the Persian language signifies the sun, for he brought light and healing to the church of God, and was an eminent type of Christ the sun of righteousness." *An Exposition on the Old and New Testament* (1704-10), 3 vols. (London, n.d.). The *Cyropaedia*, I might add, was a perfect book for Walter to choose, since it was widely regarded as a romance reflecting what ought to be, not a history bound to what was. This judgment, more mildly stated, seems to date from Cicero, who is quoted directly by Moréry, s.n. "Xenophon," and by Charles Rollin in both *The Method of Teaching and Studying the Belles Lettres* (1726-28), 3 vols. (6th ed., London, 1769), 2: 389, and his *Ancient History* (1730-38), 2 vols. (London, n.d.), Bk. 4, chap. 1. See also Degory Wheare, *The Method and Order of Reading Both Civil and Ecclesiastical Histories*, tr. Edmund Bohun (3rd ed., London, 1698), p. 62; and Edward Manwaring, *An Historical and Critical Account of the Most Eminent Classic Authors in Poetry and History* (London, 1737), pp. 243-48.

Walter's borrowed theory works out so awry that one may
wonder about his source, Giovanni della Casa (Tristram's
"John de la Casse"). From a courtesy book, *Galateo*, Walter
makes a social allegory, having to do with "prejudices of
education." Tristram does not contradict his father on the
surface. When we read, however, about "advantages of
nature, which should have pricked [della Casa] forwards,"
about lying "under an impuissance," and about devils breaking "out of their holes to cajole him," we may guess that Tristram has in mind something of della Casa's a great deal less
social and proper than the *Galateo*. Later, in fact, he refers to
the *Galateo* itself as a *"nasty* Romance" (IX, 14), presumably
confusing it with other works. What these might be we can
discover by looking into Bayle, and to a lesser extent Moréry.
They both mention accusations that della Casa favored sodomy; and even more to the point, Bayle quotes verses in which
della Casa confesses his genital insufficiency.[25] If these are the
sources of Tristram's references, the double entendres that
infiltrate the three paragraphs about della Casa make perfect
sense at this sexual and surgical moment, just as does his and
Walter's image of the warrior. Neither image is apt in the way
that Walter intended: the bloody reality of window-sash war
destroys the ideal of the warrior, and the genital reality behind
della Casa's reference to the devil's temptation of writers
destroys the ideal of social education as Walter conceives it.
Through the contextual ambiguity of words, della Casa can be
labelled a genuine "parabolic" authority for the fate of the
authors, fathers and sons both.

Another, final example of the verbal manipulation of analogies shows a third sort of technique at work. In the episode

25. *The Dictionary Historical and Critical of Mr. Peter Bayle*, 5 vols. (2nd ed.,
London, 1734-38), 5: 422-23, s.n. "Francis de la Mothe le Vayer," Note E.
Della Casa, using the image of bread for his own genitals and that of the oven
for women's, excuses sodomy because *"il mio pan sia piccolino, / E'l forno
delle Donne un po grandetto."* Burton gives no anatomical details, but
simply mentions the praise of sodomy (*Anatomy* III.2.i.2).

just before the one that we have been discussing, Walter and Trim orate at the death of Bobby Shandy. Walter, soaring with Cicero, draws tears from his sympathetic brother only because the learned irrelevance of his harangue makes him look as if "his misfortunes had disordered his brain"; Trim, with a homely and heartfelt reflection, draws real tears even from the self-interested servants (V, 2-10). The episode, a pat comparison, is done with great control and brio, one element of which is of special interest here. That is Tristram's light suffusion of Trim's speech with sexual references. Walter, we must remember, has ended his oration with anecdotes of the deaths of great Romans, rearranging the order of his source, Bacon's essay "On Death," so as to end with Augustus Caesar, who died "in a compliment . . . to his wife." The innocence of this phrase does not last long, for he exploits its ambiguity by continuing (V, 4) with one further anecdote meant to "crown all" like "the gilded dome that covers in the fabrick." The praetor Cornelius Gallus, he tells Toby, died in coition. This is, in all senses of the word, an anticlimax. A mere praetor, no more than a namesake and kinsman of the notable Cornelius Gallus (the erotic poet), ought not by rights to be the dome for a fabric of bold emperors, as in Walter's list. Nonetheless, Walter has acted quite according to type in placing above all wit the wit of death in the moment of sexual union; and Tristram has acted likewise by confronting witty Walter with an unforeseen analogy in the person of his own wife, who bursts in, with suspicions of adultery, to lay low his oratorical splendor (V, 12-13). Mrs. Shandy's vanity makes her think that Walter is talking about her when he mentions wives, and of course she is paradoxically right that "every word my father said, was accommodated either to herself, or her family concerns." He *is* orating over her son Bobby. Nonetheless, she manages to modify his classical analogies—she becomes a suspicious Xantippe (V, 13)—so as to join sex and death once more, and spoil proper feeling at the end of the episode.

Sandwiched between the trenchers of Cornelius Gallus's sudden death in the act of generation is Trim's speech about death. Trim does not mention sex, which would be inappropriate here for him. Sex is never inappropriate for Tristram, though, and he is able to make the structural analogue complete by using his narrative voice to insert double entendres into the episode. Thus Tristram alters the green gown that Susannah covets into the green gown of tumbles in the grass, and Trim's grave hat into the "old hat" of the pudenda. By the next chapter, when Trim proclaims that all flesh is dirt, and everyone makes the metaphor literal by looking at the fat scullion who has been scouring a fish-kettle, the context makes one suspect, rightly, that "fish-kettle" itself is a double entendre.[26] This infusion of sexual suggestiveness works so well that Trim's affecting lament in fact tempers grief by the hint of joy and renewal. Walter's cribbed harangue tries to swamp the experience of sorrow with bucketsful of Cicero, Burton, Bacon, and Pliny. Trim's generalities proceed from the actual event, faced honestly, and are so much better in Tristram's eyes for their empiricism. By adding the servants' responses, and sexual puns between words and objects, Tristram also gives "the powers of the living" an immediacy denied by Walter's speech in its use of ancient history, its connection of sex and death, its plagiarism. Trim and Tristram combine to offer us not only a structural analogue but also an answer to Walter's performance, a modification of it from material that Walter himself employs. Similarly, Tristram modifies our understanding of the Widow's passion for Toby by using the same images (hat, heat, head, devil) to express his own, quite different passion for Jenny; or he modifies his father's use of Giovanni della Casa and the image of the warrior, showing both to be just, but not as Walter intended.

Volumes of *Tristram Shandy* include a series of short epi-

26. Farmer and Henley, s.n. "fish" and "kettle."

sodes, directly juxtaposed or parted by a shorter discursive transition. I propose, without more ado, to examine one volume as an example; Volume VI, where the narrative line is rather thin, will serve the purpose. As in *Rasselas*, we may begin with the chapters, perhaps surprisingly in view of Tristram's playing so fast and loose with the stock forms of authorship, chapters included. Nevertheless, if we do begin with the chapters as a convenience, their feckless appearance turns out to be deceiving. Volume VI has forty chapters, with an introduction and a double conclusion framing equal numbers of chapters more or less about Baby Tristram (2-19) and about Toby (21-38); in the middle (20) stands a transition which begins, openly enough, "We are now going to enter upon a new scene of events," and then takes essential leave of the persons who have appeared in this volume, save for Toby, Trim, and—of course—Tristram. Each half of the volume holds four episodes separated by single chapters of transition. Here the balance ends. Two long episodes of five chapters dominate the first half: the tale of Le Fever (6-10), and Walter's putting his son in breeches (15-19). Each is preceded by a retrospective short episode. The two chapters about Slop's battle with Susannah (3-4) look back to the circumcision in Volume V, and the two about Le Fever's son (12-13), to the death of Le Fever. In the second half of the volume, a more even rhythm reigns. We have an episode of four chapters followed by one of three, both about Toby's green (21-24, 26-28), then one of three chapters (the end of war) followed by one of four (the start of love). This last pair of episodes (30-32, 34-37) leads in turn to one chapter of transition and one that tries to unify the halves of the volume before the conclusion. To the reader of Volume VI, things look less tidy. Sterne takes as much care to hide the arithmetic of his structure as Dr. Johnson takes to push his to the threshold of recognition. In both men's books, however, the rhythms of that structure make themselves felt. Derived as they are from waves of meaning, they change content into form and in turn affect the way we apprehend that content, the way the ideas and events mean what they do.

In the first half of the volume, the two long episodes are the centers of attention. First comes the death of Le Fever, with its earnest pathos, its tender relations between fellow men (master and servant, captain and lieutenant, father and son, innkeeper and guest), its conflicts between the brave spirit and the dying body, between social duty (of servant, of soldier, of curate) and personal feeling. This small monument of caramel stands, in tone and in meaning, opposite the tale of Tristram's breeches. Tender human relations, represented by husband and wife who can be connubial even in a tent on a battlefield (7), turn into the kingly compulsion of a contentious and sexual *lit de justice* (17-18). Le Fever's own battle of body and spirit in bed becomes the Shandys': Walter makes his wife agree with his notions before he agrees to her desires. Walter's research into Roman dress parodies both Le Fevers' real pride in a soldier's uniform; and the nice balance between rank and equality, held throughout the story of Le Fever, reappears in the empty token of the *"Latus Clavus,"* which marked Augustans of "quality and fortune . . . when the slave dressed like his master, and almost every distinction of habiliment was lost" (19).

If young Le Fever, like a true Roman, fights for glory and patriotism, wounded young Tristram is barely a Roman in costume, for Walter does not know that the *latus clavus* was a purple stripe. Hooks and eyes, his way of updating it, create an absurd version of the tokens for young Le Fever's manhood, sword and scabbard (19, 12). Hooks and eyes are also feminine. They were not used for breeches in the seventeenth or eighteenth centuries, but were a characteristic closing for bodices in Sterne's England and for women's tunics in Augustan Rome.[27] Walter Shandy is right that under Augus-

27. C. Willett Cunnington and Phillis Cunnington, *Handbook of English*

tus, the *latus clavus* and the *toga virilis* were assumed by boys at the same time. This fits in well with Tristram's manly breeches. The *toga virilis*, however, was also known as the *toga libera*, because its wearers "enter'd on a State of Freedom, and were deliver'd from the Power of their Tutors and Instructors."[28] Tristram in breeches is, at the age of five, delivered to, not from, his tutor, a post for which young Le Fever is proposed only six weeks before Tristram's accident (VI, 13). Young Le Fever, himself, of course, does leave school before assuming his *toga virilis*, a soldier's uniform with its real *latus clavus*, presumably, of braid. Thus the contrast is extensively and elegantly worked out.

The pair of long episodes, Le Fever's death and Tristram's dressing, are more than foils for each other; they also fit with every other chapter of the half-volume, 1-5 and 11-14. Precocity and courtesy in Tristram's education (2, 5) have to do with the childhood works of charity we see in his proposed educator. Sterne enlarges the analogy through the name Le Fever, which suggests something besides zeal or illness. The French Le Fevres, Protestants, were one of the greatest scholarly families of the seventeenth century: Tanneguy Le

---

Costume in the Eighteenth Century (London: Faber and Faber, 1957): on bodices with hooks and eyes, pp. 121, 130; on buttoned breeches, pp. 66-69, 211. The one use of hooks and eyes for men's clothing that I have discovered in the Cunningtons' handbook is as a closure for heavily embroidered waistcoats, p. 63. Albertus Rubenius, Mr. Shandy's source about Roman dress, says that clasps or latchets were feminine: "hae fibulae . . . quibus muliebres solum tunicae quandoque connecti solitae." *De re vestiaria veterum . . .* (Antwerp, 1665), p. 5.

28. Basil Kennett, *Romae Antiquae Notitia: Or, the Antiquities of Rome* (1696) (11th ed., London, 1746), p. 311. Kennett says on the same page that the donning of the *toga virilis* "capacitated" a young man to serve in the army, which fits Le Fever directly and Tristram the Shandy warrior ironically. Kennett also says that the *toga virilis* was assumed at the age of seventeen; Le Fever must be in his early twenties when he goes to fight the Turks, but Sterne has him leave in "the spring of the year, seventeen" (VI, 12; for his age, cf. VI, 6), perhaps to make the Roman allusion as best he can.

Fevre had a considerable reputation of his own as an editor
and professor of Greek, and—still more impressive—taught
his son-in-law and his daughter, André and Anne Dacier.[29]
The connection with the episode of the *latus clavus* is plain and
is picked up once more in the description of young Le Fever's
education and career under Toby's aegis (12-13), where Greek
and Latin pale before the Christian cause. Of the other
chapters, Slop's and Susannah's lack of charity over their
patient (3-4), and Slop's later slander of Tristram's powers
(14), tie in respectively with Toby's charity to his patient Le
Fever and Walter's attempt to make public proclamation of
Tristram's powers by putting him in breeches. The reviewers'
slander of *Tristram Shandy* (1) leads into these motifs, and is
biographically countered by Tristram's account of his education, formal and sentimental, which the two long episodes
provide. In this sense the half-volume is a defense of the
author. Finally, in the middle of this half-volume (11) comes
Tristram's own concern with his artful rhetoric in describing
Le Fever's death at the end of the previous chapter. Tristram's
historical activities in this chapter, as he examines and describes a pile of manuscript sermons, stand just between the
chronicling (Toby's mode) that marks the history of Le Fever,
and the search for meaning (Walter's mode) that marks the
survey of Roman dress. Yorick's learning and self-approving
oratory point to Walter; his "hussar-like" sermons, which
"skirmish lightly and out of all order, [but] are still auxiliaries
on the side of virtue" point to those good warriors Toby and
the Le Fevers—young Le Fever, in the very next chapter,
leaves the classics to fight the Turks.

---

29. Moréry, 2: 765, s.n. "Fevre," testifies to Le Fevre's genius as a teacher,
not only for explication of texts but also for finding "des agréments infinis"
and for inspiring a true love of belles lettres. Sterne may have been reminded
of this Protestant scholar from his possession of a book by another Le Fevre
(Jacques) about Protestants in France (item 743 in the *Catalogue of Laurence
Sterne's Library*).

As far as one can tell, the first half of Volume VI supplies most of the thematic matter for the second half. I say "as far as one can tell" because by the end of Book V not much new thematic material is left to be introduced, and one cannot prove the provenance of the motifs. None the less, the reader perceives continuity partly in terms of closeness in the process of reading, and in this sense the first part of the volume is of prime importance in understanding the second. All four episodes seem to be parallel to, or to grow from, episodes in the first half of the volume. The relationships become looser, in general, the further the reader gets from the first twenty chapters, with three exceptions. The anti-aphrodisiac breeches that Walter contrives for Toby (36) allude directly to the dressing of Tristram, with a camphorous stench making Toby's breeches as dubious a sign of his manhood as were Tristram's of his. The Shandys hold counsel once more in a "bed of justice" (39), in telling about which Tristram specifically mentions "the affair of the breeches." And there is an attack (38) on critics, followed (40) by squiggly maps of the novel's progress; this looks back pretty directly to the first chapter of the volume, in which Tristram attacks critics with the metaphor of the novelistic journey: "How they view'd and review'd us as we passed over the rivulet at the bottom of that little valley!—and when we climbed over that hill, and were just getting out of sight—good God!" These relatively direct references come at the very end of the volume and seem to be intended to give it coherence as an entity. The same sense of the volume as an entity is implied too by the squiggly maps, which treat each volume as a discrete unit. We have all the more reason, then, to look for analogies within each volume without wandering outside it.

The first two episodes in the second half of Volume VI, dealing with Toby's hobbyhorsical dressing of his green, correspond in general to the preceding episode, Walter's hobbyhorsical dressing of his son. For Walter's ersatz history,

his willful conversion of the public to the private, we have
Toby's staging of the letter and spirit of history. Toby, unlike
Walter, achieves accuracy by being personal, and his use of
clothing humanizes war, mingling the personal with the objectivity of the *Gazette*. Le Fever's legacy, his sword to his
son and his coat to Trim, have been brought from Ireland for
the Flemish campaigns that his death keeps him from joining.
On the Shandy green, Toby uses those clothes to help pursue
those same campaigns to victory. Similarly, Tom's legacy to
Trim, a Montero cap and tobacco pipes, passes into Toby's
scenic stock to outfit his troops and artillery. So dominant is
the image of clothing the green that other garments enter the
text incidentally, to complement these legacies and the comparison with Tristram's breeches. Thus we watch Toby accou-
ter himself in his Ramillies wig (what else?) and regimentals
(24). Thus the buying of the sentry-box replaces an annual suit
of clothes (22). Thus the place is "invested" (21) and given
mortars made from the Shandys' historical jack boots (23).

   The later episodes in the second half of the volume, those in
which Toby gives up war for love (sex and affection), have a
still more complex parentage. Slop's and Susannah's battle of
cataplasms over Tristram's torn prepuce (3) joins war and sex,
as do the Shandys' Sunday night disputes—if "sex" in the first
case, "war" in the second, are taken loosely. Mrs. Le Fever,
conceivably, died at a moment when an act of sex was an
expression of married love, "killed with a musket shot, as she
lay in my [Le Fever's] arms in my tent" at Breda (7). The
fanning out of the motif of sex and affection has its nonsexual
end in the character of Toby, who turns his military relations
with Trim into those of mutual love and respect, who would
nurse Le Fever "as a sick brother officer" (8), who sends young
Le Fever to war with tears and guineas and a father's blessing
(12). The affectionate clothing of the bowling green follows
from these episodes, as does Toby's "apologetical oration" for
war but not for its sufferings (32). Through such a reiterated

association of ideas, built up in our minds by these two blending patterns, war and sex, war and affection, Tristram can make natural to us the transition from the military to the sexual pipe and sentry-box: "You might have . . . shot my uncle *Toby* ten times in a day, through his liver, if nine times in a day, Madam, had not served your purpose" (29). The loving and creative warrior Toby, besieged in the seat of the passions, excites his nephew to more innuendos and his Widow to more expropriations. Tristram plays on the sexual senses of "mole" and "harbour" (34), before "the trumpet of war" is finally dropped for the "sweet instrument" of the Widow Wadman (35). These patterns are rounded off with another Sunday night session of the Shandy *lit de justice*, in which Walter, turning to a military image, says that his brother "may as well batter away his means upon" marriage as anything else. As we have seen earlier, the linkage between war and sex is stock in *Tristram Shandy*. Volume VI shows how the energy of the narrative makes connotations of various sorts cling in differing degrees to such stock ideas and images, a form of discriminated variety.

The long episodes in the first half of the volume are discrete, sharply separated in subject and narrative mode, and set up as antitheses. The four episodes in the second half, however, drift rather easily into one another. Different rhythmic patterns result, augmenting the effect of the change from a section with two long dominating episodes to one in which all four episodes are about the same length. Another development, in the nature of Tristram's presence, further clouds the focus on individual episodes in the second half of the volume. When Baby Tristram is a topic of discussion or a prospective tutee, a patient waiting for his cataplasm or a candidate for classical breeches, then Tristram the Narrator more or less holds his peace. We can barely sense him behind the smooth continuity of chapters. They are regulated by his mind, to be sure, but by a mind with which long acquaintance has made us familiar. At

this point in the book, Tristram's narrative energy strikes us
veterans only when he speaks in his own person. He begins to
do that more as the volume moves on, as though he were
willing to hold back his "opinions" only while he gives us his
"life." For example, after the first chapter, with its attack on
reviewers, Tristram speaks of his own book and abilities only
twice in chapters 2 through 19. He claims that his pen governs
him (6), and that he writes both full and fasting (17); once (11)
he treats the same subject indirectly in discussing the sermons
of Yorick. After Chapter 20, however, in which he announces,
"I must go along with you to the end of the work," he keeps
recurring to the subject of his "flimsy performance" (21), his
inspiration (25, 26), his learning (30), his insertion of a document (31), his strange story and badly woven brain (33) that
leaves him "entangled on all sides of this mystick labyrinth"
(37), his malicious and ignorant reviewers (38), and the
mapping out of his plot (40).

None of these references in chapters 20-40 has anything to
do with characters other than Tristram himself, unlike those in
the first half of the volume, the tacit parallel with Yorick, the
"full and fasting" parallel with Walter's beds of justice, and (to
strain a point) the would-be parallel with Toby in the self-
conscious pathos at the death of Le Fever. These three earlier
comparisons all express Tristram's skill as an author in terms
of those whom he loves or imitates. As he becomes an
independent subject, however, he alters this tone, in part by
shifting to a new objectivity. He begins to look at his tactics and
talents as he looks at those of others, in several different lights.
Thus in the first half of the volume, he teases himself ironically
only once (6); the second half finds him neither so gentle nor so
consistent. One instance may suffice to show what I mean.
Chapter 25 finds his impassioned plea for divine afflatus:
"—Gracious powers! which erst have opened the lips of the
dumb in his distress . . . when I shall arrive at this dreaded
page [the death of Toby], deal not with me, then, with a stinted

hand." Chapter 26 seems to call for inspiration from human flatus: "I would give the shirt off my back to be burnt into tinder, were it only to satisfy one feverish enquirer, how many sparks at one good stroke, a good flint and steel could strike into the tail of it. —Think ye not that in striking these *in*,—he might, peradventure, strike something *out*? as sure as a gun.—" Tristram, in short, treats himself with the same friendly ambiguity as that with which he treats the subject of the surrounding episodes, Toby's bowling green.

Tristram's erratic image of himself is part of a battle plan for the second half of Volume VI, a battle by twilight. Modification becomes so much more pronounced that the clear judgments of the first half of the volume, about Trim's loyalty to Toby or Slop's to himself, for example, melt into an unstable flux of appraisals and emotions. A typical element of the second half has multiple values. Although Walter's amused chagrin and Tristram's amused tenderness channel our reactions to the bowling green, for instance, we cannot help but see it as a happy illusion, a pathetic one, a necessary one, an agent for the deepest friendship, a burden made a thing of joy, a childish obsession, and so on. A mixed list like this could be made for Tristram's memoirs, and by transference, for Toby and Tristram themselves, whom the hobbyhorses express. Analogies yield most of their inferential strength before such a high degree of modification. We can, if we like, draw a formal analogy between the treatment of the green and of the memoirs as Toby maps out his field of combat and Tristram graphs his. Or, as Toby's already equivocal defenses fail before the Widow's assault, we can see Tristram's strong defenses against the critics crumbling and being dismantled as the volume ends. From such analogies, though, unlike those in the first half of the volume, we learn little about either man or either hobbyhorse. No interesting patterns of images or ideals develop; and uncle and nephew are so much alike, at least in this section, that our responses to them overlap markedly.

If we did not have the first half of the volume, the second would represent order without inquiry. Because we do have the first half to make motifs familiar, the second in fact represents a complement to it. A simplicity of emotion subserves precise assessments in chapters 1-19; in chapters 21-40, the same motifs receive an emotional treatment as comprehensive in its way as the earlier judicial treatment is in its.[30] The very nature of our judgments itself is modified as we pass to the second half of the volume. Correspondingly, the nature of Tristram's mental experience, which he is recording for us, is modified, and his announcement of "a new scene of events" in mid-volume represents a pivot not only for the narrative but for Tristram too. By showing his credentials, his education, he has waged war against the critics. Now he chooses to compound with them, albeit truculently, by playing on analogies between his foibles and those of the paragon Toby, and by promising that "by the help of a vegitable diet, with a few of the cold seeds"—like the regimen proposed for Toby in Chapter 36—"I make no doubt but I shall be able to go on with my uncle *Toby's* story, and my own, in a tolerable straight line" (40).

To what extent is Volume VI a structural paradigm in *Tristram Shandy*? Each volume does travel its own route, as the loops and whorls of plot in VI, 40, suggest. Their procedures, however, are akin. Volume V, for instance, has a formal structure quite different from that of VI. Here Sterne has arranged the volume in thirds. The first third (chapters 2-14) explores the Shandys' reaction to Bobby's death in episodes

30. Some awareness of construction along these lines is evidenced by the French rhetorician J. M. Lambert, who prepared debate charges and responses for his students of Virgil. To the charge that the second half of the *Aeneid* lacks the lively interest of the first, the students were to answer that "Virgile intéresse le coeur dans la première partie; dans la seconde, c'est l'esprit." See [Ernest Jovy], *L'Etude d'Homère et de Virgile au Collège Parisien de la Marche en 1757* (Vitry-le-François, 1911), pp. 19-20.

that we have already discussed. Our attention is fixed on familiar themes: learning, true and false sentiment, death and sex, tears and passion, and travel. The final two-thirds of the volume repeats these themes in different ways, with Tristram's circumcision taking up the middle part (16-26), followed by the resulting debate among Walter, Toby, and the military men (27-43). As in Volume VI, the episodes of plot come near the start of the volume, to serve as a new foundation for the old hods of motifs trundled by Sterne from earlier parts of the book. The long episodes in Volume V, again like those in VI, support sections of lesser comic and formal appeal, which refer back to the episodes of plot as well as to each other. We have already examined the rival orations over Bobby's life's being cut short. Walter's learning about his other son's being cut short (27-28) and the faithful son Trim's catechism of the heart (32) repeats this schema in a new vein, as does the discussion between Walter and Trim on radical heat and moisture. We have structural analogies that work according to the ideal of a discriminated variety.

Both VII and VIII have interpolated stories as pivots to join half-volumes. Tristram's flight from death takes up the first nineteen chapters of VII, presenting the usual themes (principally the formulas of art, travel, and the play between sex and death) with great urgency. Then, the story of the abbess of Andoüillets (20-25) parodies Tristram's concern: the ladies, using their formulas to keep them going on their flight from sickness (and a fate worse than death), feel a panic like Tristram's. He and we suddenly become objective, faced with a parallel that provides insight into a sort of spiritual malingering, so that we cannot go back to the tone of the beginning of the volume. Instead, the narrative becomes diverse, and themes recur in a new key. The abbess's mules turn into the sentimental ass (32), her relics into the mummies of Auxerre (27), Tristram's race against time through a foreign land into a search at Lyon for a clock and a history of China (30, 39), sex and death into the story of Amandus and Amanda (31, 40), and so on, until the frustrations of the trip are drowned in the sunlight and eroticism of the final episode, the Provençal dance (43), eighteen chapters after we bid the abbess farewell.

Volume VIII, published with VII, has a prefatory section of seven chapters, during which Tristram toys with his subject. The rest of the volume is divided as evenly as VII, with twelve chapters before, and thirteen after, the tale of Trim and the beguine (20-22). This tale is the pivot of the narration about Toby and the Widow in the volume, unlike the tale of the abbess in VII, which is an ideological (or emotional) pivot. None the less, no one can miss the similarity in technique here, or in the use of the seven prefatory chapters to set up themes— health, plans of procedure, masks, heat and cold—that come up both before and after the crucial account of the beguine. Nor can one miss, once alerted to it, the pattern of five-chapter and four-chapter episodes after those seven: 8-12 and 13-16 provide the beginning of the affair and the sentry-box siege; after a transition, 17 (the pricked map and St. Rada-gunda), come 18-22 (Trim and Toby: stories of the King of Bohemia and the beguine) and 23-27 (the Widow's second assault and victory); and then 28-32 (this courtship viewed by the Widow, Toby, and Walter) and 32-35 (Walter's discourse on love and women). Readers of my analyses will, I hope, be curious to test my brief comments against the novel; I think one will find that each volume has a different structure, but that the basic procedures with episodes, rhythms, analogies, and modifications govern all.

The individual volumes are, I believe, the largest units of consecutive structure, although the first six volumes follow in chronological order, as do VIII and IX. VII develops from the metaphor of the journey and the analogy between Tristram and Toby in the second half of VI, so that Tristram's campaign against official France, frustration, and failing health—in all three of which he copies Toby—gives us a loosely complementary resolution to that worked out in VIII and IX. Volumes do follow in thematic sequence, as the story of Slawkenbergius links III and IV, and education links V and VI. Between volumes not published at the same time, like II and III, the links are understandably less complex; and, in fact, Sterne's serial publication offers an excellent reason to suppose that continuity, given the weakness of the narrative line, is loose from volume to volume. Readers could not recall, much less feel, precise analogies or incremental repetitions from a volume published one year to another volume published the next year. Sterne might have written in two-volume units, but even that seems unlikely because of the little maps in VI, 40, the different structures of the individual volumes, and the unwieldiness of a unit as long as two volumes. A final possibility is that the whole novel is pegged to an external scheme, in the manner of *Ulysses* or even the *Faerie Queene*. No one has ever found such a scheme or the logic for it. A divorce of the system of order from the system of inquiry, moreover, would not jibe with what we can see of Sterne's practice in the rest of the novel. In short, even if the memoirs are studded here and there with small abstract devices for order, I very much doubt that any large abstract or allusory pattern has been imposed upon them. Sterne would hardly have cared "to twist his tale (like men of lore) to serve a system" (VIII, 19).[31]

As the summary at the end of the first section of this chapter claimed, Sterne's system, like Johnson's, twists to serve his tale. We have now seen how, in episodes and volumes, covert order, again like Johnson's, reinforces the visible system of order Tristram provides us, so as to achieve equilibrium within a growing set of unresolved forces. The eventual subject for

31. I would accept patterns of the very limited sort suggested by Harold Love, "A Shandean Number Game," *N&Q* n.s. 18 (1971): 339, but not of the elaborate or occult sort claimed by Douglas Brooks, *Number and Pattern in the Eighteenth-century Novel* (London: Routledge & Kegan Paul, 1973), pp. 160-76.

both men is a complex condition to be presented, toward which the illusion of formal negligence renders the purposeless particulateness of ordinary life, the life which the central character tries to clarify with his deductive system. Beneath this surface, Sterne and Johnson keep formal control, developing episodes with internal structures and rhythms, working with incremental repetition and fulcrums (the pivots in *Tristram*, the peripeteia in *Rasselas*), and in contriving natural emblems that embody a complex of values. The chief procedures for these means of control, as for those in the visible system of order, are analogy and modification, which depend in turn on associationist and epistemological principles. These same principles and systems reappear, as we shall see, in *Humphry Clinker*. Perhaps that is only to be expected, since *Humphry* combines the journey of *Rasselas* with the subjectivity of *Tristram* and augments its system of inquiry by offering, alone among our five novels, a protagonist who really goes through a process of change. The "great Cham of Literature" and Smollett "were never cater-cousins," and Yorick did not like Smelfungus; but all, as different as they really are, may be brought to a rapprochement.[32]

---

32. The "great Cham" and "cater-cousins" come from Smollett's letter to Wilkes of March 16, 1759, No. 58 in *The Letters of Tobias Smollett*, ed. Lewis M. Knapp (Oxford: Clarendon Press, 1970), p. 75. Smelfungus and Yorick are, of course, Sterne's names for Smollett and his own hero in *A Sentimental Journey*.

Humphry Clinker

I: THE ARMATURE OF CHARACTERS

Within the picaresque, of which Smollett was a master, lies the capacity for complex statement: a novel that must scan widely diverse areas of experience can connect phenomena that a work more strictly preconceived would, by its nature, bar. But complexity of statement also demands what few picaresque works offer, conceptual breadth and subtlety. Smollett achieved that for the first time in *Humphry Clinker*, by using a Richardsonian model to temper his old practice. "Richardsonian" does not mean "epistolary." The bulk of the letters in *Humphry*, Bramble's and Jery's, barely keep up any pretense of being responses to specific recipients. Once the convention is established, very early, only the three ladies really write to the people to whom their letters are addressed.[1] Nor are the letters, like those in Richardson, important as physical objects. Except

1. Letters in a travel book did not, in any case, have much Richardsonian ring to them; they were a generic convention of their own, as George M. Kahrl notes, p. 101, in *Tobias Smollett, Traveler-Novelist* (Chicago: University of Chicago Press, 1945). For the ways in which Smollett does in fact maintain a novelistic letter convention, for the sake of individual psychological depth, see Paul-Gabriel Boucé's extraordinarily fine *Les Romans de Smollett* (Paris: Didier, 1971), p. 245.

for actual letters from "Wilson" to assure us that real sealed
paper is passing through the post (Jery, April 2; Lydia, April 6,
to Mrs. Jermyn and Miss Willis; Bramble, April 17), the letters
as objects have no structural importance. The Richardsonian
model I mean is the use of a compound eye, so to speak, in
whose multiple vision the authority of the novel consists.
There is no other overt shaping of events. The world is solidly
external, and events are determined by the natural logic of a
trip to spas and to cities the travellers are curious to see. One
does find the urbanely unchallengeable voice of the omniscient narrator, but finds it in Jery, who is not omniscient and
who affects the plot, such as it is, the least of all the letter
writers. Even the narrator's function as observer is split. Jery
and Bramble, who share it, are, in different degrees, implicated speakers, parts of the armature of characters around
which the heterogeneous world of *Humphry Clinker* is shaped.

Any discussion of inquiry and order in *Humphry Clinker*
ought to begin with Matthew Bramble, the man and the
author. Man and author (of travel commentary) can be differ-
entiated, but as with the Shandys the public role must also be
taken as a branch of the private, thus changing the value we
put on it. If we do differentiate man and author, we, like Jery,
find ourselves willing to give Bramble the man allegiance and
then affection. Bramble the Welsh Juvenal, however, wins
neither. Because of his emotional investment in what he feels,
his voice does augment what we learn from Jery's urbanity. He
also speaks with the vividness that in Smollett always demands some sort of acceptance. Nevertheless, we cannot give
any specific level of credence to Bramble's excursions from
Jery's sane tone, because we must suspend meticulous judgment to admit them at all. Controlled satirists present anath-
emas like his as an almost aphoristic kind of truth, absolute but
implicitly confined. However sweeping the King of Brobding-
nag's statement may sound, we do not believe that Swift
thinks Englishmen in all ways "the most pernicious Race of

little odious Vermin that Nature ever suffered to crawl upon the Surface of the Earth." The angry verdict implies conceptual terms with a certain understood vagueness of application. Bramble does not know this. His personal statements have "aphoristic truth," but he treats them as if they were literally true. For the contexts that contain and control his unstable, emotive statements of value, we must therefore turn from him to the patterns of value in the novel as a whole. Only when modified by context can his tirades have precise meaning, except to irked members of the Bath Corporation or prospective tourists to Ranelagh.

If we do not differentiate man and author, we have more reason to take our Bramble with a grain of salt. Most obviously, Smollett shows us that the bad temper of the satirist comes from a sick body and mind, not necessarily from the disorders of society. Bramble's peevishness, so often excused as benevolent misanthropy,[2] calls up literary antecedents like Lord Ringbone in one of Smollett's putative sources, *The New Bath Guide*. That "reprobate gouty old Peer" (Letter 5) rages at Sim Blunderhead's dance to the airs of Bath fiddlers with "their d-mn'd squeaking Catgut that's worse than the Gout." Anstey makes his bad temper plausible, but not sympathetic: Sim, and the reader too, I suppose, reply to Ringbone, "I don't care a Damn/ For you, nor your *Valee de Sham*." The satire is double-edged, and Blunderhead or not, Sim gets the last word.[3] So does Nicholas Babble, the persona in the *Prater*, who hears the complaints of an elderly visitor to London:

"Before I turned the corner of the street I lodge in, I was overtaken by two rascally barbers boys, who jammed me between them, and besmeared me with powder; and while I was endeavouring to brush

2. See, for example, Thomas R. Preston, "Smollett and the Benevolent Misanthrope Type," *PMLA* 79 (1964): 51-57.
3. Christopher Anstey, *The New Bath Guide* (Kensington: Cayme Press, 1927), pp. 25-26.

it off, a son of a gun of a chimney sweeper covered one side of my coat
with soot. . . . A little farther, four or five labourers spread themselves across the foot path, and would not budge an inch, tho' I very
civilly entreated them not to stand so thick; so that I was obliged to go
without the posts in order to avoid them, by which means I was
splashed from head to foot by a pair of mettlesome coach horses, who
trotted by me as fast as they could. About twenty yards farther I
unluckily trod on a loose stone; and caused a great deal of dirty water
(for you know it rained hard last night) to fly into my face, and almost
close up my peepers."

This man also complains about a beetle in his morning choco-
late, and "such a collection of filthy smells in the streets of
London that I wonder the air is not pestilential." Nicholas
Babble gives this man little sympathy. He comments that the
peevish are self-tormentors and social pests, although, he
allows, "when a man's temper, indeed, has been soured by
sickness, and a series of real calamities, he is not an object of
contempt but of pity; and his little starts of choler, pishes,
pshaws, and discontented interjections, should be patiently
borne with."[4]

Bramble, although "soured by sickness," has suffered no
"real calamities." He is sick because of his physical excess
when young and emotional excess when old (Jery, August 8).
However accurate his judgment—and the man in the *Prater*,
not to mention Lord Ringbone, is accurate enough—he remains in his cantankerous moments a figure of some fun.
Smollett makes the point clear by his treatment of the satur-
nine Lismahago, who has much more right to a soured temper
than Bramble. While Bramble has enjoyed wealth and land in
Wales, Lismahago has had to be squire of the Miamis, sachem
and spouse to Squinkinacoosta. Bramble has dependents and
honor, Lismahago not even a captaincy. Despite his advan-

4. Hugh Kelly (?), *The Prater* (2nd ed., London, 1757), pp. 104-06 (*Prater* 14;
June 12, 1756).

tages, Bramble has made himself gouty and splenetic, but Lismahago has scars earned in foreign lands "in the course of two sanguinary wars [in which] he had been wounded, maimed, mutilated, taken, and enslaved" (Jery, July 10). Nor can one doubt Lismahago's shocking history, since tales like his were current from many sources at the time of the Seven Years' War. One book of 1757 contains tales of burning and scalping, cannibalism and burning of prisoners, scalped men who lived, and grotesque Indian costume; the author concludes bitterly that "for want of a Certificate from my *Colonel*, or some other *necessary Qualifications* I am ignorant of, I could not get any Provision made for me, by Pension, or otherwise. Indeed, as a *Reward* for my Sufferings and Services, I had the Favour of a PASS allowed, and the *Sum* of SIX SHILLINGS paid, to carry me to *Aberdeen*, about *eight Hundred Miles* ONLY, from the Place whereat I was DISCHARG'D." In November 1758, Smollett's *Critical Review* discussed another such account; and there are others very much like Lismahago's.⁵ In this light, Lismahago's life might have been part of a tragic narrative. But *Humphry Clinker* denies him even the right to be vinegary. His gruesome adventures are treated with humor, and his ridiculous behavior is stressed. This analogical treatment comments a fortiori on Bramble, who violates civility for assaults on his person far slighter than those suffered by Lismahago.

5. Peter Williamson, *French and Indian Cruelty* (York, 1757), p. 103. Louis L. Martz, *The Later Career of Tobias Smollett*, Yale Studies in English, 97 (New Haven: Yale University Press, 1942), discusses the common opinion that Lismahago's original was Captain Robert Stobo, and offers a closer parallel from the *British Magazine*, January 1760-March 1763. Other references to Indian cruelty may be found in Robert Donald Spector, *English Literary Periodicals and the Climate of Opinion during the Seven Years' War* (The Hague: Mouton & Co., 1966), chap. 7, pp. 241-311 passim. Whatever Smollett's source or sources may have been, there can be no doubt that Lismahago's account of his adventures could have been accepted more or less at face value, at least up to his becoming a sachem—that is more along the lines of Gulliver's becoming a Lilliputian Nardac or the success of Paltock's Peter Wilkins (1751).

Another modificatory method for checking Bramble, and incidentally for containing what I have called his "unstable, emotive statements of value," is to refer his satire to matters that stand outside the created world of the novel. Especially in the earlier parts of *Humphry Clinker*, before the group leaves London, we find a division of satiric labor. Jery writes about characters and events within the novel, which are not open to public challenge, Bramble about places and customs with which the vast majority of Smollett's readers must have been independently familiar. Almost everyone could have judged what the diatribes about London and Bath were worth, and could have balked without impugning the substance of the novel. We know, biographically, that Smollett himself would have disagreed with Bramble on some points, for example, that he admired the architecture of the elder Wood and the efficacy of Bath water.[6] Moreover, in a book that thrives on "originals," those seen directly in their letters and those about whom Jery writes, Bramble damages his character in our eyes by his comparative inability to respond to his fellow human beings. We know from Jery, and from bits of what Bramble says, that he is charitable and capable of close friendship. What remains closed to him, though, is the expanse between love (or pity) and disgust, a vast gray area of appraisal which appears in his letters only unintentionally, as Bramble reveals his own mixed portrait. Such a man may draw upon our qualified affection, but not our confidence. As a satirist, he is too unaware to trust.

Moreover, Smollett lets us see that Bramble is considerably less alert in other ways than his assertive tone presumes. He

6. Some differences between Smollett's views and Bramble's are noted by Martz, pp. 127-29, and André Parreaux, in his edition of *Humphry Clinker* (Boston: Houghton Mifflin, Riverside Editions, 1968), pp. 322, 324. In addition to the differences they mention is Smollett's admiration for Wood, "to whose extraordinary genius [Bath is] indebted for a great part of the trade and beauty of the place." *Essay on the External Use of Water* (1752), ed. Claude E. Jones, *Bull. Inst. Hist. Med.* 3 (1935): 76.

informs Dr. Lewis (April 20) that "every man of tolerable parts ought, at my time of day, to be both physician and lawyer" to himself, and spends the rest of the letter preening himself and scoffing at quackery, ending with the note, "my right ancle pits, a symptom, as I take it, of its being *oedematous*, not *leucophlegmatic*." These two conditions are much of a muchness; and Chambers's *Cyclopaedia* (1738) specifically mentions pitting ("easily giving way to the touch, and preserving the impression made by the finger for some time") as a symptom of leucophlegmatia.[7] Bramble's failure as a diagnostician comes just after the letter in which we are told of his contretemps with Tabby caused by his imprudent method of giving the widow twenty pounds. The next letter tells of his being one of those duped by "Wilson's" disguise as a peddler of eyeglasses, which gives a sudden symbolic sense to his—no doubt—presbyopia. These incidents, with the widow, the ankle, and the peddler, directly precede Bramble's main spate of satiric, as distinct from grumbling, letters. When Bramble's vituperative shower begins at Bath, we have already seen him blundering, henpecked, arrogant, and gullible.

These characteristics themselves have been pointed up by the single episode at Hot Well that satirizes someone not of the Bramble entourage (Jery, April 18). The "famous Dr. L[inde]n" is the pedant who delights in talking about stench and filth, then about his cure for the pox; Jery tweaks his nose and badgers him into applying a caustic to a wart on it, thus inflaming and swelling it into a "tremendous nozzle." The scatological and sexual jokes, ending in the great red double entendre of the doctor's nose, plainly set the tone for much of the narrative, and play off against Bramble's complaints about

7. S.n. "leucophlegmatia." Cf. William Salmon, *Synopsis Medicinae* (London, 1681), pp. 141, 313; and Robert James, *A Medicinal Dictionary*, 3 vols. (London, 1743-45), s.n. "oedema," which mentions pitting in oedema and says that an oedema of the whole body "assumes the Name of . . . Leucophlegmatia, or Dropsy."

the filthy exhalations of the spa and Liddy's amorous moon-
ings about "Wilson." But the episode also comments on those
who have self-important pretensions, who blunder into pre-
dicaments, who zealously avoid the appearance of dishonor,
who believe that the way to heal is to lay on "caustics"—in
short, on traits we presently see in Bramble himself. Like the
doctor, Bramble has his swellings, which Linden suggests may
be the result of the *"lues venerea"* (anticipating Jery's similar
suggestion about the swelling on Linden's nose), and which in
fact have come from Bramble's "excesses." In no way do we
make a Linden of Bramble, but his satirical position, with
which we concur, suffers a series of modifications.[8]

We have, then, a number of reasons, a priori and empirical,
for allotting the high voltage of Bramble's satire a low amper-
age. Another reason for modification, in terms of theme the
most important of all, is related to the last one: Bramble's
principles logically should condemn him to the degree that
they condemn society. He works with a sort of behaviorism,
seeing the inner meaning of a society in its external appear-
ances. The disorder and filth of England become presumptive
evidence for moral disaster. Thus Bramble's violence about
trivia reflects not only his lack of proportion but also his
diagnostic assumption that trivia are symptoms of something
more general and deadly. His descriptions insist on a reciprocity between the sensory and the moral. This method has
affinities with medical diagnosis, so much so that Bramble is
open to the charge of looking at others in a way that is self-
derived. The form of his satire, then, would itself be a
symptom of his egoism, especially in contrast to Jery's taking
the world at its face value.

The charge can be made still more precise if one notes that
Bramble's own disease resembles a "hypochondriacal" affec-

8. A full account of Smollett's satire of Linden appears in G. S. Rousseau,
"Matt Bramble and the Sulphur Controversy in the XVIIIth Century: Medical
Background of *Humphry Clinker*," *JHI* 28 (1967): 577-89.

tion (versions of which are hysteria, the spleen, and "vapours"). This disorder, as Sydenham described it, manifests itself in whatever symptoms are fit for the part of the body in which they appear: headaches, scurvy, a dry cough, diarrhea, dropsical swelling of the legs, and so forth. Sydenham also says that its immediate cause is the violent motion of the passions.[9] Presumably, then, Bramble is familiar with it, since he is curious in medical matters. His social analyses, in any case, make use of its syndrome. Each particular that he observes seems to him at least an implicit sign of some central rot in the social Leviathan.

When Bramble applies principles of order to society, relating particulars to the general, he angrily finds those principles neglected. Distinctions that ought to be kept are not; the part is taken for the whole; the fanciful takes illicit precedence over the just. Thus "Vauxhall is a composition of baubles, overcharged with paltry ornaments, ill conceived, and poorly executed; without any unity of design, or propriety of disposition. It is an unnatural assembly of objects" (May 29). In Bath (April 23), new houses are "stuck together with so little regard to plan and propriety, that the different lines of the new rows and buildings interfere with, and intersect one another in every different angle of conjunction. They look like the wreck

9. *The Entire Works*, ed. John Swan (3rd ed., London, 1753), pp. 409-15 ("An Epistle from Dr. Thomas Sydenham to Dr. William Cole; treating of the small-pox and hysteric diseases" [1681], secs. 60, 78). This description was still current in Smollett's time. It appears in 1779, under "hypochondriac affection, or passion" in Chambers's *Cyclopaedia* (Rees's edition), and it was specifically endorsed and enlarged upon by the great Robert Whytt, President of the Royal College of Physicians in Edinburgh from 1763 till his death in 1766. *Observations on the Nature, Causes, and Cure of Those Disorders which are Commonly Called Nervous, Hypochondriac, or Hysteric* (1764) in *Works* (Edinburgh, 1768), pp. 530-32. The always unreliable Michel Foucault has observations about the relationship between the physical and moral strength of the organs in hypochondria, in *Madness and Civilization: A History of Insanity in the Age of Reason*, tr. Richard Howard (New York: New American Library, 1967), p. 125.

of streets and squares disjointed by an earthquake." The collections in the British Museum lack order and connection, the worlds of politics and literature suffer the specious distinctions of parties, the capital of the land is a "chaos," "without head or tail, members or proportion" (June 2, May 29). For the same reasons, he condemns the mob and the parvenus. And logically enough, when Bramble has come upon Humphry Clinker preaching, "the first thing that struck him, was the presumption of his lacquey" (Jery, second letter of June 10).

Yet this disorder against which Bramble inveighs is his own. The social deformations reflect some of his diseases, which deform him inside and out: the gout, dropsy, constipation. His splenetic "vapours" parallel those steams that overcome him in the baths or the assembly, that "high exalted essence of mingled odours, arising from putrid gums, imposthumated lungs, sour flatulencies, rank arm-pits, sweating feet, running sores and issues, plasters, ointments, and embrocations, hungary-water, spirit of lavender, assafoedita drops, musk, hartshorn, and sal volatile; besides a thousand frowsy steams, which I could not analyse" (May 8). These "frowsy steams" overcome his head; but so, repeatedly, do his own inner vapors subject his reason and his health to the mob rule of the momentary, the striking, and the low. Within his own establishment, he has long yielded reason and rule to an ignorant woman, Tabby, who epitomizes the self-interest which he so despises in the world at large. Smollett uses analogy to provide a symbol for this disorder in the dog Chowder, who like Bramble is constipated (Tabby, April 2) and dropsical, for which he likes the Bath waters "no better than the squire" (Win, April 26). Chowder's currishness suggests Bramble's bad temper, of course, and perhaps, etymologically, his cynicism; by onomatopoeia, "chowter" means "to grumble," which may contribute to Chowder's representative function. There is no doubt in any case that Jery sees an emblematic scene when he looks into the coach at "that animal sitting opposite to my uncle, like any other passenger. The 'squire, ashamed of his situation, blushed to the eyes" (May 24). Equally emblematic is that Bramble's first act in restoring order is to demand Chowder's departure and Tabby's submission, ending this reductio ad absurdum of matter over mind.[10]

We have two related conditions here, which Smollett develops suggestively rather than precisely. First, the sick Bramble and society each reveal and cause the appearance of disease in the other: he reveals to the extent that his satire is accurate, and causes to the extent that it is not; society reveals Bramble's bad temper and raw nerves by prodding them with noxious stimuli, making them worse yet, and so causing further disorder. Secondly, society's and Bramble's disorders have, as I have said, the same symptoms, and the same reciprocity between body and spirit—the sickness of one aggravates that of the other—so that in interacting, the man and the world reflect one another. Bramble's social satire diagnoses for us, as well as records for us, Bramble's state of health. Smollett also wants us to feel by analogy that the process of Bramble's regeneration becomes a social progress, not only in the narrative that grows steadily more benign, but also in a hypothetical future where its typical, "universal" meaning offers a way of redeeming the land from chaos. That redemptive way is not the way of Juvenalian fury. In this novel violent satire informs us, perhaps gratifies us, but does not make anyone better. We in part admire Bramble's rage as an ultimate self-lacerating testimony that chaos and brutishness have a devoted foe, but that same rage, barely controllable, testifies to the grip that the chaotic, brutish passions have over that same foe. Inflamed reason becomes bodily passion that destroys the balance of the humours and the norms of reason—holism, hierarchy, a sense of proportion—so that in his letters, in his entourage, and in

10. Beverly Scafidel provides a full discussion of Chowder in "Smollett's *Humphry Clinker*," *Explicator* 30 (1972): item 54.

his own body, Bramble often seems a symptom of what he attacks.

For a half-dozen reasons we modify our acceptance of Bramble's bristling attacks. Unaware of himself, despite his pretensions, and of others, despite his vividness, he not only selects and interprets reality so as to force it into his own self-derived system, but also unwittingly condemns himself by the same laws he uses to condemn others. Since the places he visits earliest, Bath and London, are those about which he is most virulent, and also those with which Smollett's reader was most likely to be familiar, external as well as internal means existed for checking the truth of his satire. Our old companion, the principle of modification, is well fed. As usual, the modified statements have a limited utility: they are not simply false, and they extend and complement Jery's and the girls' in varying degrees, so as to give us a complex equilibrium of values continually reestablishing itself with our help as the novel moves on. The pattern is close to Sterne's, with Bramble himself as a sort of unplayful Shandy, whose claims about the world around him become, like Walter's, elements of auto-biography. As to the means by which we judge him, Linden and then Lismahago, they are the rough equivalents, in Smollett's scheme of analogies, to Slop and Locke in Sterne's.

The same kind of analogical equivalency appears in a more important scheme of analogies, referable not only to Bramble but to all the business of the novel. The five letter writers, as we shall see, form a kind of circle of shared characteristics, moving from Jery to Bramble to Tabby to Win and Liddy, and thence to Jery again; or, alternatively, the other way around. The relation between Jery and Bramble is the most important of these because the two men are the rhetors of the novel. To maintain his favored position, Jery must carry on most of what is good about Bramble, like his alertness, and discard his vitriol and self-deception. Smollett uses analogy to let Bramble "feed into" Jery, so that Jery can be a valid alternative without damaging his uncle by too sharp a contrast. We migrate from

Bramble's exposé to Jery's calm recognition by sensing the rapports between the two, thus lending them a sort of interchangeability. Only in his first letter (April 2) is Jery allowed to condemn his uncle, and even there he admits that gout may have soured Bramble's temper. "Perhaps," he says, "I may like him better on further acquaintance." By the next letter, he does; his third relates Bramble's generosity to the widow, which moves Jery's feelings and respect. At the same time, we note a growing number of similarities between the two, from hot temper or embarrassment at seeming charitable to distressingly amorous sisters or cooperation in roasting Dr. L[inde]n. Jery's fourth letter finds him following Bramble's advice, based on prior experience, in dealing with Miss Blackerby's claims of his paternity. This rapport and similarity have a thematic function, to be consummated at the end of the book as Bramble symbolically regains his youth; but in these early pages their effect has more to do with helping us transfer Matthew's revelations into Jery's fond context. We hear "the lamentations of Matthew Bramble" (Bramble, April 23) with the *savoir vivre* of a laughing Jeremiah.

For Jery to have this sort of relationship with Bramble, he must be a character as Bramble is, with a personality, a past, and obligations; but for Jery to be authoritative, he must have a kind of narrator's impartiality. Smollett contrives this by giving Jery a limited past, represented by Oxford, and limited obligations, represented by Liddy. In his first three or four letters, Jery protects his good name at Oxford and makes schoolboy puns.[11] Then this context dims, naturally enough, once the fascinations of the tour begin. All that is left, like the

11. The learned pun was an especially easy means of marking a collegian. In *Terrae-Filius* 39 (May 29, 1721), Nicholas Amhurst calls the universities the "fond nursing mothers" of the "antient art of PUNNING": "they have . . . brought it into that flourishing state, in which, amidst the decay of other sorts of learning, it at present continues." *Terrae-Filius; Or, the Secret History of the University of Oxford* (3rd ed., London, 1754), p. 203. The specific pun having to do with the drowning of Jery's dog Ponto, of course, adumbrates one of the major motifs of the novel.

smile of the Cheshire cat, is the aloof tone of a slightly
precocious sophistication, which has been fixed as Jery's
idiom. Free from the pedantry and conceit that mark collegians
in most eighteenth-century novels and plays, this voice continues to provide us with a candid and civilized way of looking
at events. Similarly, in the very early part of the novel and only
sporadically thereafter, Jery has the obligation to save Liddy
from "Wilson." This genuine familial tie and the violence of
temper it elicits hold Jery to a group of persons, and like his
Oxford life, support claims for his individual personality.
Through Smollett's arrangement of events, however, Jery's
rash temper largely drops from him like his academic wit. He
remains a character in the book, but one who has paid his debt
to the temperamental demands of being a character, and who
has bought his freedom to be detached. More exactly, Smollett
has bought it for him by deceiving our expectations, just as by
deceiving us into expecting real letters, he has bought freedom
for Bramble and Jery to be commentators without depriving
them of the credit of having friends worthy of and willing for
so long an exchange of letters.

Tabby has no such friends; and so, if Jery offers us a civilized
translation of Bramble's energy and sensory sharpness, all she
can do (especially with her complement, Chowder) is underline the hazards of Bramble's egoism. Subsidized by Bramble
himself, she presents the spectacle he deplores but, as we have
seen, also exemplifies: pretension, self-absorption, ignorance,
fancy, and subverted values. Her care for Chowder is a
warped version of Bramble's charity. Her lechery and primp-
ing point to her intentness, like his, on the body. In writing the
housekeeper Mrs. Gwillim about cleanliness, austerity, and
propriety, she reduces her brother's ideals of hygiene and
social order to their most jejune. Her rustic provincialism,
twenty years out of date (Lydia, May 31), measures all
experience for her, as in her asking Lismahago whether

Squinkinacoosta was high- or low-church or her giving Quin the Welsh name "Gwinn" (Jery, July 13, April 30). I need hardly underline the way in which Smollett again uses analogy. Tabby's traits merely push to extremes Bramble's self-absorbed misanthropy, his topsy-turvy household, his hatred of filth and disorder, his complacency about Wales, and his willingness to become the Horatian type of the *senex*: "difficilis, querulus, laudator temporis acti/ se puero, censor castigatorque minorum" (Bramble, June 2).

Jery and Tabby are different sorts of outriggers for Bramble, but both help balance his assets and deficiencies. Jery sets an example of urbanity which puts Bramble's furor to shame but which also gives the reader a means of accepting Bramble's satire on some level without also accepting his savagery. Tabby's relation to her brother is like that of the Catholics to Walter Shandy. She suggests the painful consequences latent in his behavior but also reminds us that Bramble is nowhere nearly so extreme in his views as his violent prose and fits might imply. Aside from their functions in regard to Bramble, however, Tabby and Jery have no connections with each other. They are kept in coherent relation through the use of the other two members of the travelling party, Win and Liddy. The two girls act as a unit in the thematic structure of the novel, both agog at what they see, both in love with obscure figures who turn out not to be quite so obscure. Until the final haughty letter from Win, which tops off the entire book, the two have the same number of letters, the last three of which are written on the same dates and concern the complementary topics of the ladies' swains in their various apparitions and metamorphoses. Although their earlier letters are not so precisely complementary, these too deal with romance and superstition (veiled as Methodism at times), even when Lydia is describing Ranelagh (May 31) as "like the inchanted palace of a genie" where Tenducci's singing makes her think herself in paradise,

or Hot Well, which wanted only Miss Willis's company to
make it "a perfect paradise" (April 21). Lest Bath feel left out, it
too qualifies (April 26) as "an earthly paradise" with "enchanted castles." Upon this verbal background, as well as on her
own delighted experiences, are built Win's romantic pieties
about the paradise promised by Humphry. Similarly, Liddy's
conventional romance with "Wilson," her gentleman in disguise, leads to Win's with Humphry, whose alabaster skin
(Jery, May 24) might conventionally testify to his gentility,
though the portion that Win sees is not usually called upon as a
witness. Humphry's fidelity, too, not only contrasts with the
ingratitude of Paunceford and Prankley, and the venality of
the common people, detailed in the five letters before Hum-
phrey appears, but also parallels the romantic fidelity of
"Wilson," who trails his Liddy throughout the book. Smollett's development of Liddy and Win, then, works by analogy,
the familiar analogy between master and servant. The girls
begin in collusion and end each with her own level of success.

As a structural unit, their openness to experience ties them
to Jery, their amorousness to Tabby. Although in these regards
their interests are narrower and more naive than Jery's and
Tabby's respectively, they draw the expression of those interests toward fantasy and romance, a modification that is to
become increasingly valuable as the novel goes on. If Bramble
augments the urbanity of Jery by his excursions into Juvenalian rancor, so Liddy and Win augment that urbanity by their
excursions into romance. The parallel works rather closely:
rancor and romance are both silly, but also, up to a point,
undefinedly and perhaps inconsistently valid ways of seeing
the world. *Humphry Clinker* gives both their due, rancor nearer
the beginning of the novel, romance nearer the end, where it
serves as the touch of sfumatura that lends a mystery to the
clear pictures that reasonableness paints. Symmetrically—and
this needs little explanation—as Bramble offers a more admirable version of Tabby's temper, Liddy and Win offer a more

admirable version of her amorous rapacity. The augmentation of what Tabby stands for is as much plainer than that of what Jery stands for, as the imperfections of the one are than those of the other, but Smollett's mode of operation is the same for both, analogy, modification, and discriminated variety.

In addition to this circular pattern of analogy (Bramble–Tabby–girls–Jery–Bramble) there is a convergent pattern, in which each of the other characters comments on Bramble, who is central. "Circular" and "convergent" patterns coincide, of course, for Tabby and Jery. Liddy and Win have no temperamental connections with Bramble, but do modify his satire by concession: they exemplify a society set upon trifles and the lures of the moment, the subject of his rage, in such a way as to make his deep animosity seem misplaced. If all of England's offenders are Win Jenkinses, Bramble's emotion is excessive; so, for that matter, is his diagnostic method, for Win's and Liddy's foibles do not seem to imply any deep moral corrosion. One may say the same for the Methodism to which they both fall prey, for Clinker's version of it is too well-meaning, comic, intriguing, and above all too vulnerable to be dangerous in Bramble's terms. Thus Win and Liddy counterbalance Bramble's satire by making us happy to discount it, as Jery counterbalances it by making us wince at its tone, and Tabby by showing us the logical extension of the ill nature and egoism that enter into it. Obviously both girls are needed for discounting Bramble's satire. Their different social functions and classes, made both more and less discrete by Win's affected gentility, respond to his social inclusiveness and love of hierarchy. Their different personalities prove how broadly appealing are the tinsel and whimsy he alone damns. Their position is given psychological bulk by the sum of their letters, while the qualitative differences in it, caused by the sharing of duties, precludes our tiring of it.

Win also, through her malapropisms, expresses—as Liddy in all decency cannot—the relation of the body to romance and spirituality, so as to parody Bramble's obsession with, and imperfect understanding of, the relations of body and mind.[12] The prior condition for this is that she should have a body; Liddy's is never mentioned, and Tabby's and Jery's only implicitly through their wished-for or real promiscuity. Win's is frequently on exhibit. Thus (April 26) she drops her petticoat into the King's Bath while standing "up to the sin in water"; her upturned "nether end" serves Bramble for a stepladder from the overturned coach (Jery, May 24), just before her inamorato Clinker shows the world his fair posteriors; Clinker admires her bared "beauties" as she climbs from the window at Harrogate (Jery, July 1); still later (September 7), Sir George Colquhoun sees her march by him in her "birth-day soot."

Smollett strips her mind—as he has exposed her body—through accidents, her famous malapropisms. The most amusing of these, and those that are most nearly psychological, concern Win's romance with Humphry. In her first letter after seeing him and his alabaster hindquarters (June 3), she begins with a simple pun, that the new footman is "a good sole"; and then, after having put in a maxim that involves hairless buttocks, launches into a paragraph that includes "sitty" (for "city"), "coxes" (for "coaches"), "paleass" (for "palace"), "hillyfents" (for "elephants"), and "pye-bald ass" (a zebra). Even later, her first sight of Humphry stays with her. On October 4, her hope of marrying him is "suppository." By October 14, her situation is no better, and she avoids giving "unbreech" to Humphry by remaining solitary and taking "ass of edita," even though she has heard Tabby's and Liddy's banns called with her "own ars" and must reflect that "there might have been a turd." This kind of extension of subjectivity, of which one can easily find more examples, fits in perfectly with the device of giving us various points of view.

---

12. Boucé's discussion, pp. 381-87, is the most interesting of the many treatments of Win's and Tabby's misspellings.

As to the specific subject of these misspellings, it forms an inverted complement to Liddy's seeing the face of a lover wherever she looks: "Wilson" in her first two and last two letters, O'Donaghan in April, Barton in May and June, and "Gordon," after she ends three months' silence, in September.

Win thus expresses, without indelicacy or cynicism, the relation between romance and the body. More satirically, her malapropisms express the reality behind the spiritual concerns of Methodism, to which she complacently or self-consolingly keeps returning. Here she (and Tabby) comically confirms Bramble's method of diagnosis. Since the Methodist movement began, its literature had met with scorn because of the demotic style and metaphoric extravagance with which men like Whitefield aroused mass piety. Shamela's malapropisms and double entendres are one of the earliest literary exploitations of what became a standing joke. A proximate source of Smollett's, *The New Bath Guide*, contains Prudence Blunderhead's Methodist letter in which an "Apparition" strangely like her friend Roger announces, "I must fill you full of Love" (and then does so); Anstey appends a footnote referring the curious reader to a book where "He will find many Instances (particularly of young People) who have been elected in the Manner above."[13] There was nothing new, then, in having Tabby wish that Humphry "may have power given to penetrate and instill his goodness, even into your most inward

13. Anstey, pp. 86-88. On Methodism and its general context, see Albert M. Lyles, *Methodism Mocked: The Satiric Reaction to Methodism in the Eighteenth Century* (London: Epworth Press, 1960); pp. 389-95 of my "The Framework of Shamela," *ELH* 35 (1968); and Raymond Bentman's introduction to Evan Lloyd, *The Methodist. A Poem*, Augustan Reprints 151-52 (Los Angeles: William Andrews Clark Library, 1972). Lloyd's poem of 1766 takes a Smollettian view of Methodism; as Bentman notes, p. vii, Lloyd saw it as symptomatic of "an essentially disorderly world in which chaos spreads almost inevitably, in which riots, corrupt ministers, arrogant fools, disrespectful lower classes, giddy middle classes, and lascivious upper classes are barely kept in check."

parts" (September 18). This confusion or interplay between
mind and body leads to Win's converting the terms of piety
back into those of matter, such as food ("grease" for "grace,"
"pyehouse" for "pious") or finance ("mattermoney" for one
of the sacraments). The man who puts forth Methodism for the
health of the human spirit, accordingly, is an animal doctor,
the farrier Humphry. As a result, spirituality becomes as
dubious an article in this novel as is romance. Accompanied on
the plot level by such absurdities as a belief in ghosts and
predictions, it is expressed by Methodism and given a verbal
coup de grâce by having its cant turned into materialism by
way of Win's blunders. It can only return as a genuine value
within *Humphry Clinker* when it has been translated, as Jery
translates Bramble's satire into a reasonable form.

The modificatory structural pattern of our entourage, then,
is roughly this: Bramble and the girls, he with his complexity of
feeling and they with their simplicity of feeling, augment
Jery's empirical rationalism and Tabby's rigid cycle of convention and instinct. Jery and Tabby in turn set the upper and lower
limits respectively for Bramble and the two girls; if this seems
like a paradox—how can Jery set upper limits for someone
who is augmenting his point of view?—it is only logically so, as
I have indicated above in talking of rancor and romance as
indeterminately valid, silly and useful at the same time, like
Toby Shandy's bowling green or the mad astronomer's moral
gravity in *Rasselas*. The perspective of each of the characters
also offers a reason for skepticism about Bramble's satire. The
internal economy of the Bramble party, then, is like an additional normative character added to the five or six (eventually
seven) real ones, a "character" who defines the values of
inquiry and order. From the party emerges the process of
Bramble's healing. He moves closer to Jery in tone; as he grows
more tolerant, the plot opens to accommodate reasonable
versions of the girls' romance and spirituality; and Tabby, his
caricature, softens as Chowder goes and Lismahago comes.

For us, too, the party defines a progress. A given time-frame near the start of the book has a great deal of tension among the five points of view and within Bramble himself, where anger, misanthropy, pain, thorny charity, and Schadenfreude jostle. As the tensions diminish, the party progressively brings us greater breadth and harmony of perspectives, like that to be achieved in the plot.

The sharp depiction of the Bramble party, then, is crucial for Smollett. Expectably, he reinforces its details through analogy during the expository part of the novel, before Humphry appears. To this end, all the incidental characters contribute, Sir Ulic and the charity-seeking widow too obviously to mention. We have already discussed one of the less obvious thematic analogues Smollett employs, Dr. L[inde]n, who is a parodic index, like Tabby, of Bramble's own faults. "Wilson," a practicing actor associated with Liddy, enforces illusion and romance on Jery through action, the near duel. His opposite number, Quin, a retired actor associated with Bramble, enforces disillusionment and misanthropy on Jery through observation, particularly of the women's brawl (Jery, April 30). The remaining are Paunceford and Serle, and Prankley and Eastgate (Jery, May 10, May 17). In both stories, a rich man proves ungrateful to a former friend. The snubbed friends, Serle and Eastgate, know Bramble and Jery respectively, and accordingly their respective stories end ill and well. Serle's misfortunes carry Bramble's point of view into the objective world, and there show the perils of two of Bramble's weaknesses, false delicacy and Quixotism. Eastgate's cleverness ratifies Jery's normal tone, especially (once more) in regard to Jery's own Quixotism (the challenge to "Wilson" and other acts to recover "honor" in this section). In short, the early incidental characters all support or directly call into question the fixed values of Bramble's entourage. We shall see that as the novel proceeds, and these positions become less fixed, analogy and modification become dynamic rather than expository.

II: THE FABRIC OF *HUMPHRY CLINKER*

Until the travellers come back from Scotland, too much
happens in *Humphry Clinker* for Smollett to develop his
plentiful analogies incrementally. Lismahago, for example, is
elaborately anticipated by two Celts dear to Tabby, Sir Ulic and
Mr. Micklewhimmen. These men, a dubious knight and a
deceitful lawyer with a wounded head, lead naturally to
battle-scarred, disputatious Lismahago. His maimed body
and grievances about pay and promotion repeat what the
crippled admiral and colonel have shown and told us at Bath.
His freethinking and chauvinism appear in Bramble's portrait,
six days before Lismahago shows up, of the whimsical deist
H[ewe]t, who has performed a "Giro or circuit" of Europe, but
"neither in dress, diet, customs, or conversation, did he
deviate one tittle from the manner in which he had been
brought up" (July 4). Lismahago's union with Tabby starts
with his appearance: both he and his bride-to-be are tall and
stooped, with greenish eyes, big noses, wide mouths, bad
teeth, and shrivelled faces (Jery, May 6, July 10).[14] Despite
these and anticipatory analogies with other characters, however, we nowhere find a train of analogies growing more
intellectually or emotionally complex, such as we found in
Rasselas.

The same holds true for image-connected motifs, the most
important of which is that of the four elements, fire, air, earth,

14. For Lismahago, there is another sort of continuity: Tabby in her finery
is a second Squinkinacoosta, if one is to believe a poem of 1747 about the
Dublin stage:

The BOXES then, *America* display,
With naked charms, and painted feathers gay;
Where ev'ry fair one deck'd in paint appears,
While gaudy Gewgaws gravitate their ears.

The verse is quoted by Esther K. Sheldon, *Thomas Sheridan of Smock-Alley*
(Princeton: Princeton University Press, 1967), p. 36. A similar comparison is
made by le Père Yves Marie André, *Essai sur le beau* (1741), in *Oeuvres
philosophiques*, ed. Victor Cousin (Paris, 1843), pp. 19-20.

and water. All four occur medically in the novel, as gout, flatulence (tympanum), constipation, and dropsy (edema, leucophlegmatia).[15] They also appear in other forms, natural and metaphoric. Fire is a favorite weapon of Lismahago's Indians, and it reveals, at different times, the hitherto hidden virtues of Winifred, Micklewhimmen, and Lismahago; it is also the New Light of Methodism, the "hot and hasty" temper of Jery (Bramble, April 17) and of Bramble himself, and even the flame—or, as Win says, "flegm" (April 26)—of love. Water, the most important element in this book, wells up in the spas and runs through the landscapes, for drinking,

15. The four elements had lost much of their scientific primacy by Smollett's time, but by no means all. Boerhaave awarded them a place of pride as "instruments" in the most popular single text in chemistry until the time of Lavoisier. Stahl, the founder of the phlogiston theory and "a chemist . . . unrivalled in his day," gave them a "bienveillante" reinterpretation as instruments of chemical process. In Smollett's later years, Joseph Black, Professor of Chemistry at Edinburgh from 1766, was recommending as a beginning text Andrew Reid's translation (1758) of *Elements of the Theory and Practice of Chymistry* by Pierre-Joseph Macquer, Professor of Chemistry at the Jardin du Roi in Paris; Macquer considers the four elements "as simple homogeneous bodies, and the principles of the rest." I am indebted for information on Boerhaave to Robert E. Schofield, *Mechanism and Materialism: British Natural Philosophy in an Age of Reason* (Princeton: Princeton University Press, 1970), pp. 146-48, and also, on the elements, pp. 127, 139, and 228; on Stahl, to Hélène Metzger, *Newton, Stahl, Boerhaave et la doctrine chimique* (Paris: Alcan, 1930), p. 109; on Black and Macquer, to J. B. Partington, *A History of Chemistry*, 3 (London: Macmillan, 1962): 80-83, 130-31. The claim that Stahl was "unrivalled" comes from *A New and General Biographical Dictionary . . .*, 15 vols. (London, 1798), 14: 142, s.n. "Stahl."

The relation between the disorders and the elements is obvious save for gout and fire. Richard Mead, *Medical Works* (London, 1762), p. 541, says gout is owing to a "fiery humour"; and the empiricist Thomas Thompson, in *An Historical, Critical and Practical Treatise of the Gout* (London, 1740), says (pp. 107-08) that gout is an "Inflammatory Fever": "An Inflammation acts, and is subject to all those Variations [of location] in common with Fire, even the words Inflammation and Fire are synonimous Terms. There is such a Resemblance between them that most Nations have used these Words as synonimous; nay, more, the most learned *Boerhaave* will have that Heat and Burning in an Inflammation to proceed from real elementary Fire collected in the Body."

bathing (therapeutically and otherwise), travel, irrigation, drowning or near-drowning, eliciting a poem, and so forth. These clusters, along with the putrid vapors and heavenly inspiration of Air, and the excrement, the city filth, and the farmlands of Earth, maintain an inobtrusive continuity within the book, as the reflective reader will see. Through them, the internal or medical, the social, and the scenes of physical nature are interconnected, without Smollett's straining for analogies or contriving special circumstances. These advantages do not require—in fact, they rather militate against—any consistent change in the nature of the images.

Within any given section of Humphry Clinker, Smollett's method is like Sterne's: he breaks down an episode into components and then works them out, through analogy and modification, in the manner of a musical theme and variations. Still more than Sterne, he gives every particular its proper place through augmenting and correcting our initial data about it. We can see in some detail how he proceeds by looking at a section of the novel, for instance the two weeks of events that follow the embarrassment of Tabby and Mr. Barton (Bramble, June 12). Barton has been involved in a case of mistaken identity, courting Liddy intentionally and Tabby unintentionally. When he actually gets ready to ask for Liddy's hand, he discovers what has happened, retreats, and sends Lady Griskin with a message to clarify all; there is bad blood between Tabby and Lady Griskin as a result, and Liddy and Bramble must interpose. In developing this episode, Smollett divides it into two sets, the declaration of passion and the contretemps. Each set consists of the same three elements, which appear in the episode: mistaken identities, a letter, the threat of violence despite intercession. The episode with Tabby is comic; there follows a variant from the first set (the declaration of passion), which involves not Barton but Liddy's more serious suitor "Wilson," and is commensurately more serious in tone; there then follows a variant from the second set (contretemps), which involves not Barton's comic breach of promise, alleged through Tabby's self-interest, but the far more serious false accusation of guilt, also through self-interest, that leads to Humphry's arrest for highway robbery. To be specific, the first set is the one in which Bramble and Jery learn that the disguised "Wilson" (mistaken identity) had appeared to Liddy at Hot Well and had sent her a letter; Jery's hot temper flares, despite Liddy's promise to carry on no private correspondence with admirers (threat of violence). The second set is the one in which we find an error about Humphry's identity, explanatory writs (letter), and his jailing despite "his" victim Mr. Mead's and the highwayman Mr. Martin's intercession (threat of violence). These analogous sets end, still in Bramble's of June 12, with Barton's, "Wilson's," and Humphry's (and Martin's) lives imperilled, to different degrees, and Bramble's imperilled too, also equivocally, by a "dreadful cold" and a likely attack of the gout.

The episode of Humphry's imprisonment leads in turn to five analogous levels of salvation and concord, affecting the body or spirit or both. These are the social reconciliation of Tabby and Lady Griskin, the spiritual redemption of the felons whom Humphry converts, his regained physical freedom (and conviction of an actual thief), the renewed physical health of Bramble, and Bramble's renewed mental health too, for his letter of June 14 is the first in which he recognizes that his sickness is psychosomatic. The other two letters of the same date, Win's and Tabby's, also connect body and spirit, in the form of earth and heaven, as Humphry's Methodism permits. Win tells Mary Jones that "the whole family have been in such a constipation" over Humphry, who has now been magically freed by "Apias Korkus, who lives with the ould bailiff, and is, they say, five hundred years ould, (God bless us!), and a congeror." Tabby, in parallel, promises Mrs. Gwillim divine reward for good management of Brambleton-Hall in a superb parody of the carnal metaphors favored by Whitefield, "you

know, you must render accunt, not only to your earthly
master, but also to him that is above." These three versions of
the body-spirit connection, from Bramble's new intellectual
health through Win's and then Tabby's increasing degree of
Methodist benightedness, lead to two kinds of salvation in the
next letter, Jery's of June 23, which tells first how Humphry,
saved from being jailed for Martin's crime in London, now
joins with Martin to save the Bramble coach from highway-
men, and then how Martin asks Bramble to "save [a] poor
sinner from the gallows" by giving him employment. Loyalty
of spirit and ableness of body combine, and bring us back to
the motif of identity: Humphry's has been slightly redefined,
as Bramble's "life-guard-man on the highway," and Martin
asks to have his redefined too, from highwayman to Bramble's
"house-steward, clerk, butler, or bailiff."

Although this density of structure, sufficient for me to have
doubled the length of my discussion here, is somewhat greater
than that in parts of the novel which dwell on Bramble's
complaints, the passage is typical enough of Smollett's manner. As with Johnson and Sterne, the high degree of formal
control is not visible on the surface. Smollett's is, if anything,
less visible because he surrounds every analogue in his woven
fabric with a good bit of circumstantial realism, so that each has
its own individual value. Although early on he does juxtapose Bramble's acid and Liddy's sugar, he generally avoids
sharp contrasts even more than Johnson and Sterne, whose
episodes, at least, tend to be discrete, set off by direct contrast
from the episodes around them, and cumulatively shaped. In
making the general serve the particular as much as he does,
Smollett is more "realistic" than they, and the conceptual
whole that he implies is less defined than theirs. Nevertheless,
his procedure is as closely organized as theirs, in terms of the
same system of order and inquiry, working by the same
methods of analogy and modification.

His close organization and his differences from either John-

son or Sterne show up clearly if we turn from the weave of the
novel to its pattern, the growth of harmony within Bramble
and his correlative, the plot. Smollett never tells us how
Bramble gets better; his improvement is a fact we witness,
sometimes directly.[16] For example, we see that he has under-
gone a glorious revolution when he, who has raged at Bath
bells, can commend those of Edinburgh, and can be mild about
luxury and filth: he cheerfully writes that Edinburgh "is full of
people, and continually resounds with the noise of coaches
and other carriages, for luxury as well as commerce," although
its excellent water is "I'm afraid not in sufficient quantity to
answer all the purposes of cleanliness and convenience;
articles in which, it must be allowed, our fellow-subjects are a
little defective" (July 18). These outcroppings of his inner
change are supported by a progressive loss of rancor in his
letters, and by a redistribution of descriptive chores. Jery takes
over some of the discussion about places, like Scarborough
(July 1), and Bramble some of the discussion about people, so
that he begins to seem more personally humane and closer to
Jery's healthy interests. Smollett reinforces our sense of Bramble's change by making us respond to events in ways that
presuppose such a change. The best example is Humphry's
dragging his master naked onto the beach (Bramble, July 4).
The scene is funny, wryly and touchingly funny, but funny
nevertheless. Yet we could not respond to its humor if we did
not suppose, even before we learn, that Bramble's developing
tolerance would remove any chance of the humor's being
cruel. To see what I mean, one need only imagine how

16. This is not to say that a psychosomatic cure was implausible.
Sydenham prescribes tranquillity and freedom from worry for the gout ("A
Treatise of the Gout," sec. 53, in *Works*, pp. 496-97; and see the note on
p. 496). For Bramble's mental disorders, exercise and "the Entertainment of
the Mind," as George Cheyne puts it, are just what the doctor ordered. *The
English Malady: Or, a Treatise of Nervous Diseases* . . . (London, 1733), p. 181.
Smollett does not tell us how Bramble can allow himself this healthful
distraction.

unpleasant the scene would be if the rigid Tabby rather than her brother were the victim.

Bramble's progress is also marked, like Rasselas's, by structural means. *Humphry Clinker* breaks naturally into four parts roughly even in length. The first, ending with Jery's letter of May 24, contains the exposition and the adoption of Humphry, the first assertion of Bramble's authority and the first change in the travelling party. As we saw, all the incidental characters in this section respond directly to the fixed positions of Bramble's entourage. Humphry does not, and the second quarter of the novel, as we have just seen in sampling a section, broadens its themes in London and on the road toward Scotland. The third quarter, starting with Jery's of July 10, introduces Lismahago and takes our friends through Scotland; and the fourth, starting with Jery's announcement of September 12, "once more I tread upon English ground," carries us to the end, with exceptional intricacy. These four sections do not, I believe, have the inner shape of Johnson's groups or Sterne's volumes. They are as natural as Johnson's: a casual reader would divide the book first after Bath or Humphry's hiring, or at entering London; second at meeting Lismahago or entering Scotland; and third at reentering England. The sections are too multiform to do what Johnson's do, but they establish climates or tonalities for the events within them. Bramble and the plot change in nature, and the way in which we look at Bramble and the plot changes too, partly in direct response to them and partly in response to these climates or tonalities.

What I mean will be clearer if we examine the functions of the two men who enter at the junction of the first two fourths and two halves, Humphry and Lismahago respectively. They—Humphry when he appears, Lismahago three-fourths through the book—both become members of the community of travellers because they have no community (and thus, of course, no correspondents) of their own. They both act, therefore, only on the internal economy of the travelling party. The similarity ends there, for Humphry and Lismahago have different functions. Humphry's is emblematic, less precise and more complex than Lismahago's. The expedition is his, as the title of the novel says it is, because what he represents is set free, "expeditum." Bramble's spirit of charity sets the man Humphry free from bondage to "sickness, hunger, wretchedness, and want" (Jery, May 24), his animal necessities; thereafter, by analogy, Humphry's spirit in various forms sets Bramble free from crippling animality. Sickness of body and mind, and at one point death, lose their mastery over him. In part, then, master seems to double servant. Bramble, a cynical Don riding after an enthusiastic Sancho, finds his cure in the climate of feeling made emblematic in Humphry. As Ronald Paulson remarks, Bramble moves from his own zeal for reform by invective to something more like Humphry's zeal for reform through persuasion.[17]

Yet Humphry's model is essentially metaphorical, not literal. He does not convert Bramble, although he signals and to some extent occasions Bramble's conversion. His fundamental level of operation in the novel is that of Chowder, who is a measure of Bramble's ill temper and subjection. Humphry replaces Chowder, to whom Tabby and Win compare him, the one calling him a "mangy hound" and the other declaring that "a hound [may] be staunch, thof he has got narro hare on his buttocks" (Jery, May 24; Win, June 3). Bramble, because of his own act in replacing selfish dog with selfless man, can tell Dr. Lewis for the first time that he is feeling better (May 29), but Humphry himself does not directly cause the improvement. Nor is his job throughout the novel that of source or model for Bramble's growing health, although his virtues, his inner equilibrium, and his belief in redemption do introduce formal

17. Ronald Paulson, *Satire and the Novel in Eighteenth-Century England* (New Haven: Yale University Press, 1967), p. 198; the Cervantean comparison is his.

patterns in terms of which the progress and denouement of
the novel take their shape and meaning. As these patterns
develop, they transcend him, because Humphry's "expedition," unlike Bramble's, does not imply his education.

As Bramble is both man and rhetor (source of a tone and
formal patterns), Humphry is both man and source of a tone
and formal patterns. We accept the tone and the patterns, but
modified from the specific naive form in which Humphry
presents them. His actions, therefore, must be such as to be
admired and discounted simultaneously. Thus his innocence
depends on an ignorance and comic nakedness that cost him
our serious respect. His Methodism and farrier's physic suit
"brute beasts" rather than "rational creatures" (Jery, June 2),
even if the one temporarily cures the felons (Jery, June 11) and
the other brings the almost drowned Bramble back to life. He
converts Win and Tabby only to pious affectation and cant, but
his presence, when set against the external show of the
Frenchified footman Dutton, shames those vices. When he
saves Bramble from drowning, he makes us forgive but not
forget his folly in his earlier "rescue" of his master from
drowning at Scarborough. Our relationship to Humphry the
man undergoes constant modifications through analogy and
contrast; our attitude toward his goodness, which is what
affects our sense of tone and of Bramble's progress, does not.
Clinkerism, so to speak, becomes detached enough from
Clinker for it to serve, as I have suggested it does, tonally and
formally. As we learn to know Humphry, the energies on
which Bramble must draw to be cured gain a local habitation
and a vital spokesman.

Humphry transfuses new blood into the Britain Bramble
sees; Lismahago drains old toxins from Bramble himself. He
does so obviously by pulling Tabby from her brother, and less
obviously but analogously, by filling Bramble's role as Knight
of the Woeful (or Dour) Countenance. We have already seen
the care with which the stage is set for him, and commented on

the relation between his spoiled temper and Bramble's. Given the limelight through analogy, the lieutenant stands in lieu of Bramble as a willing agent of social reproach. He also inherits some of Bramble's arguments. Welsh chauvinism shifts its coat and becomes Scottish. The attack on luxury and dietary follies, on political corruption and the loss of rural simplicity, now recurs in Lismahago's body of dogma just before he leaves the party and just after he returns to it (Bramble, July 15, September 20). If Bramble is satiric and quixotic, Lismahago is equally so, even to the point of "answering, with his horse, the description of Don Quixote mounted on Rozinante" (Jery, July 10). If Bramble has been henpecked by Tabby, Lismahago plainly will be in the same peril, even if he eases her old-maid's frustrations. But Smollett deprives Lismahago the touchy misanthrope of two pieces of novelistic ballast that Bramble has enjoyed. The first is an active disposition toward charity and change for the better. The second is the chance to speak in his own person rather than through a narrator. As a result, we at this point in the book reject in Lismahago what we had been willing to suffer in the earlier harangues of Bramble. Lismahago's appearance therefore aligns Bramble himself with a more moderate position. He stands in respect to Lismahago's vision almost as Jery had once stood in respect to Bramble's. When the group arrives in Scotland without the lieutenant, we find ourselves left, like them, without any angry and immoderate man.

After a hundred days of travel, then, Bramble has moved far enough that he can plausibly lose his bitterness through Lismahago's surrogacy. The rest of this quarter of the novel, the adventures in Scotland, tests his new health within a national capital (like London in the second quarter) and a bucolic nature (like that in Wales where he presumably grew ill). The last quarter is to bring Bramble the harder test of personal involvement, with Oxmington, Bullford, Baynard, and Dennison, not to mention Lismahago, whose cure (as

analogue) must parallel his own. He is spared that as yet in
Scotland. As a result of his fresh blandness and detachment,
Scotland seems to many readers a place of rather too much
repose. The prickliness and dourness of Lismahago the stereo-
typed Scot do not reappear; the Frenchified Dutton gets no
more than a mile or so into Scotland, when he is replaced by an
old soldier, Archy M'Alpin; the letters after the party leave
Edinburgh move away from the ordinary themes we have
discussed, so that the texture of the novel grows less complicated, further and further from the disorder and artifice that
have been the source of its richness. All this can easily be
defended in theory. In practice, it looks thin, at least to a
modern reader for whom the workaday world of eighteenth-
century London is as exotic as the romantic wilds of Scotland.
For Smollett's readers, the land "that Ossian wont to tread"
(Jery, September 3) would have had its own magic, its own
suggestiveness, and therefore its own novelistic richness.
Bramble's fascination with it would, for the first time, have
brought his response into line with his readers'.[18]

His response is certainly in line with Smollett's own, for his
letter of August 28 lifts into lyricism with Smollett's "Ode to
Leven-Water." The once bitter, reckless old satirist of Bath and
London has precisely right feelings in his praise for a Scots
Arcadia. Feelings become judgment, judgment becomes feelings in this letter and that of September 6. The "Ode," that
union of Bramble and Smollett, repeats in sequence Bramble's
prose references near the end of his letter of August 28, to "the
Arcadia of Scotland," "pure water," and "delicious fish"; and
its poetic mode of procedure, from recollection to description
to moral comment, is one particularly associated with Bramble

18. The cultural marriage between England and Scotland, which carries
out familial and educational themes to lead to the denouement, requires that
each partner in the marriage have a strong individual personality. Cf. B. L.
Reid, "Smollett's Healing Journey," in *The Long Boy and Others* (Athens:
University of Georgia Press, 1969), p. 93.

during the novel. All three—the past, the present, and the moral—are gathered up in the person of "the admiral" (Bramble, September 6), who stands in contrast to the lame Admiral Balderick in Bath. He is the symbol of this "Scottish paradise" "who has lived near ninety years, without pain or sickness, among oaks of his own planting," "in great health, peace, and harmony." "Knowing no wants," he and his wife "enjoy the perfection of content." That Clinker takes this man to be a spirit suggests the admiral's almost supernatural state, suspended in time as are the ancestral customs and land about him. Bramble's physical decay, the continuous change of England, the sadness of the *laudator temporis acti*—these are not universal conditions. Just as the travellers in *Rasselas* pass from one level of personal complexity to another, Bramble passes from one level to another of alternative tone—the exposition, the English trip with Humphry, Lismahago and Scotland—until he, like the prince, can comprehend (in all senses of the word) what he has seen and felt.

The spiritual privacy, so to speak, of Scotland has shown us the health of Bramble the observer. Social England must now test Bramble the participant. Therefore, the movement of plot in the concluding fourth of *Humphry Clinker* develops the final obstacle course for him intricately and ingeniously, through analogy and modification. The events before the weddings can be divided in half, each half including three subdivisions, which also present formal repetitions. The first of these halves involves the three successive letters about the near-duel over Lord Oxmington's rudeness (Jery, September 28), the first visit to the Baynards' (Bramble, September 30), and the visit to Sir Thomas Bullford's (Jery, October 3). Each of these three incidents turns on ideas of honor and on an aristocrat's, or would-be aristocrat's, prerogatives. Each also draws upon the theme of hospitality, which recurs while the party is in Scarborough and (tacitly) during their congenial trip through Scotland. The two earlier episodes threaten the equilibrium

reached in Scotland, Lord Oxmington openly by causing
Bramble to reengage himself in a Quixotic rage for honor,
Mrs. Baynard covertly by her use of illness—"delicate nerves"
and "imbecility of spirit," as her husband puts it—to throw her
estate into self-aggrandizing disorder. One tests Bramble by
goading him, the other by caricaturing his motives. The old
Bramble was able to handle neither kind of test. A slight like
Oxmington's would throw him into uncontrollable fury.
His former advice to Baynard, to "carry [Mrs. Baynard]
abroad . . ., where he might gratify her vanity for half the
expence it cost him in England," proved as disastrous as
Bramble's own case has taught us to expect when physical
remedies alone are applied to a psychological and moral
problem. Now, to some extent, the new Bramble passes both
tests. Oxmington is handled with some forbearance, and
Baynard is given not only better advice but also a personal
commitment of some depth. None the less, both episodes
leave a bitter taste in the mouth. Both experiences must be
purged.

A partial purgative comes in the third subdivision of this
half, the visit to Sir Thomas's estate. The scenes at Sir
Thomas's are built on a half-dozen elements from the Oxmington episode: the insult to Lismahago, payment for being
entertained (Bramble's guinea at Oxmington's; Sir Thomas's
gift of a snuff box to Lismahago), dousing in a pond, retri-
bution for injuries, asking pardon for malfeasances (Oxmington and his servant; Frogmore), and the brutish host (*Ox*ming-
ton's brain is "very ill timbered"; *Bull*ford is "of moderate
intellects"). Smollett adds to these repeated elements two
reminiscences of the scenes with Lismahago's predecessor,
Micklewhimmen (Jery, July 1). Frogmore's "poisoned" mush-
rooms elaborate on the deserved sufferings of the young
clothier who drinks Micklewhimmen's claret, down to the
"double evacuations" of both men. The fire scene, in which
the barely clad Lismahago saves himself by a nighttime

descent down a ladder, yokes Win's similar descent with Micklewhimmen's saving himself (and revealing his powers) at Scarborough. As Win showed her "beauties" to Humphry, Lismahago proves his "parts and mettle" to Tabby. His display, moreover, confirms his match with Tabby, while Micklewhimmen's display, in pelting down the stairs toward safety, destroyed his. Smollett's technique is as plain as it is shrewd. The elements of the Oxmington episode have taken on a charge of nastiness of which Smollett rids them by reassociating them in a purely comic context. The Bullford episode is lighthearted in itself, and Smollett amplifies this tone by reviving for us an earlier comic episode, that with Micklewhimmen, to reinforce the new association of ideas. The internal proof that he succeeds is the difference between Lismahago's retributive triumphs at Oxmington's and at Bullford's, the former vicious and the latter both controlled and amusingly apropos.

Smollett carries his formal ingenuity still further in leading to the meeting with Dennison, who discharges through direct contrast the unpleasantness of the meeting with Baynard. Baynard has a willful valetudinarian (or so she claims) for a wife, a spoiled son, and bankruptcy hanging over him; Dennison is prudent, uncompetitive, successful in his wife and son, and able to be the model for Baynard's recovery in reforming his land, dispelling his household ghosts, and creating order and tranquillity. Smollett brings us to his purgative contrast by giving us third versions of two incidents already represented in both the Oxmington episode and its comic counterpart, the stay at Sir Thomas Bullford's. These are the duel (a duel of wits in the Bullford version) and the ducking in a pond. If the Bullford episode has repeated and reformed Oxmington elements, we now have those elements reversed: Jery's near-duel with the real Wilson (October 4) is serious and brings an offer of hospitality; Bramble's near-death is still more serious and brings a still more joyous hospitality with it. Thus the events between Scotland and the denouement are divided into two complementary halves, Oxmington–Baynard–Bullford and Wilson–accident–Dennison, which set up a progress from a threatened disruption of the Scottish equilibrium to a new and richer equilibrium of recovery and love.

Under Dennison's roof, finally, Bramble acknowledges his past, his identity, and his son—Humphry—lost through egoism. Scotland had been a symbol of natural order; Dennison is a symbol of the moral order derived from a knowledge of oneself, and as such he embodies a completeness of ideal that encompasses both the romantic and the valetudinarian plots of *Humphry Clinker*. The events in this last quarter of the novel have been, in fact, moral tests; by responding to them, Bramble has earned the right to be a lesser version of Dennison. He gains a son, admittedly no George Dennison; and the surrogate acts of revamping Baynard's life (Bramble, October 26), and being called "father" by Liddy when he recovers from drowning, complete this reform and bring the personal and social into line. To go one step further, and to realize that his acknowledging Humphry and his past is to atone for an irresponsible class-proud dishonor done Humphry's mother, is to see how the "duel" for Liddy's honor and the arrogance of aristocrats are also germane to the central matter of the ending. The experience of the novel, then, is compressed and focused through analogy, modification, and epitome, and brought to bear upon the restoration of order—holism and hierarchy—to the represented world. The dialectic of plot gives us back the complexity that seemed to have been lost in the virtual merger of Bramble's and Jery's narrative voices.

Such a denouement, thematically, fulfills what has been latent; mimetically, it risks being at cross-purposes with Smollett's realism. Sudden discoveries of identity, after all, especially those that knit together families and friends, properly belong to romances, not to narratives that insist, like Bramble, on seeing the world as it is. Imlac cannot turn out to be Rasselas's father, or Falkland Caleb Williams's. Therefore, if reality is not to snuggle into the forms invented by desire, Smollett has no choice but to make the forms invented by desire parts of the reality he has depicted all along. Bramble's holism and hierarchy serve this purpose, for they claim, as principles, to be able to give each particular a fit place within a worldly and humane outlook. Rejected objects, like the romance that Liddy and Win represent in their different ways, like Humphry the orphaned outcast, or like the sins of the past, must be accommodated once more within Bramble's world, his mind, and within ours, the plot of the novel. As he broadens his view of things, we are trained to secularize the miraculous and bring it within the confines of "nature" as we understand that norm in this sturdy imitation of nature. He and we are helped by the intrusion through Liddy and Win of superstition, fantasy, and romance into the sensible urbanity which Jery and, increasingly, Bramble establish. No novel devoted to finding everything its just place can reject these attitudes, voiced by two of the small troupe. If Smollett had wanted to reject them, he would merely have left them out: he offers us the illusion, not the fact, of comprehensiveness, and he could have contrived that illusion without allowing the girls a foothold in our tolerance. Not only does he accept their vagaries, but he sets up an entwined series of incidents which emotionally reinforce what the girls represent. For this procedure of strengthening by analogy we encounter a group of people whose identities are redefined; we also encounter a group of revenants. The groups are not mutually exclusive, and they merge in the denouement.

The definition, or the redefinition, of identity is a theme ready at hand for technical reasons. Any novel that depends as heavily as this one on analogies between characters runs the risk of blurring the characters' individuality. Smollett counters this risk by making them individually vivid, by placing them within a tight thematic structure, and—this being the point at issue—by making their identities a matter often and openly referred to. Furthermore, the letter writers themselves keep defining what they see, sometimes objectively and rightly, sometimes not; and in this way too, since each character who appears is seen and described by at least one other, identity keeps being defined and redefined in the normal process of the novel. I have already mentioned some examples of this, like the contretemps with Barton, Humphry's imprisonment, and Bramble's helping Martin to redefine himself. Jery's valet, Dutton, makes himself into a Frenchman and Maclaughlin into a tailor (Jery, July 18), Grieve turns out to be Count Fathom, and Lismahago is interpreted by each of the characters. Jery's rash notions of honor make him define Wilson as a scoundrel and blunder into two abortive duels. "Wilson," in turn, poses as an actor playing a young man (Aimwell) who poses as an heir, which is precisely what "Wilson"—George Dennison— was in the first place. Lismahago, that fighting man with his "genus et proavos" from a primitive nation, Scotland, be- comes "first warrior" and sachem (by adoption and election) among the more primitive Indians. Win Jenkins, who tries to imitate her inimitable mistress, ends up as her mistress's niece (with a bar sinister) by marriage. Most of these examples are plausible enough to anchor in a realistic context the redefini- tions of identity near the end of the novel. As my grouping of examples suggests, George Dennison's, Lismahago's, and Win's new identities work by analogy with their old. The amusing poetic justice for each helps induce us to accept the coincidences more willingly.

The theme of revenants has roots in nature too: if a well- travelled ex-Oxonian landowner who has been an M.P. takes a trip around England, he is likely to meet old friends, some on purpose, some by accident. Bramble finds Serle, Quin, and the valetudinarians in Bath, relatives and Hewet in Yorkshire, Baynard and Bullford as he travels south; young Jery has met Eastgate in Bath, and Barton and Dick Ivy in London; what then is more natural than that Bramble should meet his old friend Charles Dennison? A second level of this theme strings out some less probable meetings, such as that between Count Fathom/Grieve and the Melvilles, or the return of the pavior's son (Jery, September 12). Here we have more accent on the recovery of the past, as in the pathetic incident (Jery, July 10) in which Humphry, working at the forge of the dead smith, is taken by the smith's mad wife for her husband mystically come back. Lismahago is taken twice for a ghost, once by Tabby after his presumed drowning at Solway Sands, once by his horsewhipped nephew (Jery, September 12; Bramble, September 15). In the same letter of Bramble's we hear about one man's use of "second sight" to anticipate a visit from a friend whom he had not seen for twenty years; the letter before that, Jery's, tells about the pavior's son and the recovery of Lismahago; the letter before that, Win's, calls Scotland "the land of congyration" because of lights, lamentations, "a mischievious ghost," fairies, and an old witch; these aberrations of Win's come up in the letter directly preceding hers, Liddy's account of "the sudden apparition" of "Wilson" at the hunters' ball; and finally, the next letter back, Bramble's of September 6, tells about Humphry's fear of the admiral, as a spirit. This thematic cluster between September 6 and September 15 permits the sudden appearance of a son for Bramble, and a suitor for Liddy, in early October. Smollett brushes away the superstitious incrustations from the revenants and gives us a range of probabilities in his variants on the theme, so as to make the novel look seamless and sensible. His hardheadedness diverts us from the dubious train of happenstance, so that in supporting Bramble-like skepticism he makes us swallow marvels that no novel-reading Bramble could be expected to stomach.

The rising up of the past, and the intrusion of the spiritual world upon the world we know, have obvious connections with Methodism. Once again, Smollett prepares his climax by pretending to be a man of moderation. He makes Methodism a form of superstition, useful for the classes who can be duped by it, and corrupt in the cant of a Win or a Tabby. Even Liddy— compare her letters of June 10 and September 7—has her doubts about it. Tough-minded Lismahago may be a free-thinker, and his rational Indians do well to stew the missionaries (Jery, July 13). Bramble objects to his own apostolic name as a relic of "canting hypocrites." Nowhere does he show much interest in religion of any sort, but mocks the fanaticism of the Scots and the Cromwellians (July 18), and declares his preference for living safely over relying for rescue on Providence (Jery, August 8). The secular equivalents to religion are nominal: our attention is called to "Matthew" and "Obadiah" as the biblical names of two lukewarm Christians; Bramble has begotten Humphry on a barmaid at the Angel; Bramble and Jery happen to be alumni of Jesus College, so that Jery's closing "Pray, remember me to all our friends of Jesus" (e.g., June 23) is a nominal equivalent to the Methodist cant we get from Win and Tabby.[19] And Bramble's inveighing against a newly fallen world is a mundane and empirical version of the Methodist emphasis on universal sin; his hyperbole argues a fortiori in opposition to theirs.

Against this sort of background, Smollett presents us with Bramble's secular conversion, in which "the Methodist doctrines of the new birth, the new light, the efficacy of grace, the insufficiency of works, and the operation of the spirit" (Jery, August 8) have their counterparts. Humphry bears his master from the water "as if he had been an infant of six months" and bleeds him like an animal with a farrier's fleam. From this loss

19. As Parreaux points out, p. 320, "Jesus College, Oxford, has since its foundation maintained a special relationship with the Welsh." John Macky, writing at about the time that Bramble would have entered, goes so far as to call it "Jesus College for the Welsh, in *A Journey through England*, 2 vols. (3rd. ed., London, 1732), 2:81. Welsh students were given priority for a large number of the fellowships offered. Once again, Smollett refuses to compromise the plausible, but instead exploits it.

of humanity, followed by incoherent words, Bramble revokes forty years—the proper biblical period—to confess, repent, and atone for "the sins" of his past that "rise up in judgment against" him. We certainly have a revelation following, but not caused by, an act of charity. After this, Bramble, through being able to accept his blessings, can imitate his erstwhile "fellow-rake at Oxford," Charles Dennison, in "that pitch of rural felicity, at which I have been aspiring these twenty years in vain," ever since the shady birth and desertion of Humphry, who is "about twenty years of age" (Jery, [October 6]; Bramble, October 8; Jery, May 24). We are never encouraged to call all this providential, as convention might dictate. But our reservations about Providence, at least for the duration of this novel, make us ready to accept coincidence and the mechanics of second causes. That is precisely what Smollett wants us to accept, and what he exemplifies, all the time reminding us through religious parody that we have chosen to follow rationality down the line.

Effectually, the structure which we have been considering makes real each person's romance, permits each to convert reality into a form arranged by personal desire. The marriages take place auspiciously, Bramble finds himself cured, Humphry has new bonds to his master, and so on. Romance elements like apparitions, wonderful reunions, rejuvenation, and true love translate into objective terms what the subjectivity of the letters implies. As usual, Smollett treats various elements with varying degrees of seriousness and emphasis, to give each its place in the represented world and in our feelings. The marriage of Liddy and George Dennison, for instance, is serious, because we need the sense of refreshment which it alone of the weddings can provide. At the same time, a marriage based on a disguised heir's slinking about England after a featherheaded girl, each of them growing feverish in the other's absence (Bramble, August 8, October 11), ought not to be blessed in the wry world of *Humphry Clinker*. Smollett, therefore, shields it by making much of Tabby's and Win's weddings, with their abundance of comic detail and carefree spirit.[20]

Or again, matters ought not to proceed to their happy conclusion quite so steadily as the dialectic of the book requires. Smollett breaks the sense of steady progress while he maintains the progress itself. To the usual petty accidents and injuries of the novel, he adds comic reductions of disaster, which remind us of and rephrase certain threats. We have talked about the way in which the practical jokes at Sir Thomas Bullford's reduce to comedy the themes of sickness, fire, drowning, and dangerous bathing for the gout. Later the wedding festivities include farces about Harlequin Skeleton and "Death in pursuit of Consumption," and Wilson uses a cat to make Humphry believe "that Satan was come to buffet him in propria persona" (Jery, November 8). With such devices, Smollett manages to broaden his joyful tone, to present a world of common sense and yet to pry it wider with crucial, though never dominant, forces of romance.

The process of epistemological broadening resembles that in Johnson and Sterne. *Rasselas* works through layers of realization, in that we progressively enlarge our understanding of a given situation. Johnson could have stopped sooner, as he did in the tale of Seged or as Juvenal did in his Tenth Satire: the idiom of *Rasselas* does not entail the ending we get. *Tristram* introduces its layers at once, but the procedure is the same. The elder Shandys alone might be the subject of a Pickwickian novel; they, revised by Tristram the man and the author, are the subject of Tristram's memoirs; Tristram's memoirs, and his process of contriving them, become the subject of Sterne's novel. Similarly, one could have a book with an unreformed

---

20. Sheridan Baker notes the displacement of wedding jokes from Liddy to other characters in his "*Humphry Clinker* as Comic Romance," *Papers of the Michigan Academy of Science, Arts, and Letters* 46 (1961): 645-54.

Bramble, on the model of Smollett's own *Travels through France and Italy*.[21] Bramble's recovery of his son solves nothing in the plot, negates nothing we have accepted as true. Humphry's identity, after all, has not been an absorbing mystery, "Wilson" could have been any rich man's son, Bramble's health has been pretty well established. The secular version of Providence that rewards its grudging apostle comes as a charming bonus, as the best ending that the novel could have, but not as an inevitable, or worse yet, a forced ending. The inevitable ending calls "only" for the world, with its empirical diversity, to be reconciled within Bramble's mind. Thus the conclusion does not revoke the continuing force of the filth and affectation he has seen, but enlarges the context in which that seeing, an act of the mind, takes place. This is not very different from the "presentational" mode one finds in Johnson and Sterne, although the three authors handle the problem of a fit ending differently.

Bramble's utopia, pastoral Wales and the *tempus actum*, fails him as the Happy Valley and Shandy Hall fail Rasselas and Tristram, because of human frailty, in this case Bramble's own and Tabby's. Nonetheless, he derives his system of inquiry from it and from his own condition, still in the manner of Rasselas and Tristram, so as to search for earthly happiness. Tristram's happiness or fulfillment can come only when he

21. Recent criticism has stressed, not always convincingly, Smollett's deliberate assumption of a splenetic persona in his *Travels*, a proto-Bramble whom we need not always believe. See, e.g., John F. Sena, "Smollett's Persona and the Melancholic Traveler: An Hypothesis," *ECS* 1 (1968): 353-69, and Scott Rice, "The Satiric Persona of Smollett's *Travels*," *Studies in Scottish Literature* 10 (1972): 33-47. I prefer Gardner Stout's interpretation, that Smollett is playing a role we are basically to admire; but in either case, my point about the presentational nature of *Humphry Clinker* is strengthened by the parallel between Bramble and the speaker of the *Travels*. Gardner D. Stout, Jr., "Introduction" to his edition of Laurence Sterne, *A Sentimental Journey through France and Italy by Mr. Yorick* (Berkeley and Los Angeles: University of California Press, 1967), p. 37.

redeems the past by satisfying the familial and interpretive demands his heritage imposes on him. Bramble too, as events prove, must find happiness in redeeming the past by satisfying certain familial and interpretive demands. He begins by defining the state of happiness negatively, as the absence of pain; so, for that matter, might Rasselas, although his mental pain has no effect on his body. Both men find a sort of cure in distraction, the process of search itself becoming the product sought for. In this condition, they resemble Tristram, whose form can be adequate only in motion. This medicine they presumably must continue taking, but in addition, Bramble and Rasselas find a resolution of another kind, one which revokes the temporal process. As Johnson does, Smollett uses a logic of form and of emotion, through varieties of incremental and associative repetition, for instance, or through connotative elements (e.g., ghosts and spirits in both books), to give us a dialectic progress of our own. The form, for us and for the protagonists, satisfies us as process and also allows us to revoke temporal process and confront the total presented world of the novel: events are generated through analogy and modification, and cohere retrospectively in terms of the same procedures. Thus particulars are bound together for us precisely, without any shrinking of the empirical breadth that mid-eighteenth-century fiction demands.

We have seen at length how *Humphry* combines inclusiveness and control, through tying visible order to Bramble's system of inquiry and creating covert order through procedures of inquiry like analogy, modification, and grouping. Incremental repetition of events, surrogate characters, the use of the travelling party as a unit—these techniques of order, familiar from Sterne's system of order—recur here. The translation of Clinker's Methodism or Bramble's nosology into more nearly satisfactory forms closely resembles analogies and modifications which Sterne uses to rehabilitate the Shandys. Finally, both novelists remind us, through insisting on multiple perspectives, that one must be an epistemological skeptic.[22]

For neither Sterne's nor Smollett's comedy, nor for Johnson's apologue, does this skepticism really blight crucial inferences. Sterne's and Smollett's characters do not do well at prediction—that would be running counter to the whole temper of these novels—but the novelists are much less concerned with the consequences of that sort of failure than with failures of assessment. The unexpectedness of the ending of *Humphry*, for example, does not make us feel trapped in a treacherously impenetrable world. Yet that sort of effect is implicit in the system of order and inquiry we have been describing, and becomes explicit in the novels of Fielding and Godwin to which we shall now turn. *Amelia* and *Caleb Williams* share several traits with *Humphry*. The three novels concentrate on social satire. Their endings take one by surprise. Their protagonists undergo great change. To juxtapose them with *Humphry*, to see how they use the system of order and inquiry that Johnson, Sterne, and Smollett use, is to expand radically one's sense of the emotional and cognitive range of their common mode.

22. Smollett's epistemological interests have been singled out by John M. Warner, "Smollett's Development as a Novelist," *Novel* 5 (1972): 148-61. He has much that is interesting, especially about Smollett's earlier fiction; but he seems to think that Smollett was ahead of his time in being concerned with epistemology, a "Romantic" or "Pre-Romantic." If this book of mine can not only prove something about the eighteenth-century novel but also help discredit such verbal tinsel as "Romantic" and its prejudices, I shall be delighted.

Amelia

The epistemological concerns that have been a source of fascination for Johnson, Sterne, and Smollett become something close to a matter of life and death in Fielding's *Amelia*. In Johnson, nearly all thought is speech; in Sterne, when thought is not speech or unambiguous gesture, it is part of a familiar (familial) system; in Smollett, we know, and only we need to know, what the characters are thinking. Unlike these men, Fielding makes the hiddenness of thought, and therefore of motives, a major concern. He subsumes under it his study of the patterns of individual thought, patterns only brokenly perceived despite the efforts that we, not to mention the characters, are forced to make. The novel itself has as tight an organization as we expect from him, along lines familiar from our analyses of Johnson, Smollett, and Sterne; but as I remarked in the Introduction, and as the analyses have shown, the rules of inquiry for artifacts do not work equally well for experience. In his earlier novels, Fielding makes the rules work acceptably for both, as far as the reader goes, through the use of a helpful narrator who gives clues (sometimes obscurely or misleadingly) and sets the limits of possibility. *Amelia* lowers us almost to the level of the characters, strips us of comedy and comfort, and creates in us what one might rather lumpishly call "epistemological empathy." More than ever before in his novels, Fielding returns to a theatrical mode in which all we know is what we can witness. outward action, objective and largely undoctored reality, "flat" characters whose confrontations give the drama shape, unreliable speakers, economy of playing time—predominantly, in *Amelia*, we get a "realistic" version of what goes on when spectators, at a play or in real life, apprehend what takes place before them and with their own unaided wits try to draw inferences from it.[1]

This new mode of Fielding's implies a double program, the retreat of the narrator and the potential frustration of our attempts to deal with the represented world. The narrator, of course, retreats entirely from the sort of aesthetic commentary that marks *Tom Jones*. He shuns it because that Ariostan mode would import too much of the epic into theatrical *Amelia*, because renewing it would become repetitious or trivial, and most of all because we are not to be reminded that *Amelia* is a willful artifact: it is a "Model of HUMAN LIFE," in which we can and should study causal relationships (I, 1). The narrator retreats from exuberance and irony, too, because he is no longer blazoning the truisms of worldly good will for our reaction, but giving facts full play and prominence for analysis. He speaks, most of the time, with calculated neutrality, or takes a choric role, to express our supposed feelings or our bewildered attempt to order facts.[2]

---

1. Perhaps this why Fielding went back to his plays for models, such as *The Modern Husband* for the Trents and the Noble Lord, or Mondish in *The Universal Gallant* for James and the tone of *Amelia*'s "secular" ending. Sheridan Baker, following prior discussions by Wilbur Cross and Charles Woods, mentions other plays of Fielding's that seem to have contributed to *Amelia*, among them *The Temple Beau, The Coffee-House Politician,* and *The Author's Farce.* "Fielding's *Amelia* and the Materials of Romance," *PQ* 41 (1962): 437-49.

2. In "Nature's Dance of Death. Part II: Fielding's *Amelia*," *ECS* 3 (1970): 491-522, C. J. Rawson has shown how the narrator's lack of witty command

He even retreats from omniscience. In the earlier novels, he likes to play baffled, offer a choice of explanations, or present us with mock-lessons; but the narrator of *Amelia* prefers grave moral generalities that detach themselves from the total situation or character to which they are supposed to apply, like maxims in *Rasselas*. No doubt Colonel James really is generous "to the highest degree," but the narrator misleads us when he asks leave "to stop a minute, to lament that so few are to be found of this benign Disposition" (IV, 4), a sentiment undercut not only by James's later actions but also by the narrator's implicit contempt for his indiscriminate giving (VIII, 5). When he lays down the "general Rule, that no Woman who hath any great Pretensions to Admiration is over-well pleased in a Company where she perceives herself to fill only the second Place" (V, 3), he implies falsely, or at least simplistically, that envy is Mrs. Bennet's motive for dispraising the Noble Lord as against Atkinson. Three books later, we have no reason to believe that Mrs. Ellison's reputation was much damaged by Amelia's discovering her perfidy, or that any such damage would be widespread. Yet the narrator insists that "loss of Reputation, which is generally irreparable, was to be her Lot; Loss of Friends is of this the certain Consequence" (VIII, 3). The reader of Fielding, where evil is always baffled, can hardly grant that "it is almost impossible Guilt should miss the discovering of all the Snares in its Way, as it is constantly prying closely into every Corner, in order to lay Snares for

---

augments our sense of his inability to affect what happens, and of the separation of systematic aesthetic procedures from the obscurity and untidiness of life. I agree, although I would place more stress than Rawson does on the cognitive importance of the presented facts' being free from significant outside intervention. Other critics have preferred to think that the equivocal handling of the narrator is a mark that Fielding, of all novelists in English, was technically inept. See, e.g., Anthony J. Hassall's "Fielding's *Amelia*: Dramatic and Authorial Narration," *Novel* 5 (1972): 225-33.

others" (VIII, 9). In *Amelia,* as in Fielding's other novels, the homilist emerges for local effects; but for the first time, his words seem to pretend to a universality which they do not have within the novel itself. His maxims participate in the general instability of the world of *Amelia.*

We do not even know how to take the exordium on the art of life, because the world from which the "most useful of all Arts" might emerge has been left an enigmatic paradigm by the narrator. In the plot of *Tom Jones,* the most important job of the narrator is to lead us to balanced appraisals of characters and events. Only when these become redundant, in the last book, does he desert us. We can see how far the narrator of *Amelia* retreats from this role, and the consequences of his retreat, by comparing two episodes, one from each novel. In prison, Booth is robbed by Cooper the Methodist and (perhaps) by Robinson the gambler. We are granted our inference of Cooper's villainy from his predestinarian cant: the Methodist, says the narrator, had "as the Phrase of the Sect is, *searched* [Booth] to the Bottom. In fact, he had thoroughly examined every one of Mr. *Booth*'s Pockets" (I, 4). Therefore, by Fielding's favorite logic of analogy, the gambler Robinson, who claims to believe in a universe of fatal chance, should cheat. A "strapping Wench" charges him with that very crime. Yet he is able to rebut Booth's suspicion and confirm the rebuttal by proving that he has not stolen Booth's snuffbox, despite the strapping wench's charge that he is also a pickpocket. Robinson then proceeds to win all Booth's money at cards, an event qualified by the narrator's remarks on lucky gamesters' being thought cheats, and to refuse to lend Booth any of it, which the narrator again qualifies by talking about "the Rascality, *as it appeared to* [Booth], of the other" (italics mine). We never discover whether Robinson the gambler has bilked Booth; when he returns to the story at the end of *Amelia,* he returns as a thief, the very role of which he had proved his

innocence in the matter of the snuffbox. Analogy and inference have been blocked at every turn.[3]

The significance of an episode like this may be made clearer
by comparing it with the treatment of Jenny Jones, who pleads
guilty to Mrs. Wilkins's arraignment of her as Tom's mother.
Both Jenny and Robinson are accused by at least partially
interested and noxious characters early in the respective
narratives (*TJ*, I, 6; *A*, I, 5); both charges can be put in proper
focus only when Jenny and Robinson themselves bring about
the respective denouements. Jenny's confession uncorks the
sarcasm of the village women, which she bears patiently,
"except the malice of one woman, who reflected upon her
person. . . . Jenny replied to this with a bitterness which might
have surprised a judicious person, who had observed the tranquillity with which she bore all the affronts to her chastity; but
her patience was perhaps tired out, for this is a virtue which is
very apt to be fatigued by exercise." The irony here is three-
fold. Most obviously, it is directed at Jenny, to whom looks
are far more important than chastity, so much so as to surprise
"a judicious person." The innocent wonder of the "judicious
person" marks him as a novice in human nature, causing us to
laugh at him and consequently to be surer of Jenny's fault. Our
amusement at Fielding's specious and witty excuse for Jenny's
lack of patience further confirms our opinion. The second layer
of irony is, of course, that we are mistaken about Jenny, who
merely gets angry at the accusation that is true—she is
homely—and can be patient in the face of those that are not,
and for which, besides, she has braced herself. The final layer
of irony is that the second makes very little difference: our
assessment of Jenny, albeit made for the wrong reasons, is

---

3. Cf. Leo Braudy's acute comment about Fielding, that "the elaborate
patterns we make of history are only retrospectively ironclad and knowable."
Narrative Form in History and Fiction: Hume, Fielding, and Gibbon (Princeton:
Princeton University Press, 1970), p. 167. Knowable, but not always known.

right. It is borne out by Jenny's later promiscuity, which follows perfectly from her negligence about her reputation.

The procedure that Jenny's "trial" exemplifies is very different from that in the Robinson episode, where Fielding gives one ambiguities instead of precision. Robinson's defense sounds reasonable and high-minded. His philosophy, although perniciously like Cooper's fatalism, is close enough to Booth's that we cannot damn its professor out of hand without damning our hero. Then, too, victimization pervades Newgate so thoroughly that we cannot infer Robinson's part in it. As a result, we can guess neither what Robinson is likely to do nor how crucial a role he is likely to play in the plot. This might not matter much in *Tom Jones,* where a Lucullan feast of elaborate rhetoric and complex appraisals would slake our appetites until the revelations of plot were ready. *Amelia,* however, interlaces appraisal and prediction so closely that our immediate reactions to characters and events have only a minor interest in and of themselves. By the time that we really can appraise a Robinson, we already know him well enough to make appraisal superfluous, a sort of moral pedantry. Why belabor the venal perjurer with petty charges of being a card sharp? Here in Book I, the ambiguity of Robinson's guilt is simply left unstated as we slip quickly to the affairs of Miss Matthews. The quiet pressure of uncertainty helps, however, to bring us a personal sense of the difficulty of making prudent choices when empathy has brought us to feel how urgent it is that they be made.

For such a quiet pressure to be effective, it must be sustained. Fortunately for Fielding, he does not always have to sustain it as fully as he does his treatment of Robinson, by leaving something unsolved. In one other case, though, he does leave something hanging. We never find out who sent the anonymous letter to Amelia, telling her of Booth's illness in Gibraltar (III, 6). Here, as with the Robinson episode, Fielding hides his slight slipped stitch from us in the ensuing pages. He presents us, as distractions for our curiosity, with some analogues or surrogates, anonymous letters whose authors we quickly know or guess, like Mrs. Atkinson's warning verse to Amelia (VI, 9), or Dr. Harrison's epistle to James on adultery (X, 2). He also drops the issue of the Gibraltar letter per se in favor of interest in the two men suspected of writing it, James and Atkinson. The energy of plot is thereby diverted to the examination of character. Fielding performs the same sort of maneuvers in concealing the Robinson episode. He several times shows us Booth losing at play to men in luck or to sharpers, so that the honesty of the gamblers seems less important than Booth's repeated imprudence. When the honesty of Robinson the gambler becomes a trivial question at the end of *Amelia,* Fielding succeeds in hiding, and yet in making effective, the unresolved episode ten books earlier. But, as he might have interpolated, "Hic labor extremus, longarum haec meta viarum" to keep such minor turns of the plot from lapsing into messiness. To sustain "a quiet pressure of uncertainty" in more important matters, he cannot conceal and therefore must limit himself to obscuring facts and delaying resolutions. These techniques become central to his strategy in *Amelia.*

By far the clearest example of obscured facts is the unhappy history of Mrs. Bennet, which takes up almost all of Book VII. We never discover to what extent Mrs. Bennet is telling the truth. As John Coolidge points out, "an alternative story can be constructed by reinterpreting the events she relates. Was she, for instance, really the pitiable victim of the machinations of the young widow who became her stepmother? Or was she the perhaps equally pitiable 'only darling' of her father, fighting desperately and even viciously to drive out a rival for his love?"[4] Coolidge's suspicion about an alternative story is

4. John S. Coolidge, "Fielding and 'Conservation of Character'," reprinted in *Fielding: A Collection of Critical Essays,* ed. Ronald Paulson (Englewood Cliffs, N.J.: Prentice-Hall, 1962), p. 171; I am generally in debt to this essay.

natural enough, because Fielding has deliberately made us
wary. He has given Mrs. Bennet her dramatic self-accusation as
"an adulteress and a murderer" so as to compound ambiguities by calling to mind Miss Matthews's earlier confession
that *she* is an adulteress and a murderer. The reminiscence,
with the memory of Miss Matthews's dubious and partial
penitence, is given strength by Mrs. Bennet's quick shrinking
of her crimes, within the space of one paragraph, to "Indiscretion," of which (she says) Amelia's candor may well be ready
to acquit her. Mrs. Bennet's first having chosen to warn
Amelia with a bit of coy doggerel, vague in application and
painfully unspecific, has already thrown her serious intentions in doubt. The narrator then lays a third or fourth heavy
straw on the camel's back by telling us, after several passages
of Mrs. Bennet's coyness about beginning her story, that she
has teased Amelia into hearing her whole life so as to establish
her good character before her anecdotes of her "indiscretion."
"This," he says, "I really suppose to have been her Intention:
For to sacrifice the Time and Patience of *Amelia* at such a
Season, to the mere Love of Talking of herself, would have
been as unpardonable in her, as the bearing it was in *Amelia* a
Proof of the most perfect good Breeding." "Good breeding,"
we may suspect, is a polite way of saying "curiosity," but even
that note of teasing irony only supports the narrator's innuendo that Mrs. Bennet cares as much for dramatizing as for
justifying herself. Neither conduces to an unvarnished
account of the facts.

Mrs. Bennet's story, once she begins it, remains under
subtle attack. At the first chance for real pathos, Fielding not
only implies that Mrs. Bennet's mother fell into the well
because she was mildly drunk—"we were all," says Mrs.
Bennet, "in a high Degree of Mirth"—but also has Amelia
react to this account of a drowning by asking, of all things, for a
glass of water. Ambiguity of tone joins the hint of hidden facts
to spoil this climax; and the same techniques seem to reappear

later, to spoil the sexual drama of chapters 7 and 8. If we are inclined to doubt Mrs. Bennet, we can start with her decision—this is not *Clarissa*, where we are told everything— that the Noble Lord slipped an aphrodisiac drug into her small punch, which did alone what high spirits, late hours, vanity, Ranelagh refreshments, and persuasion had no part in. More plainly, just as she reaches her most dramatic juncture, her having poxed her first husband, we learn that her second is the beloved paragon Atkinson. Fielding has distracted our sympathy from her in the most tonally ambiguous of ways.

Some obvious parallels also impugn Mrs. Bennet. The widow who replaces her mother is, Mrs. Bennet claims, a hypocrite for having denied that she was to marry Mrs. Bennet's father (VII, 2); but we have shortly before (VI, 7) seen Mrs. Bennet herself denouncing remarriage, with great bitterness and learning, at a time when she is, or is about to be, remarried. The widow, with "the Spirit of a Tigress," is said to "have broken the Heart of her first Husband"; soon we learn that Mrs. Bennet's first husband died of "a Polypus in his Heart," and that her temper at times runs high (VII, 2, 9).[5] Nor is Mrs. Bennet's partially undigested learning, first used falsely to attack remarriage, clear of the stigma that she puts upon her aunt's affectation of "understanding." What is most striking about her story—the seduction and the sight of Mr. Bennet weltering in blood—recalls, challengingly, what is most striking about Miss Matthews's.

This archipelago of analogies and modifications puzzles us. As Fielding sails off into the main subject matter of the book, we join him or stay marooned with barren suppositions and innuendos. As a result we do not learn the precise faults of

5. Mrs. Bennet's doctor is kind to her in telling her that she had no part in her husband's death. Polyps were thought to come from the blood's standing still, which might result from violent passions like anger, fear, grief, and sudden terror. Mrs. Bennet causes all these in her husband. See Jean-Baptiste Sénac, *Traité de la structure du coeur, de son action, et de ses maladies,* 2 vols. (Paris, 1749), 2: 461-62 (Bk. IV, ch. x, sec. 6).

Mrs. Bennet, as in *Tom Jones* we learn those of Mrs. Fitzpatrick, who tells a story in some ways similar. We have instead a widening of receptivity, an awareness of a range of potential motives for, and potential reactions to, certain actions. As a corollary, we cannot appraise Mrs. Bennet's acts in the terms familiar from the earlier novels, namely, the character's motive, the action's result, and our aesthetic distance. Our pleasure or resentment about the results of actions in Mrs. Bennet's story—her expulsion from her father's house, say—often depends upon the unclear motives of the characters in that subjective story. Aesthetic distance is still more confusing. Because it is not an integral part of the idiom here, as it is of the earlier (comic) novels, its functions vary markedly from one situation to another. When Amelia asks for water, we do not feel that we are being reminded, as the narrator of *Tom Jones* might remind us, that amusement should temper sympathy. Nor, of course, are we expected to enjoy the jarring of tones for its own sake, as we might do in *Tristram Shandy*. We think we are being told something about this episode itself, but precisely what we are being told remains veiled even from our alerted eyes.

The same principles operate when Fielding delays resolutions. The startling events of *Amelia* do not provide coups de théâtre. One's reaction to the "madman's" rifling of the Booths' rooms (VI, 4), the announcement that Booth's arrest is at the suit of Dr. Harrison (VIII, 1), or the imminent death of Atkinson (XI, 6) is to weigh contingencies. On these contingencies, in turn, hangs our sense of the characters' frailty, of the degree to which the genre and tone will let them be hurt. As R. S. Crane has pointed out, the comedy of *Tom Jones* rests upon our being able to discount tragedy.[6] *Amelia*, in contrast, works

6. "The Concept of Plot and the Plot of *Tom Jones*," in *Critics and Criticism, Ancient and Modern*, ed. R. S. Crane (Chicago: University of Chicago Press, 1952), pp. 616-47; see especially pp. 634-36.

by enlarging the realm of real possibilities, so that when the plot evokes some sort of lurking disaster, we do not know to what extent it can be discounted.

Finally, the fog through which we see the characters and assess the idiom of *Amelia* is thickened by a psychological density not hitherto typical of Fielding. In this novel as in Fielding's others, of course, richness of character remains defined not by what goes on in the mind—Richardson's definition—but by what goes on in the plot. The ways in which a Colonel James can impinge upon the thematic systems of motive, the ways in which those who inhabit his world may apprehend his acts, are what matters. None the less, within this mode Fielding can let us know, for a purpose, that there is a mind the sum of whose actions exceeds the character's pragmatic effects on the plot. For example, the effects of the Noble Lord on the plot could be traced to his being a lecher or a man eager for possession. Fielding in addition makes him pathologically obsessed with novelty, as happy with a whore (to judge by his diseases) as with a model of chastity. Mrs. Ellison, who seems to Amelia an earthy matron with airs, turns out to be a woman whose hobby or job is to be a version of Clarissa's Mrs. Sinclair. But for no reason given, she also treats her dupe, Mrs. Bennet, with great generosity, including gifts of money and lodging, and influence toward an annuity of £150 from my lord. Is it that she simply likes to indulge in both intrigue and officiousness? Has she something to gain? If she appeared in a novel by Richardson, we would find out the facts; but in Fielding, who is interested in exploring the conditions of life, not of psychology, we do not find out. We do, however, feel the force of the ominously irrational affecting our sense of what may happen within the plot. From Fielding's point of view, the pains of the Old Man of the Hill safeguard Tom Jones from having to experience those pains in a full world; but the smiling pathology of Mrs. Ellison simply implies that there may be more Mrs. Ellisons to threaten

Amelia, and that she (and we) had better keep a sharp eye out for them. Like the Old Man, Mrs. Ellison develops the represented world, but her effect chiefly reinforces that of ambiguous characters, unclear events, and a loosely defined tone.

The narrator of *Amelia* has retreated, and our attempts to deal with experience put us on the same level with the characters, who fumble blindly. Most simply, they legislate their personal humours into universals: Bath declares that a man who will fight can never be a rascal (V, 6), and Amelia decides that only the best of men are fond of children (VI, 1), or that "a Woman's Virtue is always her sufficient Guard" (VI, 6), or—about Mrs. Bennet, with scarcely less naiveté—that "there must be something uncommonly good in one who can so truly mourn for a Husband above three Years after his Death" (VI, 3). If such a character is right, as Amelia is about the Jameses (VI, 6), he makes his judgment on unreliable grounds, based once more on personal wishes. Amelia, for example, criticizes Colonel and Mrs. James because they have slurred the Noble Lord, whose love of children attests his purity. Even sophisticated characters, though, wander blind outside the limits imposed by their personalities or preconceptions. James, for instance, misestimates Miss Matthews, Amelia, and Atkinson. We are conscious of the effort we must make not to follow his example.

From our being on the characters' level, Fielding draws not only empathy for them but also his plan of action for the novel. He begins with a hero, Booth, who claims to believe that every man acts according to the passion that happens to be uppermost, and who therefore calls into question the possibility of virtue, prudence, and order. If "Men . . . act entirely from their Passions, their Actions [can] have neither Merit nor Demerit" (XII, 5), can be neither good nor wise. Unable, in accord with his philosophy, to order his own life or to perceive an order that might be divine, Booth finds himself oppressed by the order of others, the law or his friends. Fielding thus

translates the moral problems of *Amelia* into the epistemological terms to which his narrator's retreat and our own inadequacy make us especially sensitive. The action of the novel
then follows a process correlative with a process by which
Booth might learn to abandon false philosophy and false doubt
and to join with the reasoned doctrine of Harrison and the
faith of Amelia. We do not see that process any more than we
see the process in Rasselas or Bramble. We see local evidence
of it, more than in Rasselas and less, I think, than in Bramble,
but the order of events, developed by analogy and modification, remains, as it always is in Fielding, the chief index for the
growth of the hero.

Through his growth Booth discovers one kind of truth at the
end of the novel and gains an anchorage in virtue and order.
His conversion gives him and his friends the only possible
guarantee of his future prudence in a stormy world. The
discovery of another kind of truth by another kind of method,
of Betty Harris's having cheated her sister Amelia, leads to his
being rescued from the world in a blaze of divine derring-do.
The rescue, in fact, is made general. Within *Amelia*, we see that
the civil law is imprudently put together and is executed by the
laws of fortune, sometimes fairly, sometimes not. The
denouement tells us that all fortune, in the civil law or outside
it, lies within the jurisdiction of God. As a result, the world of
reality is transformed into the world of desire. All the main
characters, in any case, get what they want: death on the field
of honor for Bath, money and polite entertainments for his
sister, a doting lover for Miss Matthews, Miss Matthews
herself for Colonel James; and genuine happiness for our
friends. As divine logic, this world has an objective basis, but
as the reward of human hopes, it makes real what had
appeared subjective. As soon as Booth is converted, as soon as
he personally begins to see how desire can become reality
through God, *Amelia* moves toward this sort of ideological

resolution. Near the start of the novel, Booth's shortcomings are plain in the way he shapes his past for sentimental and apologetic reasons; at the end of the novel, he triumphs by shaping his future. Our desires too, for we are good-natured readers, find a reward.

Yet the baffling world of *Amelia* is too black for this resolution to awaken the unequivocal joy we feel at *Humphry Clinker's* mingling of reality and desire. Theologically, no doubt, the order of Providence encompasses all mundane truth; but practically, Fielding's use of it announces that the mundane solution has failed. Like the conclusion of *Clarissa* or of *Rasselas,* though not so thoroughly, the end of *Amelia* admits the vanity of human wishes in a tawdry and dangerous world. Society claims all men as victims, attacking them if they differ from it, corrupting them if they do not: "Bad Education, bad Habits, and bad Customs," Harrison tells Amelia, "debauch our Nature, and drive it headlong as it were into Vice" (IX, 5). Under such circumstances, no practical answers exist for the Booths until they acquire, through a fortune, the magical freedom of an Abyssinian prince. Moreover, the public and private themes of the novel, which Fielding has kept in cybernetic flow, fork apart. Redemption is the only spiritual alternative to despair or complicity. But since no mass conversion is to be expected before the apocalypse, redemption must be individual. The personal revelation of order puts an end to the process of social inquiry, the only end that this frustrating and embittering process can satisfyingly have in *Amelia.*[7]

7. The analyses by Ronald Paulson and Cynthia Griffin Wolff, which concentrate on the separation of private and public themes, suggest some of the discomfort *Amelia* causes if it is not read as Fielding's version of the pattern common to *Clarissa* and *Rasselas,* written in a "theatrical" mode that makes the narrator neutral or choric. Paulson, *Satire and the Novel in Eighteenth-Century England* (New Haven: Yale University Press, 1967), pp. 157-64, "The Public and Private Worlds of *Amelia.*" Wolff, "Fielding's *Amelia*: Private Virtue and Public Good," *TSLL* 10 (1968): 37-55.

II: BOOTH'S SYSTEM (BOOKS I-VII)

If we are to follow Booth's progress, we must start where he
starts. Therefore, books I-III of *Amelia* emerge from Booth's
"philosophy," and through episodes in the prison yard and
with Miss Matthews, embody it in different ways. The
philosophy itself, of course, is not important. It is so inconse-
quential that Fielding gives Booth's abjuration (XII, 5) short
shrift, a single paragraph of dialogue. It makes no claim to
reason, for on his own showing Booth can only have chosen
that doctrine that appeals to his passions of the moment. It has
no claim to being a serious creed, for Booth himself does not
believe it. He continually blames and praises people, even at
times himself, although as we have seen and as Booth recognizes, his philosophy denies the merit and demerit of actions.
He also often assumes consistency in character, one might say
rather too often, although by his theories only rare men, the
obsessed and the torpid, should have passions so steady as to
make such consistency likely. Nor has Booth's philosophy a
claim to objectivity: since no one can tell what passion is
"uppermost" in another man, causal statements of this sort are
either tautologous or baseless. No doubt Booth may have
reasoned from himself, the sole place where he might have
access to causal relationships between passion and action; but
his implicit claim that others behave as he does depends on an
unprovable guess. Finally, Booth's philosophy has no
pragmatic value in making predictions about behavior. Nonetheless, Fielding does not want to play it down, for he makes it
worse by the declaration that his hero denies Providence.
Booth is a freethinker, "a Doctrine which, if it is not downright
Atheism, hath a direct Tendency towards it" (I, 3). The
novelist who could idealize a promiscuous bastard in 1749
might be capable of anything by 1751—but not even Lovelace
had been a freethinker.

Booth is one, even if trivially, because freethinking has a

common bond with his philosophy, the bond of egoism. Systems of inquiry are moot if all action results from the unpredictable self; systems of divine order are moot if appraised only by the self, weighing what one can see of actual rewards and punishments against a personal notion of what they should be. Booth the victim makes men and society versions of himself, so that he is at once scapegoat and paradigm.[8] Too feeble to be taken seriously as ideology, his "philosophy" and freethinking, denials of human and divine responsibility, must be taken seriously as symptoms, dramatic emblems for a complex state of spiritual disease. For this reason, Fielding can let the theories fade as the novel moves on: they are the result and the accessory of Booth's flaws, not their source. Booth's conversion, in this context, is not only a religious change of heart but also a symptom of his having gained the moral strength to evaluate himself and thus to face the world with courage and intelligence. Because that is a

---

8. Fielding does what he can to soften the charge against Booth, by having him unjustly imprisoned, and by adducing arguments from Claudian and the life of Marcus Brutus. The unjust imprisonment is only emotionally germane, and the arguments mislead us. Claudian and Brutus doubted because they had seen vice triumphant, as Booth has seen Thrasher triumphant; and thus, Fielding implies, moral feeling has led Booth astray, like Claudian and Brutus. That implication is false: Booth's doubts arise not from disinterested justice but from his sense of his own worth, his "imagin[ing] that a larger share of misfortunes had fallen to his lot than he had merited." If one follows Rader's suggestion that a passage in Cudworth may have been Fielding's source for this passage, one discovers that in Cudworth too, Diagoras Melius and "innumerable others" deny a providence because the wicked remain unpunished, not for Booth's reason, their own "misfortunes." Fielding is this gentle with Booth, is willing to lend him this kind of rhetorical dignity, so that he will seem more worth redeeming; but his redemption paradoxically depends on his system's being too trivial and ignoble (unlike Claudian's and Brutus's) to serve him. No novelist has ever surpassed Fielding in the art of having one's cake and eating it too. Ralph Cudworth, *The True Intellectual System of the Universe*, 3 vols. (London, 1845), 1: 131; Ralph Rader, "Ralph Cudworth and Fielding's *Amelia*," *MLN* 71 (1956): 336-38.

gradual process, its first crest, the conversion, needs no more fanfare than the announcement of his freethinking has here.

More immediately in Book I, motives, order, and egoism all come to the fore in Thrasher's court and the prison yard. Booth's theory, then, is a social as well as a personal symptom. We find a series of systems of law, predictive and judgmental, in these chapters. Those of prudence and of fortune (or fate) come up in the first chapter, the exordium. In the second chapter, the narrative proper begins with an ironic version of prudence and fortune, in the system of civil government. Thrasher's court, like the artists of life whom the first chapter praises, conquers Fortune through Prudence, to establish causal relations. Bigotry and greed form Thrasher's firm principles, as he turns that Hobbesian holiday on which his court opens, the first of April, into a universal condition. But if he seems to be following all too well the advice of the narrator's grave exordium, to conquer Fortune, his victims can neither follow nor believe it. For them, his prudence is their blind fortune, his solipsistic parody of universal good is their partial evil. Fielding appears to be keeping the moral tone of the exordium only by a sudden attack on its ambiguities. The tone of the exordium assumes that regulative law (the antithesis to blind Fortune) coincides with moral law ("the noblest efforts of Wisdom and Virtue"). So it does, but only from the point of view of Thrasher, with his unquestioning egoism, and of God. Thrasher's victims can hardly be blamed if they have a different notion.

Thrasher's egoistic version of the narrator's scheme in Chapter 2 leads in Chapter 3 to Booth's and Robinson's schemes. Robinson's fatalism asserts an order that precludes inquiry, since he cannot isolate causes. Booth offers causes (motives) after a fashion—the hazard of the passions—but cannot assert an order. He also expounds in theory what Thrasher puts forth in practice, that the law of nature is properly defined by passionate and subjective reactions to stimuli. At this point, Fielding intervenes with a brief mention of Providence, a fifth and final universal system of law in which order and cause, reason and will, are identical. He does not dwell upon Providence lengthily, but uses it at this point to remind the reader that the four alternatives—Booth's, Robinson's, Thrasher's, and Thrasher's victims'—are logically equivalent. Each of them needs a perspective that warps reality and destroys any independent check. None, Thrasher's position perhaps excluded, can be proved: how does one demonstrate chaos, or fate, or causation through chance passions?

Fielding also, however, does what he can to let us see the world as Booth sees it. The events from those in Thrasher's court to Booth's meeting with Miss Matthews are a hornbook of causes and effects, all couched as little paradoxes. We observe innocence injured, guilt lightly punished, men merry in the face of the gallows and frantic at commitment for a small felony, and so forth. Each of the paradoxes stands apart from the others so that they present no pattern from which the observer could learn to make inferences. Reading each of them from effect to cause, which is what we must do, gives relationships that are logical but teach nothing. These opening chapters, always in Fielding's novels a training ground for the reader, give Booth's view a special weight in establishing the epistemological condition already discussed. Because of what we have seen, we are less likely to be harsh with him, but we also learn to recognize the nightmare implied by his glib dogma.

If Thrasher's court and the prison yard are in a sense Booth's nightmare, the complementary episode with Fanny Matthews, that illogical daughter of Racine and Aphra Behn, may be thought of as his dream. A perfect Boothian in a Boothian setting, she continues to preach a fatality in love, to ascribe all acts to the passions, and to judge reality by her own preferred reading of events. Thus she and Hebbers always act on envy, lust, rage, and pride, whichever is uppermost. We

have every reason not to take her story at face value, played as
it is with theatrical rant before a handsome male audience, and
decorated by Fielding with mock-heroic comparisons. We are
hardly surprised to learn that Hebbers, the "Martyr to my
Revenge" (I, 6), has survived his martyrdom. Thus her
pseudonym, "Vincent," is perfect for her, since it suggests not
only conquering (vincens) but also a dupe at gambling (a
vincent).[9] Both terms apply secondarily to the swindled
soldier Booth.

By no coincidence, following an entire chapter (I, 10) on subornation and perjury, and on the (Boothian) conflation of acts
and motives "contra Formam Statutis," Booth tells Miss
Matthews a story strikingly close to hers, in a rectified form.[10]
Its hero, Booth himself, is a handsome military man who, like
Hebbers, is the social friend of a family wealthier than his own
and consisting of a widowed parent and two daughters,
Amelia and Betty Harris, who correspond to Hebbers's Fanny
and Betty Matthews. In each family there is some form of
rivalry between the sisters; there is also a rival mistress,
Hebbers's Widow Carey and Booth's (pretended mistress)
Miss Osborne, to fan the jealousy of the ingenues. Hebbers

9. See *OED*, s.n. "vincent"; Francis Grose, *A Classical Dictionary of the
Vulgar Tongue* (3rd ed., 1796), ed. Eric Partridge (London: Routledge & Kegan
Paul, 1963), s.n. "vincent's law."

10. Acts are conflated with motives because, as Murphy explains it (I, 10),
the form of the statute reads into the act an implication of motive. The law
thus deals with the hiddenness of the individual heart by adopting the sim-
plificatory techniques of fiction, such as analogy, economy, and normative
modeling: "The law by the term *malice* (*malitia*) in this instance meaneth, that
the fact hath been attended with such circumstances, as are the ordinary
symptoms of a wicked heart, regardless of social duty, and fatally bent on
mischief." Richard Burn, *The Justice of the Peace, and Parish Officer* (1755),
2 vols. (8th ed., London, 1764), s.n. "homicide," v. 7. This procedure has an
obvious bearing on the epistemological questions we have been considering,
and on the relation of Booth's story to Miss Matthews's and to the truth
(which we cannot know, but of which we can guess the complexities from
our later knowledge of the Booths, the Jameses, and Bath).

insinuates himself into Miss Matthews's bedchamber when she has drunk too much wine; Booth insinuates himself into Amelia's bedchamber—he is later shifted to a garret—in a wine hamper. The result of each ambush is, in order, exile of the lover, then a treaty of marriage, then the breaking of the treaty, then an elopement, then the lady's pregnancy, and then the lover's leaving for military quarters—Hebbers pretends that he has been called to Yorkshire, and Booth ships for Gibraltar. The separation is followed by a wound and a reunion; or, with Hebbers and Miss Matthews, a reunion and a wound. Miss Matthews's brother, whom she regards as an inveterate enemy, recurs in the form of Booth, who is accused by his sister Nancy—she is delirious—as "a Highwayman who had a little before robbed her" (II, 4). Miss Matthews's tragic rant, and love for the theatre, recur in Booth's sentimental speeches (cf. the beginning of Chapter 3, where his harangue comes straight from the tradition of pathetic tragedy), and the mutual quotation from *The Mourning Bride* in Chapter 6. Her London landlady, who entertains only "persons of character," is exalted into Amelia's old nurse, who entertains Booth and Amelia because they, like Hebbers and Miss Matthews, have pretended to be married. In short, as Booth presents his tale, he offers Miss Matthews a laundered version of her own life.

She is quite ready to accept it as such and to convert the reality of others into her own romance. Since Booth has become particularly valuable to her as the repository of all that she found lacking in Hebbers, her seduction of Booth places her in the position of her envied rival, Amelia. Neither she nor Booth, passing to sexual seduction from the emotional seduction of their passionate, sentimental narratives, see that the two women are inverted doubles. For instance, Amelia's inner harmony attracts Booth to her even before he sees the result of her plastic surgery; Miss Matthews's harmony, which has a great deal to do with Hebbers's seducing her, is material rather than spiritual—it is her skill on the harpsichord. Amelia is

faithful and tender, Miss Matthews infatuated and sentimental. Miss Matthews, as we soon learn, has "distributed her
Favours . . . to those she liked" (IV, 5), but Amelia's only connection with sluttishness and its results is the superficial token
of a lost nose.[11] This parodic relationship between the women
clarifies for us the nature of the exchange desired by Miss
Matthews and accepted by Booth. Nothing, of course, is
clarified for them. Booth has won Miss Matthews's "heart" by
letting her imgine herself an Amelia; she now wins his body by
playing on the same traits in him that Hebbers had played
upon in seducing her. These are lust and pride, the first of
which I think we can take for granted, and the other of which
we find Miss Matthews tickling just as assiduously (IV, 1): "O
Mr. *Booth*," she murmurs, "could I have thought when we
were first acquainted, that the most agreeable Man in the
World had been capable of making the kind, the tender, the
affectionate Husband—the happy *Amelia* in those Days was
unknown. . . . I confess to you, I thought you the prettiest
young Fellow I had ever seen; and, upon my Soul, I believe
you was then the prettiest Fellow in the World."

These references to the past are not accidental. Fielding may
seem to have begun his novel in medias res, but he has really
begun, conceptually, with first principles—various kinds of
law, examined and developed in various ways—and with

---

11. Fielding could hardly have chosen to give Amelia a damaged nose
instead of a scarred chin or missing molar if he had not intended the
semblance, belying the reality, of lewdness. He himself refers to the nose lost
through pox in his description of Blear-eyed Moll (I, 3) and his comment, in
the very chapter that tells us of Amelia's accident, about a captain who had
"received an Injury in the same Part, though from no shameful Reason." His
critics saw the point, like the one who "thought fit to sneer the *noseless Amelia*
by his *noseless Head* from Herculaneum of the *Venus of Paphos*." Bonnell
Thornton, *Have at You All: or The Drury-Lane Journal* 3 (London, 1752); and see
Philip Stevick, "The Augustan Nose," *UTQ* 34 (1965): 110-17. Fielding
revised his text so that the nose was repaired surgically, but did not drop the
reference to it.

characters provisionally free of history. For Miss Matthews, Booth is the happy alternative to the path she has taken, so that she tries to revoke her past blunders within the "enchanted Castle" (IV, 1) that now imprisons her as a result of her past. Booth blots a past of obligations in favor of a romance which he renews in a "first Love" of flatteries and favors. In making their new starts, each cooperatively presents his old start in accord with the predilections of the other, as a sympathetic fiction leading to the future.[12] Needless to say, this sort of freedom turns out to be an illusion. Three paragraphs after her seduction of Booth, Miss Matthews gets a note from "Damon" that gives the lie to her romantic story and reveals her entanglements. Booth, in her company, suffers an even greater embarrassment when he is suddenly confronted by past and present obligations—that is, by Amelia in person. The ersatz utopia collapses.

Thrasher's court and the prison yard express the present as Booth sees it, in starkly naturalistic black and white. The episode with Miss Matthews expresses the past as Booth sees it, in rose and mauve, shimmering with pleasing desire. When reality turns into romance, a constant and sighing Miss Matthews, decked in rhetorical sequins, can be a conceivable alternative for a constant and tearful Amelia. Romance, after all, is designed to tickle the fancy, not to challenge the reason or will. Booth therefore does not, in his retrospective story, make fine discriminations among characters or present hard moral choices; his history, like his philosophy, spares him both.[13] We learn how to evaluate his judgment of characters

12. Peter V. LePage, "The Prison and the Dark Beauty of 'Amelia'," *Criticism* 9 (1967): 337-54, points out that prison represents not only the "tyranny of the social will" but also a "freeing from responsibility." Booth and Miss Matthews seize the chance to redefine themselves in mutually congenial terms.

13. As Andrew Wright says, "Booth's story, as he relates it in Book II, is neither domestic nor realistic; it is operatic and sentimental." *Henry Fielding: Mask and Feast* (London: Chatto & Windus, 1965), p. 110.

when we see that those he describes are cartoons of the people
we meet once we, and they, escape from Booth's subjectivity.
His Amelia is a stock stage heroine, James a good-natured
libertine, Bath a humours character with a warm heart, and
Miss Bath an ingenue, who "if she had any Fault, it was that of
Vanity, but she was a very good Girl upon the whole; and
none of us are entirely free from Faults" (III, 8). The real
Amelia shows a shrewdness, a tolerance, a candor, and a
strength that overweigh her romantic tears and fidelity. The
real James is a villain. Bath and his sister show how the laws of
punctilio, combative or social, have deadened them more and
more to the codes of human decency. Her self-absorption and
his willingness to butcher his friends in style threaten to be far
from funny in the treacherous England of *Amelia*. As to moral
choices, Booth makes none in his tale. Dr. Harrison appears as
a stock ideal, a friend and an agent for true love; but as a moral
advisor who offers a Christian way of scorning circumstances,
he draws only a kind of aesthetic admiration in Book III.
Atkinson's fidelity presents chances for pretty maxims (as in
III, 7), but not for imitation. Not even the fictional Booth is a
moral example for Booth. His constancy to Amelia in his story
merely makes him appealing to Miss Matthews, for whom he
destroys that very virtue.

   In the terms of our study, books I–III present two contrasted
but functionally analogous episodes, both practical explora-
tions of Booth's system. The first, in court and prison, sets up
analogous schemes of order, all so inadequate as nearly to
dissolve prudence and virtue. The second, in Miss Matthews's
room, sets up two closely analogous histories of prudence and
virtue (and their opposites), which lead to the collapse of
prudence and virtue and to the reduction of order to storybook
simplicity. The second three books then modify the first three
by showing us that the impenetrable and simple are not the
totality of the world but its horizons. Most of reality is in

between and is also more complex, since the formulas of Booth's "philosophy" and romance are really means of refusing to consider the empirical at all. The second three books permit empiricism, for they give us not life as Booth sees it but life as he ought to begin seeing it. Within these three books, therefore, the principle of modification has two logical functions, to test Booth's story by comparing it with the real Amelia, Bath, and Jameses, and to test the world of Thrasher and Newgate by letting the Booths and us meet a new group of characters whose springs of action they and we can learn to know. These new characters are Mrs. Bennet, Mrs. Ellison, and the Noble Lord.

Booth's story does not come out well when tested by the real Amelia, Bath, and Jameses. Especially when we begin to inquire into motives, as his story does not tempt us to do, we find not only that he has reduced the personalities of his friends, but also that his own personality is the source of what he has revealed about them. A version of Booth's bravery and honor appear in the central humour of Bath, a version of his romantic sentimentality in that of Amelia, of his libertine generosity in that of James, and of his vanity—but how he plays this down in his description (III, 8)!—in Jenny Bath, soon to rise to Mrs. James. Together, the dominant humours of these persons mark the gamut of Booth's. Atkinson's leading traits double his master's with a difference: he too is distinguished by bravery, honor, and romantic sentimentality, but his generosity is selflessly Christian and his vanity turns inside out to become humility. Furthermore, as we come to know him in the second quarter of *Amelia*, he is not his master's parody or ape, but a person in his own right. He is connected to both Booths, and thus to a model of behavior, Amelia herself, that finds no parallel among the various Sanchos, Sosias, and Straps.

Fielding's strategy with these five characters—Amelia,

Atkinson, Bath, and the Jameses—depends on the change in nature or in potential that they undergo when they pass from Booth's story to the real world of books IV-VI. Each of them, except for Atkinson, has two natures, one in Booth's story and one in reality. Each, therefore, indicates at least two points on a sort of moral locus that passes at some third point through Booth. Thus, the artless and good-natured *miles gloriosus* who is Booth's Major Bath, and the rather more dangerous Colonel Bath whom we later meet, give us two points on a certain locus of soldierly honor; Booth provides a third, and, as it happens, James a fourth. James similarly provides two points on a locus of friendship, with other characters filling out the range. Moreover, on each of the four loci, Atkinson appears, as one would expect from his doubling Booth's traits. He offers an unanalyzed level of simple perfection, too simple to be a pattern for Booth, any more than Humphry can be a pattern for Bramble, but too nearly perfect not to count in the appraisal of character, which is the purpose of this grouping. We have here a third variant on the armature of characters around which *Humphry* shapes events and the matrix of characters from which *Tristram* develops. The same kind of structure in *Amelia*, using the same ideal of discriminated variety, however, has relatively little effect on the plot. It instead helps us read out from the visible plot to the invisible changes in motive and moral strength of the characters, principally Booth. His reduction of his friends to his own terms, and the discontinuity we see between his images of them and the way they really are, first draws attention to the adequacy of this grouping as a gauge for him.

As the Booths' friends escape from the images Booth has assigned them, they also move farther from the Booths. The steady action of books IV-VI, as motives come into question and become questionable, is greater disappointment in old friends, except for Atkinson, and growing obligation to new. In Book IV, James's friendship for Booth is prejudiced by his pride (over rivalry for Miss Matthews), and Mrs. James's for Amelia is prejudiced by hers. At the same time, Atkinson and Mrs. Ellison appear, by contrast, solicitous, as Atkinson punishes the sentinel's mistreatment of the Booths' little Billy (IV, 7), and, in the same chapter, Mrs. Ellison's "great Concern . . . on *Amelia*'s account" (after the incident with the sentinel) produces "the first Acquaintance between the Mistress of the House and her Lodgers." (In the original edition of *Amelia*, a chapter near the start of Book V made Mrs. Ellison still more like Atkinson, for she helps save the life of the Booths' sick daughter.) Book IV ends with Mrs. Ellison's treating Amelia to the oratorio, and with promises of help from my lord, which the first chapter of Book V juxtaposes with the cold comfort for Booth from Colonels James and Bath. A bit later (V, 4), Mrs. James practices punctilio while Mrs. Ellison, once more like Atkinson, remains helpful in Booth's legal troubles. The next pair of chapters shows the punctilio of Mrs. James's brother, Bath; and so, between the generosity of Mrs. Ellison and the continued assurances of my lord, who is tainted largely by innuendos from the tainted Jameses, we work our way without much digression to the end of Book VI.

On our arrival there, as we discover from Mrs. Bennet's story, we have understood almost nothing about the three new "friends," although they first appear as early as the end of Book IV, as soon as we have had a chance to get to know Amelia, James, and the rest a bit better—in fact, before we have met Bath again. None of the three newcomers is ever tagged by the narrator's moral comments, none of them explained through action. In short, Fielding dwells on motives with the characters of whom we know enough to analyze in those terms, and leaves us to speculate about the newcomers. He provides us with all the information about them that the Booths have, and also with innuendos and analogies, which tend to raise suspicions rather than offer any kind of moral definition of the new characters.

The Noble Lord, for example, is plainly parallel with James, but how? Both appear as generous men, able and willing to help Booth. Both appear to be lecherous, James by his own as well as the narrator's account, and the peer by the Jameses' hearsay evidence. But Fielding develops this analogy to mislead us. He hints that the lord might see and covet Amelia: "the Reader, when he knows the Character of this Nobleman [as a 'passionate Admirer of Women'], may, perhaps, conclude that his seeing *Booth* alone was a lucky Circumstance" (IV, 9); we are left to mull this over in complacent innocence, not aware that the peer has already seen Amelia at the oratorio. In fact, Fielding lessens our suspicions about the peer by proceeding to make us read the analogy backwards, from the hint about the peer to a sense of satisfied expectations when the hint is fulfilled by the peer's analogue James, who does see and covet his friend's wife (VI, 1). The analogy does inform us, but with limited utility, for we are kept in the dark about the peer's and the unblemished Mrs. Ellison's true motives. Such mystification is no oddity in Fielding, a gay deceiver of long standing, but it does not surround the characters familiar from books I-III, who have a different function in the epistemological structure of the novel.

In fact, our very insight into their motives, newly developed in our learning how to reject Booth's pretty tale to Miss Matthews, deceives us. Our sense of the Jameses, for instance, is such that we tend to read their comments about the Noble Lord in terms of their own interests. James is himself a lecherous patron whose price for helping Booth is, at the moment, Miss Matthews. What is more natural for him, in this novel, than to cast the peer in the same role? In the next two chapters after his accusation, his eye hits on Amelia, which gives him a motive to part the Booths from my lord (VI, 1, 2). We may well suspect Mrs. James of having been sent by him on that errand when she suddenly appears (VI, 5) with a changed manner, "the utmost Freedom and Good-Humour," to bring up the subject of the peer by mentioning the watch he gave the Booths' daughter Emily (as James knows) and then to favor the Booths with innuendo about him. Fielding's implicit comparison of her hints to Iago's makes one wonder all the more.

Mrs. Bennet presents a still more intriguing case. She first emerges from the nondescript when she blames the peer's politeness to Amelia (V, 3), to which the narrator, continuing a reference to Roman civil war from Mrs. Ellison's mention of *All for Love*, replies with a quotation from Lucan which suggests Mrs. Bennet's envy of Amelia. Since we have just seen envy at work, in Miss Matthews's and James's treatment of Booth, we are open to such a suggestion. Another hint of analogy appears when she announces a preference for Atkinson over the peer, for this comment follows on Mrs. Ellison's, her friend and fellow widow's, in the chapter before: "A Serjeant of the Guards is a Gentleman, and I had rather give such a Man . . . a Dish of Tea than any Beau *Fribble* of them all."

To these two potential analogies we must add the one that most interests Amelia, who compares her own condition to that of Mrs. Bennet at the beginning of Chapter 4, and who is further confirmed in her projective sympathy the next time Mrs. Bennet is mentioned, a book later (VI, 3), when she reads that lady's pathetic letter about a dead husband and famished child. Nothing could hit a more responsive chord in someone whose husband has courted her with a warning of her "starv[ing] alone, deprived of the Tenderness of a Husband," "entailing Beggary on" her children (II, 3), and who herself can cry that the barbarous world hates her husband and is "endeavour[ing] to starve" her "poor little Infants" (IV, 3). Fielding plays with this analogy once more, when he has Booth grow pleased with Mrs. Bennet because of her sudden "Gaiety; and Good-humour [that] gave a Glow to her countenance that set off her Features, which were very pretty, to the best Advantage, and lessened the Deadness that had usually appeared in her Complexion" (VI, 7); this is exactly how James became enamored of Amelia a short while before (VI, 1) when "the highest Good-humour had so sweetened every Feature, and a vast Flow of Spirits had so lightened up her bright Eyes, that she was all a Blaze of Beauty," which her earlier "Vexations . . . had somewhat deadned."

Fielding's immediate handling of the possibilities opened for Mrs. Bennet is masterful. Rome, widowhood, tragedy, partiality for a soldier, perhaps (we do not know) envy for what may be Mrs. Ellison's second marriage—all these converge in her quotation from the *Aeneid*, denouncing, through Dido, second marriage. Here, of course, more problems are raised than answered. We have had two diametrically opposed uses of classical learning, Harrison's Christian and Booth's non-Christian scholarship. Dido, in this passage, is proclaiming a moral law, but, as Servius says (about the line before the one at which Mrs. Bennet starts), "bene inhonestam rem sub honesta specie confitetur."[14] She has already been inflamed with fatal love and is about to commit adultery. We may be startlingly reminded of Miss Matthews, also a "widow" of sorts, also "tragic" in her own mind, also (and especially) partial to soldiers, envious, adulterous, fatalistic, capable of "*a Look as languishingly sweet* as ever *Cleopatra* gave to *Antony*" (IV, 1) and of being compared to Dido in her rage (IV, 5). Fielding has not discouraged the reminiscence. Mysteriously, Mrs. Ellison has refused to be "seen with such People [as Mrs. Bennet] in public Places" (VI, 5), and has later warned Amelia not to "cultivate too much Intimacy" with her (VI, 8). The suspicious incident in which Amelia's visit finds Mrs. Bennet in bed and the

14. Servius's comment can be found in numerous Virgils, including the *Opera* edited by the elder Peter Burman, 4 vols. (Amsterdam, 1746), 2: 468. The Delphin edition of Virgil, which Fielding owned, and which is part of the series Mrs. Bennet quotes, remarks on the "sensus duplex" of Dido's words in a note to *Aen.* IV, 23.

household in confusion and disorder (VI, 9), leaves us at the end of Book VI with a multitude of possibilities all skillfully suspended. Admittedly, not until Mrs. Bennet has finished her story in Book VII can we really appreciate Fielding's formal brilliance, for he has realized every one of these multiple possibilities in Mrs. Bennet's, or perhaps I should say Mrs. Atkinson's, ambiguous character.

Mrs. Bennet's story, halfway through *Amelia*, is the point of convergence for the two epistemological lines that begin with the impenetrable reality of Thrasher's court and the subjectively edited reality of Booth's and Miss Matthews's stories. Fielding has used analogy and modification in books IV-VI to permit inferences about the characters who appear in Booth's story, and also to frustrate inferences about the characters who do not. Mrs. Bennet's story, in several ways a (discriminated) variant of Miss Matthews's, permits us to see and appraise, retrospectively, these obscured characters in their true light. They emerge from darkness as the Jameses, Bath, and Amelia have emerged from the false light Booth has shone on them; Mrs. Bennet, herself an "obscured character," illuminates them through a "subjectively edited" method, and thus joins the two epistemological methods and inferential processes of books I-VI. Her story comes at its logical spot in the pattern and progress of the novel, too, because she reflects, mildly or comically, the society she condemns as duplicitous, self-interested, and scheming. In and of itself, her story, with its blacks and whites, and its sharply etched individual experience, runs counter to the temper of analogy and modification. Mrs. Bennet presents herself as an innocent victim and individual paragon, forerunner of the Jane Eyres, Oliver Twists, or Benjy Compsons over whom later generations have dabbed their eyes; her foes have been sudden and sly. These are moral versions of the two epistemological poles we have seen, romance and arbitrariness, where a system of inquiry is facile or vain. By making Mrs. Bennet's account dubious in various ways, none of which impugn her warning to Amelia, and by making her mirror her society, Fielding reintroduces the gradations of appraisal and the possibility for prediction that the temper of her story denies. Our conclusions may be shaky, but our system for reading experience and our awareness of its twists and turns are enhanced. As a narrator who supposes herself innocent and who is in fact implicated in the vices she deplores, Mrs. Bennet is of course an analogue to the earlier storytellers, Booth and Miss Matthews, as well as to Bramble, Tristram the system-loving satirist of systems, and, as we shall see, Caleb Williams.

III: THE WIDENING VIEW (BOOKS VII-XII)

The mysteries of character unfold in Book VII, shockingly. While the real Jameses, Bath, and Amelia of books IV-VI slowly replace their Boothian versions, we can watch the process of modification calmly. Book VII reveals our own ignorance and feebleness at analogy, and our own danger with the world, as the prison yard far more briefly and dryly revealed them. With the loss of the comic idiom to which Fielding had accustomed us, the potentialities of danger with the novel also grow. For example, in Book IV the tone of badinage tells us not to worry that Booth's affair with the promiscuous Miss Matthews will leave him, and thus Amelia, poxed and noseless in fact. A similar affair after we have heard about the Bennets would be much graver. The Bennets' history brings genuine suffering and malice into the prospects of the Booths, because unlike Mr. Wilson's or the Old Man's stories in Fielding's earlier novels, Mrs. Atkinson's interpolated story remains within the direct experience of the novel. It concerns people we know and warns Amelia of an immediate threat. As I suggested above, we feel a new sense of the irrational in it because the personalities of these familiar people, the Noble Lord, Mrs. Ellison, and especially Mrs. Bennet, cannot really be understood.

Moreover, because of its partial resemblances to Miss Matthews's story, which foretells a good deal about Booth and his own story, one may ask if this interpolation too will look forward to Book VIII and beyond, as well as backward to the schemes of the peer and his pander. If so, we cannot predict, even vaguely, how it might do so, because of the ambiguity not only of Mrs. Bennet's character but also of her tone, which mingles apology and melodrama, parable and protestation (as, in fact, Miss Matthews's story has). As we enter Book VII, then, the system of order and inquiry in the novel has been precise, but its correlatives in the represented world have been severely battered. Book VIII offers a fresh start. If the abyss of malice now gapes on one side, the tutelary genius of Dr. Harrison now stands ready on the other. If the loss of comic safety removes a shelter for the Booths, it also removes a fictional equivalent to Providence, and thus makes the serious intervention of Providence a possibility.

Mrs. Atkinson's story has the impact it has because it is perfectly prepared for and yet unexpected. It proves that human nature among the noble lords and Mrs. Ellisons is the same as among the Jameses and Baths, with the double result of leaving the Booths nearly friendless and of casting doubt on the chances of appraising and predicting actions, for we and the Booths have been badly fooled. This is a chilly end for the second part of *Amelia*, the conceptual unit that modifies the Boothian world of books I-III. As we enter the third and last part with Book VIII, we find ourselves having to relive, with our new understanding, the events we have passed through. Thus Book VIII opens with Booth's arrest while dashing out to rescue a sick wife, as Book I began with his arrest while rescuing an underdog in a street fight. Thereafter, until the start of Book XI, almost everything that happens to the Booths repeats what has happened to them earlier in London. Booth had already been arrested, had been denied help from James (but had been offered it from Atkinson), had heard the false learning and philosophy of his fellow prisoners, had suffered from false rumors and promises of advancement, had justifiedly been jealous, had got advice about prostituting his wife (from James, V, 9), had dealt with a masquerade to which Amelia—in direct contrast to Mrs. Bennet—did not go, had been involved in a mild imbroglio in which Colonels Bath and James were mistaken for each other (V, 8), had lost all his money at play, and so forth. All this is repeated in three books (VIII-X) from three-and-a-half earlier books (half of Book I, and books IV-VI). Like Johnson, Sterne, and Smollett, Fielding relies on incremental repetition—as, like them, he relies on analogy, modification, structural forms provided by the characters, structural inferences from active readers, particulars of limited utility within complex units of value, and emblems or symbols (the prison, gambling).

Sometimes the repetitions simply reinforce the darkening of the plot. For example, James, who in wooing Booth's mistress unwittingly paid for his release from Newgate (IV, 2), knowingly refuses to pay for his release from Bondum's while wooing his wife (VIII, 8). To make the comparison plainer, Fielding has James give himself the literary airs of "Damon" in the first instance, Oroöndates in the second. Or again, Amelia would not go to Ranelagh if it were "a heaven upon earth" (VI, 5), but then, after having been to a true heaven upon earth, St. James's Church, she finds Vauxhall (IX, 9) a place which "carried my Soul almost to Heaven. . . . I could not have, indeed, imagined there had been anything like this in this World." At Vauxhall a member of the Court of St. James, who has connections with the "setter" Trent, makes advances to Amelia such as another member who has connections with Trent planned to make at Ranelagh. Or again, Mrs. James's visit to help her husband steal Amelia's honor (XI, 5), only to find that Betty the maid has stolen her mistress's clothes, may recall the earlier visit of Mrs. James (VI, 4), made for ambiguous purposes, when she finds the Booths aflutter about their being "robbed" by the "madman" through the carelessness of this same Betty. In each case the incremented repetition is more unpleasant than the original incident; it is part of a more menacing world.

We can see less obviously incremental repetition in three episodes that grow from Mrs. Bennet's story. Fielding's prior novels did not use interpolated stories as sources for the narrative, so that his practice in *Amelia* marks a special interest in developing the possibilities that repetition and variation afford, especially from so tonally ambiguous a source as this story. The first of these episodes plays upon the scene in which Mr. Bennet charges his wife with betrayal, throws her on the floor, kicks and stamps on her, and then lies in his blood after attempting suicide (VII, 8). Two books later (IX, 6) the same wife is assaulted in her sleep by her second husband, Atkinson, upon the fancy of adulterous betrayal (the dream that James was about to rape Amelia). When Atkinson wakes, "the Bed appeared to be all over Blood, and his Wife weltring in the midst of it." Here the rephrasing of the earlier scene turns out to be comic—the "blood" is really cherry brandy—just as in *Humphry Clinker* practical jokes rephrase earlier disorders for a comic idiom. Some of the role of Mr. Bennet descends upon Booth, who threatens to be in "the highest Torment" and to produce "tragical Effects" from jealousy of James; and both comic and tragic excess stand in contrast to the civilized behavior of Harrison, who has just been told about Amelia's fears of James (IX, 6, 5). The rhetorical functions of this scene in its place derive both from its context and from its reminiscence of Mr. Bennet; and its comedy is the funnier and more satiric because the smell of the cherry brandy suddenly releases us from a real fear, implanted by the Bennet episode, that Mrs. Atkinson has actually been wounded. There are wounds, there is blood, in *Amelia*.[15]

15. The comic relief is intensified if a reader, along with Sheridan Baker, sees the cherry brandy scene as a descendant of similar scenes in Apuleius

Two books later, with an echo of a second episode of Mrs. Bennet's story, our fear is released more slowly. As Mrs. Bennet's dealings with the peer drove her husband to act with the "Malice of a Madman" (VII, 8), Mrs. Atkinson's have brought hers into a "raving delirious Fit" and "high Fever"(XI, 6). We do suspect, of course, that Atkinson will survive, unlike Bennet, since Fielding's comedy gilds the announcement of his illness: Amelia keeps calling him "the Serjeant" despite Mrs. Atkinson's decided "my dear Captain" and "my poor Captain." Still, the situation is serious, and the chapter pathetic. The third echo of an episode in Mrs. Bennet's story, finally, is graver and briefer, the Jameses' talk about isolating Amelia for seduction by sending Booth out of town, to the West Indies or the North (IX, 4; XI, 1). Their comments tell more strikingly of their degeneracy because they lay plans so like the peer's successful ploy with Bennet (VII, 6). Here Mrs. Bennet's experience serves simply as a dreadful warning, made firmer by the parallel in function between the pimping of her friend, Mrs. Ellison, and that of the Booths' friends, Trent and Mrs. James, in the two stories.

From this series of three examples, we can see how wide a range of response Fielding can, and chooses to, induce by analogy from material of the same initial tone in Mrs. Bennet's story. In fact, he milks this last bit of narrative, the peer's plot against the Bennets, for two further correspondences. Mrs. Atkinson at the Haymarket masquerade turns the tables on the noble peer for his perfidy at the Ranelagh masquerade. She there barters away an iota of Amelia's honor to get her second husband the place which the peer, to lure her to total dishonor, had dangled in front of her first husband. Likewise, Trent pre-

---

and Cervantes ("Fielding's *Amelia*," p. 442); but a grimmer note of internal analogy is struck by Atkinson's nightmare if one remembers Mr. Bennet's death from a polypus: John Bond, *An Essay on the Incubus, or Night-mare* (London, 1753), remarks that the stagnation of the blood that causes nightmares may leave "the rudiments of Polypi in these parts [i.e., the heart and brain]; which may afterwards produce fatal effects" (p. 69).

tends to leave town so as to bewhore his wife to the peer for a place, that of pimp (XI, 3). Our responses to these two events, unlike our disgust at the peer's deceit of Bennet and the Jameses' of Booth, are quite complex, and again, different from each other.

The procedures we have been discussing, and which are familiar from Johnson, Sterne, and Smollett, lead to an understanding of how Fielding conceived the books of *Amelia*. One is tempted to say that most of the books are really conveniences for grouping chapters, so smoothly do they feed into each other in sequence. Perhaps so; but the groups are of real importance, like the four sections of *Humphry*, in alerting us to ways of looking at superficially similar material. In isolation, one might compare the revelation of Trent's character (X, 9), for instance, with that of the maid Betty's (XI, 5). Their contexts, however, give them quite different functions. These contexts are determined by the books, each one of which, as I see it, treats a central theme, which provides what one might call a primary resonance that directs our reading of events and analogies. In each chapter of a book, Fielding treats the central theme, supporting it with one or two subsidiary themes, and giving it special life through some elements of individuation. Within a book, while the central theme remains more or less the same, the subsidiary themes shift, and the elements of individuation change constantly. As we pass from book to book, the same material, in response to new central themes, takes on its new shades of meaning, its discriminated variety. And of course any theme may be treated seriously in one chapter, ironically in the next, seriously but with extenuations in the third, comically in the fourth, and so on.

Criteria of sequence developed from this procedure become important in the third part of *Amelia*, books VIII-XII, because of the wider world in which the Booths find themselves. Books I-III and VII have an order more or less established by the movement of narrative; books IV-VI, which do not, limit them-

selves to the seemingly fortunate growth of the Booths'
acquaintance with Mrs. Ellison (and, through her, Mrs. Bennet and the noble peer), along with a reinvestigation of their
relationships with the Jameses, Bath, and Atkinson. Only one
chapter, the "madman's" assault on their rooms (VI, 4),
apparently breaks this tight scheme, and it turns out instead to
start the renewal of the Booths' relationship with Harrison,
just as the other obvious mystery of books IV-VI, Atkinson's
marriage with an unspecified widow, starts the initiation of a
new member, Mrs. Bennet-Atkinson, into the Booths' familial
circle. After Book VII, however, too much has to be included in
Amelia for this kind of structural neatness to be possible.

Since we have seen how sequence is handled by Johnson,
Sterne, and Smollett, I do not want to go into tedious detail
with Fielding. A brief look at Book XI, and a briefer look at X,
with a suggestion of what I take to be the central themes of VIII
and IX, should suffice. There is a certain logic to the order in
which these central themes appear. Thus if the last book of
Amelia, Book XII, represents the triumph of divine and ideal
earthly justice, following upon penitence and confession, one
can see why the penultimate book, Book XI, should present
the bases on which justice, in this broad sense, rests. Therefore
Book XI portrays a series of compacts, implicit and explicit,
and a series of penitent confessions that prepare the way for
the two crucial ones, Booth's and Robinson's, in XII. First
comes the Jameses' compact to cater to one another (XI, 1),
with Mrs. James agreeing to be her husband's bawd in
exchange for money and fashionable society. We move to
higher social realms in the next chapter, in which Harrison
refuses to bewhore his conscience to a peer by supporting
Colonel Trompington for parliament, this being the price for
favor towards Booth. Like the first chapter, the second ends
with a hypocritical promise to do Booth service. The third
chapter, the history of Trent as wittol for the Noble Lord, connects being bawd for a spouse with another peer's compact for

money and fashionable society. Analogies between the Trents and the Jameses, and between personal and political prostitution, are too evident to need discussion. The Noble Lord and Trent have already done something for Booth, lent him fifty pounds for play, and the end of Chapter 3 once again deals with the hypocrisy of favors as the two conspirators arrange their beneficiary's arrest, ruin, and cuckoldry.

The events of these three chapters bring about Booth's first confession to Amelia (XI, 4), that he has lost "our little All" at cards, and his compact with her never again to play. None the less, under the influence of wine and the genuinely good but human Bob Bound, he promptly does gamble (in what Fielding later [XII, 2] calls "the Great State Lottery of Preferment"), so that the fifth chapter begins with another compact and bribe, and another hypocritical offer of service, more villainous but hardly less damaging than Bob Bound's. This effectual robbery, parallel to Trent's robbery (presumably) at cards, and perhaps to Booth's own playing fast and loose with the family's purse, recurs lower on the social scale in three successive chapters with Betty's robbery of her mistress (XI, 5) and the pawnbroker's of Betty (XI, 7), and Atkinson's now-revealed theft of Amelia's picture (XI, 6). His penitence and Betty's echo Booth's, and move us into a climate of distorted justice: Atkinson is convicted, but is the gainer thereby; Betty and the broker cannot be convicted because the law is too ill drawn; Booth's "conviction" in Amelia's eyes, after James's note (XI, 9), is unjust; and his arrest on Trent's debt is not justice that we are inclined to applaud. A further pair of compacts, one between Booth and Miss Matthews, the other implicit in James's challenge, elaborates the sort of analogical web Fielding loves. The same mode of relationship is explored through many different kinds of emotion and consequences, on several social levels.

For each of books VIII-X one could trace out the same kind of analogical web. For instance, if the stress in Book XI is on

certain elements of law, the initial topic in *Amelia*, the stress in
Book X might well be, as it is, on personal identity, the second
topic to be taken up. Its central symbol is the masquerade, in
which characters remain part hidden, part revealed (X, 2), and
the consequent discoveries that Mrs. Atkinson has played
Amelia (X, 3), that the moral letter is Harrison's and that
Amelia is wary of James (X, 4), with the further confusion of
identities between the two colonels (X, 5). One false friend
leads to another: Trent swindles Booth at cards (X, 5), Booth
breaks his oath to Harrison in charging Amelia with keeping
secrets from him (X, 6), and Mrs. Atkinson admits having bar-
tered a bit of Amelia's honor to the peer at the masquerade (X,
8) as Trent advises Booth to barter it to the peer (X, 7). The
revelation of Trent's character (X, 9) follows on the revelation
of Amelia's and Mrs. Atkinson's role at the masquerade, of
Amelia's suspicions of James, of Harrison's letter, and of the
Colonel for whom it was intended. At the same time, we have
the use of learning—Mrs. Atkinson's, Harrison's, Bath's, the
rakes' at the masquerade—to interpret the enigmas of motive
and identity. This series leads to Booth's false learning, with
which the book closes. There, Amelia quotes Terence on
empathy, while Booth (who does not "hold her [as a divine or
a philosopher] in a very respectable Light") argues that hidden
and selfish motives rule all conduct. The notion of virtue, by
these doctrines, becomes a masquerade.

This chapter carries over into the next (XI, 1), in which the
Jameses, who nicely illustrate Booth's thesis about human
selfishness, discuss the masquerade, masquerade before the
public as a fond couple, and set up their plans for hypocrisy.
Similarly, the motifs of penitence and justice at the end of Book
XI carry over into Book XII, and those of false learning and
good nature carry over into the first chapter of Book X from the
last of Book IX. Book IX, which develops notions of honor and
is dominated by Harrison's Christian treatment of honor,
picks up in turn the theme of honor-as-reputation from Book

VIII, which develops notions of worldly dependency and obligations. The groupings are not and need not be clear-cut; I dare say, too, that my rapid abstractions do not do them full justice. None the less, Fielding's procedure should be clear, with his use of analogy and modification to secure multiple perspectives on a given theme and on a given event or character.

Fielding also provides multiple perspectives through themes and motifs, as almost all novelists do, and through his double ending. I should like to look at two themes, both of which use a favorite device of Fielding's, literary allusion, although never, in *Amelia*, for what had been one of Fielding's favorite purposes, burlesque. The two themes are those I identified as central in Book X, role-playing and the use of learning. They are closely tied to the appraisal of oneself and one's fellows, and thereby to the epistemological interests of the novel; they come together in Booth's conversion through reading Barrow, and thus allow the mundane and providential conclusions. They represent, therefore, a way in which Fielding can create conditions for Booth's conversion without showing us detailed inner growth or violating his theatrical mode of presentation.

Let us begin with role-playing. No reader can miss the allusions to the contemporary theatre (rather than to the epic, as in *Tom Jones*). Although such allusions are common in Fielding, I count only four in the first six books of *Tom Jones* (leaving out the introductory chapters), two to Shakespeare and one each to Addison and Lee. The first six books of *Amelia* have over a dozen. More important, the allusions in *Tom Jones* are either serious—as in a comparison of Allworthy, tranquil on his supposed deathbed, to Addison's Cato (V, 7)—or jokingly mock-heroic, as in a comparison of Mrs. Partridge to Othello (II, 3). In *Amelia*, most of the comparisons and allusions have to do with role-playing. Miss Matthews, whose tragic rant I have mentioned, outdoes Shakespeare and Kitty Clive in her fury; later,

she twice chooses to call herself Calista after the Fair Penitent
in Rowe (I, 6; III, 9; IV, 2). Mrs. James manages to equal Miss
Bellamy and Mrs. Cibber in her distress over her husband's
duel (V, 8). Mrs. Ellison, as a jolly widow, finds her allusions in
comedies by Garrick (V, 2), Farquhar (V, 3), and Congreve (VI,
3); she scorns *All for Love* (V, 3). In contrast to the staginess of
these ladies are Amelia's two theatrical allusions. One, a passage from *Cato* quoted ironically to indict affectation, is used
specifically to tell us that she is free from that vice (VI, 4);
another is in direct harmonious response to Booth (II, 6). Her
cordial is "one of the excellent *Farquhar*'s Comedies" (X, 5), but
she keeps sharp the line between the stage and her life. James,
on the other hand, gives himself the airs of dramatic (and
romantic) military lovers, Oroöndates and Alexander.[16] He is
rebuked within the next several paragraphs (VIII, 7, 8) by two
theatrical allusions, both to military comrades of the same
stripe, Shakespeare's Iago and Vanbrugh's Don John (*The
False Friend*).

The allusions to the stage become most interesting with
Booth himself. Near the beginning of *Amelia*, as he glumly
plods through the rain after his exile from the Harris house (II,
6), he spontaneously replies to a whispered call in the words of
Alphonso, the fugitive prince in Congreve's *Mourning Bride*,
who rises from his father's tomb as Booth has risen from Dr.
Harrison's wine hamper. Despite the element of mock-heroic,
this moment is not funny, but revelatory of Booth's self-pity
(and, in retelling the incident, of his self-dramatization for
Miss Matthews). Four books later (VI, 5), the other spoiled
spot in his character, his airs of the man-about-town, is picked

16. Oroöndates, a fictional character from La Calprenède, appears in
Banks's *The Rival Kings* (1677), a play not very popular, in contrast to Lee's
The Rival Queens (1677), where Alexander appears, and which held the stage
well past 1750. Curiously, except for Garrick's *Miss in Her Teens* (1747),
anachronistically mentioned by Mrs. Ellison, all Fielding's theatrical references come from plays written before 1714.

out by an approving reference to Fainall, the adulterous villain in *The Way of the World*.

The complementary faults that these two quotations suggest come together in the train of references to *Othello*, the first of which (VI, 5) signals the beginning of Booth's jealousy, and the second, ironically, James's paradoxical pangs of jealousy over someone else's wife, Amelia (VIII, 8). The four others, in books IX and X, become the only dramatic allusions applied to Booth. We find him quoting from *Othello* when Atkinson kindles his earliest suspicions about James (IX, 6), and then, in three chapters quite close to each other (X, 3, 5, 6), having his head ache with jealousy, quoting Othello about faith and cuckoldry, and listening to Amelia with "some of *Othello*'s blood in him." I do not propose to trace the Booths' nocturnal elopement, their reunion on a besieged island (Gibraltar), or the fact that "Iago" is Spanish for "James" to this train of allusions. I suspect, however, that our hero takes his surname from the most famous Othello of Fielding's association with the stage, Barton Booth. His "Master-piece," Cibber thought, "was *Othello*, . . . [where] the Actor is carried through the different Accidents of domestick Happiness, and Misery, occasionally torn, and tortur'd by the most distracting Passion, that can raise Terror, or Compassion, in the Spectator."[17] While *Amelia* is no domestic tragedy, it treads the rim of that condition; while Billy Booth is no tragedian, his roles, both personal and social, threaten to make him one.

After Book VIII, the only dramatic allusions I find in *Amelia* are to Shakespeare, the four to *Othello* and two to *Henry IV*, in which Bath and Trent refer their own ideas of honor to the false notions of those two radicals, Hotspur and Falstaff respec-

---

17. *An Apology for the Life of Colley Cibber*, ed. B. R. S. Fone (Ann Arbor: University of Michigan Press, 1968), pp. 314-15. Some of Fielding's names may have been chosen arbitrarily: see the note by Y. Y., *N&Q* 9 S 2 (1898): 426 (November 26). On *Othello*, see Eustace Palmer, "*Amelia*—The Decline of Fielding's Art," *EC* 21 (1971): 135-51.

tively (X, 5, 7). After the cluster in Book X, I find no dramatic allusions except for an aphorism Harrison quotes from *Macbeth* (XI, 2). We no longer need them. All the roles in the novel, except for Robinson's, have been established for us. The characters themselves, however, gauge each other less well than we gauge them, and they keep plying each other with rumors and assumptions, which are a structural complement to the theatrical allusions. A great variety of roles is thus imposed upon Booth. Miss Matthews's threats to blazon his shame from her lodgings at the Pelican and Trumpet (IV, 3) would make of him a monster of infidelity; she has heard of him as a thief (II, 5); the jailer takes him for a highwayman (II, 9); and Dr. Harrison trusts reports that he is vain, foolish, and unjust (IV, 3; IX, 1). He is supposed to be the victim of a duel (V, 8) and of arrest for forgery (XII, 8), perhaps James's pimp (X, 2), certainly a liar and slanderer of his wife (XII, 2). These unchosen roles for Booth, along with those he chooses and those really forced upon him by circumstances, fill out the description of him and his social context as a complex of possibilities. In this regard, the treatment of the constant Amelia can serve to contrast with that of Booth. Throughout the novel she has only sexual roles thrust upon her, by the arrogance of James and the Noble Lord, or by the jaundiced eye of Mrs. Bondum (XII, 2). Otherwise, she is treated as what she is, from Book IV on. Other characters have two roles, the real and the hypocritical, but essentially all are defined to a degree that Booth is not. It would be fashionable hyperbole to say that his conversion gives him an identity for the first time; for us, in any case, his conversion emerges from a richness of possibility, and for him, from ineffectual confusion about himself.

The vicarious knowledge one needs for appraising the world is, roughly speaking, learning; and since no one can do without such vicarious knowledge, the theme of learning is as crucial as that of role-playing. This theme, embodied in the relation of academic learning and understanding, comes up overtly in Mrs. Atkinson's account of her aunt's distinction between them (VII, 3-5). The ladies argue about two faculties, intellect (understanding) and memory (learning), with no control of the third traditional faculty, the will.[18] Only in Harrison, who appears shortly thereafter, are all three faculties harmonious. He so dominates the latter half of the book that Fielding can launch with gusto into the motif of learning and understanding. Thus books VIII-XII contain roughly twice as many classical references, some of them protracted discussions, as books I-VI. To suit the greater seriousness and broadened moral scope of the events, many more of the references come from Homer and Virgil, just as the dramatic allusions turn to Shakespeare. Only one line of Virgil (in comment upon Miss Matthews) comes up before Mrs. Bennet raps off a half dozen with emphasis two chapters from the end of Book VI; and the first half of the novel has no quotations from Homer. Books VIII-XII, however, include five quotations from the *Aeneid* (and some additional references), with another five, plus some additional references, from Homer.[19] Livy, Terence,

18. Frances Yates discusses this Augustinian arrangement of the faculties in *The Art of Memory* (Chicago: University of Chicago Press, 1966), p. 174. For an example of its use in Fielding's time, see George Jeffreys, *Miscellanies in Verse and Prose* (London, 1754), p. 427.

19. The sporadic use of references to Virgil strengthens my belief, based largely on the inability of critics to find convincing parallels in detail between the *Aeneid* and *Amelia*, that Fielding's comments on his use of Virgil have been almost universally misunderstood. He says that *Amelia* "will be found to deviate very little from the strictest Observation of all those Rules [of writing]; neither Homer nor Virgil pursued them with greater Care than myself, and the candid and learned Reader will see that the latter was the noble model, which I made use of on this Occasion." *The Covent-Garden Journal*, ed. G. E. Jensen, 2 vols. (1915; reprinted New York: Russell & Russell, 1964), 1: 186 (*Covent-Garden Journal* 8; January 28, 1752). Fielding does not mention Virgil's story or themes. His point is that Virgil is his model for "those Rules," a structural model with "Rules" different from Homer's. Le Bossu, for example, remarks that Virgil has a more complex intention than Homer, two or three exemplary heroes to Homer's one, fewer fables and allegories,

Plato, Horace, Juvenal, Ovid, Lucan, and Lucian all come up; besides these, an earlier letter from Harrison has quoted Cicero, and, of course, the narrator has mentioned an agnostic passage from Claudian in explaining Booth's lack of faith. During the last half of the book, too, we have a chance to observe the learning of numerous characters besides the obvious ones, Harrison, Mrs. Atkinson, and Booth. Bondum hashes a Virgilian line (VIII, 1); the translator and the philosopher display their classical wares (VIII, 5, 10); Bath and Amelia do too, but in translation (IX, 3; X, 9); and Fielding goes out of his way to draw into the list minor characters like the young clergyman (IX, 8, 10), the Vauxhall rakes (IX, 9), and the ministerial peer (XI, 2). We discover that Atkinson (X, 4), Colonel Trompington (XI, 2), and Trent (XI, 3) have, alas, none to display. Still, their learning is openly made a topic. They fall in with the detailing of this generously developed motif.

Learning in Fielding's earlier novels had come up, in part, to help satirize pedantry, professional jargon, or knowledge picked out of books rather than experience. In *Amelia*, none of these is of much importance. A concern with psychology and causation in this novel refers the theme of learning, more than ever before, to the faculty of memory, and therefore to the possibility of making the past germane to the present. Learning without intellect (understanding) is pedantry; intellect without learning stumbles; and both are the material on which the energy of the will must work for prudent and benevolent action, the ethical ideal of *Amelia*. Harrison, who is perhaps the most admirable character in Fielding, comes closest to the

---

and a later introduction of some principals (Turnus, Lavinia, and the other Italians). Warburton says that Virgil, unlike Homer, made "the Machinery and Intervention of the Gods . . . an indispensable Part of the Action" to impress "the Belief of a Providence" upon his readers. These comments, in two books Fielding knew, apply to *Amelia*; no significant echoes of Virgil's story and themes appear throughout *Amelia*, if in fact any appear at all. *Monsieur Bossu's Treatise of the Epick Poem*, 2 vols. (2nd ed., London, 1719), 1: 51-60, 101-02, 180-81. *The Divine Legation of Moses . . .*, 2 vols. (London, 1738, 1741), 1: 185.

ideal. The Booths, Jameses, and Atkinsons, as couples, are versions of what he embodies.

Atkinson himself knows nothing, although his devotion is a simple bridge between past and present, and, more important, his intuitive goodness suggests the purity and purpose of his will. To this amiable limited man, Mrs. Atkinson joins her abridged learning, which stops short of Homer, and her abridged understanding, which stops short of wisdom. Her ignorance of Greek and the plainer niceties of Latin grammar (X, 1), however, count for less than her slapdash way of using what she knows. Her deceitful use of Virgil to condemn remarriage (VI, 7) is at least apposite, which is more than can be said for any of her other snippets from the Latin poets. In no case does Mrs. Atkinson pay attention to the context from which she parrots a tag. She will compare Amelia's virtue to the dust and smoke of burning Troy, if she can find three words of Virgil to do it with (VIII, 9), and for two full hexameters (XII, 8), she will congratulate Amelia on recovering her fortune by quoting an exhortation to Turnus, whose *"auspicious Day"* is soon to be darkened by Aeneas. Needless to say, the narrator and Harrison offer us a very different standard for the use of the classics.

The Jameses' classical learning is not tested, but their "learning" in the extended sense of memory is. More than any other characters in the novel, they live in a present without a past, indiscriminate and idly greedy rather than consistently malicious. Without a past to draw on for empirical fuel, they lack understanding, and so their supposed knowledge of the world keeps failing them. Neither gets anything he wants from either of the Booths. Perhaps this makes them embarrassingly ineffectual, for the Booths are naive and Booth himself is immature in all three of his faculties. We have already watched him simplify his past in the history he tells Miss Matthews; and still earlier, the narrator has associated him with irreligion through a partial use of Claudian, whose "Ad Rufinam" in fact recounts the restoration of his—Claudian's—"labefacta religio." Such distorted learning accompanies distortions of understanding and will; but at other times Booth does much better. The level of his comments on Lucan to the hack (VIII, 5) proves that he can read intelligently, with attention to context, and this display of jailhouse learning leads to another in his final captivity, when he comes to understand Barrow's divine reasoning as well as he has understood Lucan's ethical sense.

His role in *Amelia* demands such inconsistency in learning as it does in role-playing: when Booth learns to be in tune with himself, he is also in tune with his constant wife, and the novel can end with a marriage of true minds. During most of the book, Amelia's social role as dutiful wife, which permits her access to her husband's will, prohibits her from a similar access to his learning or understanding. Because he responds to events in personal rather than mutual terms, she must keep concealing what she knows or thinks from his jealous honor, his stern arguments (as at the beginning and end of XI, 5), or manly image of himself. For real mutuality, he must take the first steps and open himself to her, which he does in prison (XII, 2).[20] The Booths then become positive counterparts to the empty Jameses, who have been open with each other in the previous chapter, XII, 1. What Amelia is, and what she providentially brings to the Booths' marriage, also leads to preferment higher and more significant than anything Mrs. Atkinson can have won as a false Amelia from my lord, or that James, as a would-be Booth in Amelia's arms, can offer.

When Booth learns to define himself, he has a precondition for understanding virtue or obligation; when he learns to define the world in terms of an ability to observe and use the

20. As Allan Wendt says, "The naked beauty of virtue is a necessary but not sufficient motive to ethically satisfactory actions." Booth must reassess his actions and turn to Amelia in order to be bound by her goodness. "The Naked Virtue of Amelia," *ELH* 27 (1960): 131-48.

past, he has a precondition for prudence. Both self and past are badly distorted in his narrative for Miss Matthews, and grow less so, openly and even more by implication, during the rest of the book. Yet in the epistemologically treacherous world of *Amelia*, the preconditions for prudence and virtue are very far from guaranteeing them in action. As in Johnson, Sterne, and Smollett, no character, not even Dr. Harrison, remains fault-less and effective. The principle of modification means that any resolution in the England of the eighteenth century must be dubious. It need not, however, affect a divine resolution, governed by the law of Providence and therefore free from the need for empirical vigilance. Fielding seizes the dilemma by both horns and creates a double cornucopia, for there are two resolutions which follow Amelia's pardon of Booth (XII, 2) and accompany James's withdrawal of his challenge (XII, 4).[21]

The first of these resolutions is Harrison's decision that he will "distress his Circumstances" to bring the Booths into the country, where he can protect them till "something can be done for" Booth (XII, 3). We have here a plausible response to the three threats—physical, marital, and financial—that men-aced the Booths during the "black Despair" at the end of Book XI. James's challenge has been largely subterfuge (XII, 1), Trent can claim "only" fifty pounds, Booth has already proved some willingness to prosper "no longer [as] Captain *Booth*, but Farmer *Booth*" (III, 12). Fielding needs no sudden sweets of fortune to round off his sober fare. None the less, after the boiled beef and cabbage comes the second resolution, a provi-dential *pièce montée* that nourishes more than it fattens. Ob-viously, as in *Humphry*, this dessert has been prepared for. A series of repentences and confessions leads to Robinson's. A series of "pawnings" (real or suggested) of Amelia's image,

---

21. The double ending of *Amelia* has been recognized by Sheldon Sacks, *Fiction and the Shape of Belief* (Berkeley and Los Angeles: University of California Press, 1964), p. 261.

starting with Booth's use of her to present himself to Miss
Matthews, ends with the recovery of the real Amelia—the
heiress—through pawning the pictured one. The benevolent
judge (XII, 7) has been prefigured a book earlier by the judge
who deals with Betty (XI, 7); the suborner Murphy of the
denouement has recommended subornation on our first
acquaintance with him (I, 10); and we have had several hints
that Amelia's sister (also a thief named Betty) may be dis-
honest. Despite this sort of preparation, however, the grand
surprise of the denouement seems "unnatural" to many readers, as Fielding might have suspected it would. His plot did not
require it, yet he not only included it, he hardly palliated its implausibility. Why, in this novel of modifications, does Fielding
execute the last one this way?

   If Fielding had lifted the Booths from straw pallets and star-
vation to the heights of sudden fortune, he would have
rebuked our "art of life," prudence. Prudence depends on prediction, and prediction, on probabilities. The hand of God
moves uniquely and improbably in this novel, maneuvering
Robinson first to the pawnbroker's and then to Bondum's
house, both at the right time. It turns imprudence, conversely,
to advantage. Mrs. Atkinson's bartering Amelia's image to the
Noble Lord is imprudent, but it results in Amelia's recovering
her pictured image (through the evil of Atkinson's illness);
Booth's imprudent dithering away of the family's necessaries
results in Amelia's being recognized by Robinson (through the
evil of her having to pawn the portrait); Booth's imprudent
dinner with Miss Matthews leads to his conversion (through
the evil of his having been jailed). In short, the gratuitous end
of *Amelia* appears to rebuke the virtue of prudence that the rest
of the novel has been teaching and recommending. God helps
those who harm themselves. Analogously, our prudence as
readers, which pertains to the likelihoods and the idiom of the
novel, seems in part to be mocked by a nearly miraculous
conclusion.

A novel from which the benevolent supervisory narrator has largely retired ought not to violate the independence of its characters; an exact imitation of life cannot pop on the mask of comedy. Fielding therefore gives us his double ending, one (the prudential) plausible, the other (the providential) implausible, and both thematically prepared for. Harrison's decision to shelter the Booths takes into account, among other things, Booth's pledge not to gamble again, as well as Amelia's ability to "take an heroic Resolution." Prudence, at least for the future, is rewarded, along the principles of Harrison's decision in Book VIII to have Booth arrested when he seemed extravagant. The Booths, then, have the promise of temporary shelter by XII, 3; Harrison prevails on James not to duel in XII, 4; and this mixture of Christian charity and prudence draws us into XII, 5, in which Booth's conversion testifies to Christianity and prudence both, shoring up his promises with real principle based on understanding. In fact, as Harrison points out, one does not have to travel far from the notion that men act according to their passions to the fuller faith that he and Booth now share: "It would be fair to conclude that Religion to be true which applies immediately to the strongest of these Passions, Hope and Fear" (XII, 5). Booth's conversion, then, ends the motif of prudence in a satisfying way, even as it gives the needed impetus to the motif of Providence in the second half of *Amelia*'s double ending.

The providential ending, which complements the prudential, is implausible and meant to be so.[22] For reasons that I have

22. Cf. C. H. K. Bevan, "The Unity of Fielding's *Amelia*," *Renaissance and Modern Studies* 14 (1970): 90-110. Providence, Bevan remarks, "cannot, unlike the purely ethical theme of *Amelia*, be verified from within the novel, in terms of demonstrable relationships between known causes and effects" (p. 109). Fielding therefore draws upon the reader's faith, which must in some sense be answerable to Booth's. But the precondition of our acceptance is Fielding's implicit acknowledgment that such a stroke of Providence is something painfully rare, at least in so plain a form; and that very acknowledgment dissuades many readers from being willing to accept the stroke of Providence on any level, because it is, as it must be, implausible.

already mentioned, Fielding had to mark its separation from
the idiom of *Amelia*, and give it its own conceptual identity. He
did not want to pretend that the everyday world, for which
this Christian novel has little respect, could be redeemed far
enough to be just for the sake of justice. From the world's
standpoint, fortune still rules, and the Booths triumph by
happy accident. Nor could an exact imitation of life pretend
that the intervention of Providence, or its bold and blatant use
of second causes, was likely to be common in anyone's theology or experience. Realism insisted on its implausibility, even
while reality in the largest sense insisted on its possibility,
perhaps its symbolic necessity. Fielding did, after all, need
an ending that would continue the broadening of possibilities and knitting together of themes which forms the repre-
sentational mode of *Amelia*. In this novel we do not get or need
vicarious tragedy on the outskirts, as the story of the Old Man
offers it to us in *Tom Jones*. The leading candidate, Mrs. Bennet,
becomes Mrs. Atkinson, has a captain for a husband, and presumably spends her post-novelistic life in Horatian felicity and
quiet with her two chopping boys. A breadth of possibilities,
which increases throughout the novel, serves the same purpose as vicarious tragedy in earlier novels, that is, to assure us
that the author is representing life fully, not picking and
choosing events to fit his predilections. Given this inclusiveness throughout the first eleven books, the resolution must
embrace it. Fortune, which looks like chaos or contrivance to
profane eyes, makes its widest sweep; Providence, which
informs all reality, reveals itself most clearly.

The triumphant resolution of *Amelia* caps an ambitious and
profoundly intelligent scheme, economical and intricately
ordered in execution. Unfortunately, Fielding's very efficiency
has kept his novel from popular or critical success. His quasi-
theatrical mode of presentation denies him the cognitive and
emotional resources that Sterne and Smollett gain from our
intimate knowledge of the characters' psychology and from

the comments of partially reliable narrators, Tristram and Jery. Fielding therefore must assert the values of *Amelia* through simple, emotionally striking means, which run the risk of disgusting us as "sentimental" or arbitrary. Booth the glib philosopher and self-apologist, for example, is made eligible for redemption because we see him a brave and tactful equal with the colonels, a man of classical learning, a loving husband and father with a sense of humor and a happy refusal to be bound by the logic of his "philosophy." But Fielding has to make us see these and similar traits in him without allowing us access to a psyche in which they can be securely rooted. The result is that Booth and other characters at times seem simplistic or, if superficially inconsistent, weak.

Amelia thereby develops three flaws. One is that it asks readers to care for these occasionally simplistic or weak characters, concern with whom is at the heart of the book, now that the irony, the high spirits, and the urbane wisdom of Fielding's earlier novels have had to disappear. The second is that the texture of the novel is sometimes superbly elaborated and sometimes rather bald. The reader who takes intense pleasure in those parts where Fielding is supreme feels betrayed when the demands of the subject so strain the powers of novelistic form that Fielding must work without finesse. The third and most damaging flaw stems from the Booths' not knowing each other deeply enough. They love and accept each other, which is adequate for Walter and Toby, Bramble and Humphry, or Tom and Sophia, where "full consciousness" and "amplitude of reflexion" need not inhere in the relationship, because they inhere elsewhere in the novel.[23] For the Booths' marriage to be shallow, a compact of hearts and shared attitudes but not of minds, maims Fielding's central insistence on learning and understanding. He has, however, no good

23. The terms are Henry James's, from his famous few sentences on Fielding in the preface to *The Princess Casamassima*; in *The Art of the Novel: Critical Prefaces by Henry James*, introd. R. P. Blackmur (New York: Scribner's, 1934), p. 68.

way of making us believe they do realize each other's nature with any depth, especially inasmuch as the novel compels us to doubt the possibility of anyone's knowing others profoundly. The epistemological skepticism of *Amelia* thwarts even Fielding's technical genius from full realization of the subject.

One will not be disappointed, in any case, if one looks to *Amelia* for a consistent, complex example of the mode we have been describing. It is filled with analogy and modification; it refers them to epistemology, thus making them part of a system of procedures; it refers its visible schemes of order to a central character, Booth, whose own system is tested through broadening perspectives. It is "presentational" in spite of its providential ending, as *Humphry* is in spite of its pseudo-providential ending. In neither case does the ending solve anything in the plot, nor is it demanded by the idiom of the book. *Amelia* might all be written on the level of Booth's tale, as perhaps is Sarah Fielding's *David Simple*; of books IV-VI, as is *Joseph Andrews*, roughly speaking; or of books I-XI. The denouement, a reversal of sorts in the manner of those emotionally mixed awakenings with which Johnson and Smollett complete their books, still remains in *Amelia*, as in *Rasselas* and *Humphry*, the last and most thorough modification, the last and most panoramic perspective from which we are allowed to see the total world of the book.

The reference of order to Booth, and the presentational mode, suppose the same sort of debunking of systems, and therefore the same apparent formal negligence, that we have seen in Johnson, Sterne, and Smollett. Fielding shares with these men a high degree of organization, based on the associative methods common to the order of mind in the reader and the means of epistemological inquiry. His grouping procedures are somewhat less defined than Johnson's and Sterne's, and somewhat more than Smollett's, but are very much of a piece with theirs. The same might be said of his movement from chapter to chapter, although his combination of thematic groupings (what I earlier called "central resonances") and narrative line gives him a directness that the seeming haphazardness of Smollett and Sterne lacks, and that asks somewhat less formal cooperation from the reader than they do. By and large, then, we have a fruitful accord among contemporaries. If the accord began to die with the next generation, that was not because its fruits had all been plucked. As we shall see, *Caleb Williams* made exceptionally creative use of it.

Caleb Williams

I: HISTORY INTO ROMANCE

To the reader fresh from *Amelia,* some of the problems in *Caleb Williams* look familiar. Fielding wants to combine satire and a causal model of contemporary life, so as to expose "glaring evils" and teach the reader the rules of the treacherous game in which we are all engaged. Godwin also offers an exposé, "a general review of the modes of domestic and unrecorded despotism," with special attention, like Fielding's, to the abuses of the law and aristocratic privilege. He promises us a model of contemporary life, a faithful development, as he says in his Preface, of "the existing constitution of society" through its practical effects. In theory his principle of causality looks different from Fielding's, deductive rather than inductive, polemic rather than educative; they come closer in fact, partly because both men use the history of a private life to move their novels. A picaresque hero, as an objective onlooker, might have served the public indictment that both authors warn us to expect. Yet Fielding and Godwin alike put such value upon human relations and personal morality that neither works with a picaro. As a result, public and private plots end up at odds, at least for many readers, in *Amelia* and *Caleb;* nor do the denouements clearly keep all the energies of either novel in balance.

Godwin, being no Fielding, made matters worse for himself. His use of language is so clumsy that few inferences can be drawn from what in other writers might be subtleties. For instance, in Volume I, Chapter 3, Tyrrel is compared to Milo of Crotona, "that hero of antiquity, whose prowess consisted in felling an ox with his fist, and devouring him at a meal."[1] The next paragraph calls him a "rural Antaeus," and the paragraph after that, "this Hercules." Godwin gains nothing by this flurry of allusions except to tell us that Tyrrel was strong, which we already knew. Or, if he is in this case simply producing for us the naive pedantry of young self-taught Williams, what excuses can be found for the old hag's incredible rant (III, 4)? "Leave you! No: I will thrust my fingers through your ribs, and drink your blood!—You conquer me?—Ha, ha!—Yes, yes! you shall!—I will sit upon you, and press you to hell! I will roast you with brimstone, and dash your entrails into your eyes!—Ha, ha!—ha!" We cannot expect tonal or intellectual subtleties in the style of someone who writes like this, because the initial control of language is not there. At the other end of the scale, the conceptual end, Godwin has seemed to some so bound up with a radical ideology as to compromise his control over the mimetic texture of his novel. His Preface and his open attacks upon the legal system reinforce these doubts: doctrinaire novels—Bage's contemporary *Hermsprong* (1796), for instance—have a way of resisting anything else but crude and reductive readings.[2] *Caleb Williams*, though, deserves better. Its seeming failures, other than those of style, lead us to a plan that only a novelist of great skill and ambition could conceive.

1. This exploit is mentioned by Athenaeus, *Deipnosophistae* 412f-413a; and in Zachary Grey's note to *Hudibras* I, i, 327-28 (first edition, 1744).

2. David McCracken, "Godwin's Literary Theory: The Alliance between Fiction and Political Philosophy," *PQ* 49 (1970): 113-33, distinguishes Godwin's use of fiction from that of reformers like Bage and Holcroft.

Like *Amelia*, this novel begins with a short introduction and a long flashback. Caleb offers general exposition for one chapter, and then for fully one third of the book tells us about men and events that have nothing to do with the story of his own life, except by way of stimulus and analogy. This historical information, he says, he got from Falkland's steward Mr. Collins. The initial guarantee of verisimilitude is made through someone who had lived through the period described, and whose character is beyond cavil. Furthermore, Caleb has interwoven "with Mr. Collins's story various information which I afterwards received from other quarters, that I [might] give all possible perspicuity to the series of events" (I, 1). But this is a blind. Caleb tells us about Falkland's past dealings with Tyrrel and Emily Melvile. He transcribes private conversations and still more private feelings, and dissects motives that he could not have learned. And can we believe that men like Tyrrel's "confidential friend" (I, 4), for instance, would have gossiped to an adolescent farmer's boy, the secretary of Tyrrel's enemy? Unless Godwin was pointlessly abrogating his narrative convention at the very beginning of the novel, when most authors are trying to establish theirs, he must have been suggesting that Caleb is at the very least making free with history, after the mode of the interpolated stories in *Amelia* or the whole of *Tristram Shandy*. Caleb's subjective story is "true," like Tristram's and unlike Booth's, because in the nature of things there can be no checking it. One cannot ask the real Dr. Slop or Gines please to step forward. We know, however, that the narrator has an axe to grind, and we read with suspicion, warranted suspicion.

In any case, our doubts might be wakened by Caleb's comments on himself. He tells us in the fourth paragraph of the book that he was "a sort of natural philosopher": "I could not rest till I had acquainted myself with the solutions that had been invented for the phenomena of the universe. In fine, this produced in me an invincible attachment to books of narrative and romance." Caleb's train of logic is extraordinary, for natural science and romance do not seem to be kith and kin. He ends the same paragraph, "My curiosity however was not entirely ignoble: village anecdotes and scandal had no charms for me: my imagination must be excited; and, when that was not done, my curiosity was dormant." Ignoble or not, what Caleb says he prefers has more to do with the romantic than the true, or rather, with his notion that the romantic is the true. No one can be surprised that he tells, and embroiders, the flashback story instead of letting us see a sober body of notes and attestations, such as a real Collins could have provided for him. No one should be surprised, either, to find him shaping events in terms of the structures he knows best, those of novels that he has read. He does not tell us what these are, specifically, but he borrows the framework of the flashback story from two of the most popular novels of the eighteenth century, *Sir Charles Grandison* and *Clarissa*.[3] Godwin can hardly have thought that repeated close parallels with these two novels would slip by without setting off at least a faint familiar tinkle in the reader's mind. A thorough body of allusion must have had its own conscious rhetorical purpose.

Let me indicate how thorough the allusions are. Falkland goes to Italy, as does Sir Charles Grandison, where he teaches English to a beautiful rich Italian girl, as does Sir Charles. The result in both novels is that the Englishmen must confront jealous Italian pretenders to the girl's hand—Count Belvedere in Richardson and Count Malvesi, which sounds like a negative inflected form of "belvedere," in Godwin; in both novels the Englishman subdues the Italian by his noble behavior. Sir Charles and Mr. Falkland are involved with lovelorn wards, in

3. There were at least nine editions of each before *Caleb* was written. D. Gilbert Dumas, "Things as They Were: The Original Ending of *Caleb Williams*," SEL 6 (1966): 575-97, writes: "Godwin was, according to his journal . . . reading Richardson's *Clarissa* while engaged in writing the final 26 pages of the first version of *Caleb Williams*" (p. 578, n. 7).

both cases named Emily, and with rescuing a young lady from
an abductor who plans to rape her and thus force a marriage
(Harriet Byron is rescued from Sir Hargrave Pollexfen, Emily
Melvile from Grimes). Emily, in turn, finds herself very much
in the position of Clarissa, whose cruel and envious guardian
insists that she marry a coarse landowner (Solmes, Grimes)
although she is attracted to a dashing young aristocrat (Lovelace, Falkland). Each girl is imprisoned under a saucy servant
who torments her, menaced by hints of forced marriage, abducted at night from a garden at least semi-consenting,
rescued *en déshabillé* from the threat of fire by the dashing
young aristocrat (fraudulently in *Clarissa*), jailed on a false
debtor's charge when ill and weak, and killed by this experience. If one considers that all these duplications of Richardson's plots occur in ten brief chapters of Caleb's story, their
force will be clear. Caleb can only cast his story in terms that he
knows, the terms of books. Again, I mean to imply, not that he
warps facts, but that fact and fiction are identical, science and
romance are one and the same, because the novel is an account
of mental phenomena.[4]

    After Caleb gets past such allegorically conceived names as
"Clare" for his famous poet, he moves to "Barnabas Tyrrel,"
named after Barnabas Tirrel, a jealous would-be knife murderer in Henry Brooke's *The Fool of Quality* (1765-70).[5]
"Ferdinando Falkland" comes from the romance of English
history. The name conflates those of two heroes in the English
Civil War, the parliamentary general Ferdinando Fairfax and
the great royalist Lucius Cary, Lord Falkland. Both appear in
Clarendon's *History of the Rebellion*. A better metaphor than

4. There are obvious parallels in Blake, an almost exact contemporary of
Godwin's, or in "The Rime of the Ancient Mariner," published four years
after *Caleb Williams*. Like Godwin, these "Romantics" are very much in a tradition that this book has traced through Sterne and Smollett, and that marks
a good deal of mid- to later eighteenth-century verse.
5. *The Fool of Quality* went through numerous editions, both complete and
in John Wesley's abridgement; Tirrel appears in chap. 15.

civil war could hardly have been chosen for Caleb's internally torn aristocrat. The similarities therefore between Lord Falkland and Mr. Falkland are striking:

[Lord Falkland had] a perfect habit of unchearfulness; and he who had been exactly easy and affable to all men, became on a sudden less communicable, and very sad, pale, and extremely afflicted with the spleen. In his cloaths and habit, which he had before always minded with more neatness, industry, and expence, than are usual in so great a soul, he became not only incurious, but too negligent; and in his reception of suitors, so quick, sharp, and severe, that it made him to be looked upon as proud and imperious. . . . He was a man of excellent, nay of exceeding great and prodigious parts, both natural and acquired; of a wit so sharp, and a nature so sincere, that nothing ·could be more lovely; of great ingenuity and honour; of the most exemplary manners, and singular good nature, and of the most unblemished integrity; of that inimitable sweetness and delight in conversation, of so flowing and obliging a humanity and goodness to mankind, and of that primitive simplicity and innocency of life, as could hardly be equalled.[6]

6. The description comes from the *Biographia Britannica*, 3 (2nd ed., London, 1784): 295, s.n. "Lucius Cary." The editor, Andrew Kippis, was Godwin's tutor, friend, and associate. For speculation about names in this novel, some of which repeats what I have suggested, see pp. 388-91 in Burton R. Pollin, "The Significance of Names in the Fiction of William Godwin," *Revue des Langues Vivantes* 37 (1971): 388-99; Pollin's work is independent of mine in "Allusion and Analogy in the Romance of *Caleb Williams*," *UTQ* 37 (1967): 18-30, an expanded version of which is the substance of this chapter. I might note that Lord Falkland is used as a *beau idéal* in Coventry's *Pompey the Little* and *The Vicar of Wakefield*, and that sentimental heroes named Faulkland appear in Frances Sheridan's popular *Sidney Bidulph* (1761-67) and her son's still more popular *The Rivals*. Caleb's own name, as Ian and Heather Ousby have explained, refers by way of his biblical namesake to his "twin identity as servant and spy"—the deterministic projection of the mind's creations into the external world, in this case the world of Christian names duly registered at baptism, makes tragic what Sterne had made comic; the technique is identical. Ousby and Ousby, "'My servant Caleb': Godwin's *Caleb Williams* and the Political Trials of the 1790s," *UTQ* 44 (1974): 51.

Mr. Falkland has been a man of "frankness, ingenuity, and unreserve," "of uncommon taste and capacity," whose conduct was marked by "such dignity, such affability, so perpetual an attention to the happiness of others, such delicacy of sentiment and expression!" "The sallies of his wit were far beyond those of Mr. Tyrrel in variety and vigour; in addition to which they had the advantage of having their spontaneous exuberance guided and restrained by the sagacity of a cultivated mind" (I, 3). Like Lord Falkland, who was "little, and of no great strength," Mr. Falkland too is small and cannot contend with Tyrrel. And of course, he becomes melancholy, occasionally harsh, and solitary. The character projected into the novel again indicates the scope of Caleb's knowledge of men and manners.

The conception and history of Falkland, and the history of Emily, then, have literary antecedents; three elements in the flashback story seem not to. They are parts of the relationship between Falkland and Tyrrel, the episode involving the poet Clare, and the history of Benjamin and Leonard Hawkins. These elements do not need antecedents in Caleb's reading experience because they have analogues in his life—he is, after all, telling us everything in retrospect, from shortly before the final trial at which Caleb reveals his secret. The one thing he cannot tell us about, therefore, is the trial and defense of Falkland on the charge of killing Tyrrel, which has no analogue in his own experience at the time that he writes the bulk of the book. And in fact, when he arrives at this point (I, 12) he yields the rostrum: "I shall endeavour to state the remainder of this narrative in the words of Mr. Collins." The rest of the chapter, and of the flashback story, comes directly from Collins's mouth, as it had to.

No such rein hampers Caleb when he writes about the Hawkinses, whose situation so transparently doubles his. He is, in his own mind, the sturdy man of little property and great independence whom the law torments, the object of an aristocrat's sullen revenge, and perhaps—this memoir is written before the climactic trial at the end—a martyr. Young Leonard, agile and sagacious, "knows what is due him," and so is refused to Tyrrel's service (I, 9); young Caleb, well read and athletic, goes into service "but ill prepared for the servile submission Mr. Falkland demanded. In early life I had been accustomed to be much my own master" (II, 7). Leonard, impatient at confinement, breaks the padlocks that have made his father "a sort of prisoner in his own domains," and is falsely jailed under the "Black Act." The same elements— confinement, impatience, breaking of padlocks, false arrest— come up with Caleb, as do Leonard's escape from prison and disguised wandering.

The Hawkinses' misfortunes prove a clear case of oppression. Caleb imagines his own case clear too, although we have more than enough room to disagree with him and to refuse to apply to him the emotional pattern set up in the flashback story. The other two threads of plot—those concerning Clare, and the rivalry between Falkland and Tyrrel—are complementary projections by Caleb of his own experience or would-be experience into the form of history. Clare passes on his radiant mantle to Falkland, his executor and friend; Tyrrel and Falkland are physical and moral antitheses. These two relationships set the limits for Caleb's with Falkland. Caleb aspires to be the confidant of his patron, and he tells us how Falkland tries to "disburthen his mind" to his new secretary (I, 1), how he, Caleb, draws Falkland into conversation (II, 1) and makes him cry out, "Who gave you a right to be my confident?" (II, 2). When Falkland is overwrought, Caleb thinks "with astonishment, even with rapture, of the attention and kindness to me I discovered in Mr. Falkland through all the roughness of his manner" (II, 3). Finally, in the climactic scene where Falkland lets his "tongue . . . for the first time for several years" speak "the language of my heart," he refers to Caleb as his "confident" (II, 6). Here the malign attraction of Caleb and Falkland

for each other becomes a terrible parody of mutual love and
trust between Clare and Falkland. As to Falkland and Tyrrel,
all but the last of the narrative episodes in which the two rivals
jar, like those that have to do with Emily Melvile, go back to
Grandisonian material. For instance, the squabble over danc-
ing with Miss Hardingham and the visit to Tyrrel in which
Falkland tries to reason toward peace (I, 3, 4) both glance at
Malvesi's misunderstanding of Falkland's connection with
Lady Lucretia Pisani (I, 2). What is left of their rivalry, after one
subtracts what comes from Richardson, is their mutual fear,
mutual outrage, and eventually mutual humiliation. This nest
of emotions is precisely that in which Caleb and Falkland
increasingly find themselves. Each man endangers the other,
acting incomprehensibly except to himself, and each becomes
the agent of the other's social destruction. Not until the end of
the novel do we see this pattern fully worked out, but its
nature is quite clear at the time that Caleb writes his memoirs,
the bulk of the book.

Some inferences follow from what has been said. First, one
might expect to find that the whole book, not simply the flashback story, bears the marks of having been written by a
romancing historian. Verisimilitude should yield now and
again to more subjective versions of reality. Allusions should
give a skeleton to sections of the text, just as in the flashback
story. Second, the flashback story itself might be expected to
have a bearing, through analogy, upon the events of Caleb's
own life. Just as the sets of relationships involving the
Hawkinses, Tyrrel, Clare, and Falkland look forward to
Caleb's moral duel with his old patron, so should incidents of
all sorts from the flashback story look forward, if only to justify
their inclusion in this apology for one's self. Certainly by the
time the reader has finished the history of Falkland, Tyrrel,
and the rest, he has been urged to think analogically, by a rash
of parallels thrust at him. Falkland has aborted duels with
Malvesi and Tyrrel, aborted love affairs (real or suspected)

with Lady Lucretia and Emily, attempted rescues of Emily and the Hawkinses (he is out of town at the crucial moment for each); Leonard Hawkins and Emily are arrested innocents; and we have already noted the polar relationships between Falkland and, respectively, Clare and Tyrrel. A final inference, obliquely connected to romance and analogy, has to do with Caleb. If he has arranged events, we may be able to look beyond or through those events to a truth he himself does not see. That occasionally happens in the novels by Sterne, Smollett, and Fielding that we have discussed; it obviously happens in Richardson, and a growing body of criticism asserts that it happens in Defoe and Goldsmith. Or, to put the matter another way, Godwin's Preface tells us "that the spirit and character of the government intrudes itself into every rank of society." Why should Caleb's "rank" as an upper servant be exempt? The indictment of *Caleb Williams* is most comprehensive if it includes the narrator, who is also part of "things as they are." Thus the young man, who like so many eighteenth-century Quixotes and Polly Honeycombes tries to read life with the system of a novel, ensnares himself in a fiction truer than any he has known.

As obviously as Sterne, Smollett, and Fielding, Godwin offers us a privately shaped world, one with a built-in principle of modification, for although fiction may show us "things as they are," the reality of things as they are does not fit well into the a priori patterns of the fiction Caleb knows, into his version of Falkland's chivalric romances. At this point in the story, we are merely suspicious, as we are of the tale Booth tells Miss Matthews; it is left for Godwin, like Fielding, to create a depth of understanding from that suspicion of ours in the rest of the novel. The principle of modification must operate upon Caleb's intended analogies so as to show their limited utility within the systematic context—that of personal apologetics—that Caleb imagines for them. No doubt Godwin's job is in some ways harder than Fielding's, for he must

stay within the limits that Caleb the narrator sets and give each
particular a triple meaning, as part of Caleb's self-exculpation,
part of Caleb's unwitting self-revelation, and part of a moral
understanding that includes but goes beyond the other two
meanings.

II: ROMANCE INTO HISTORY

Volume II of the novel takes up the job of modification by
maintaining and developing what is suspicious about Caleb's
story in Volume I: the loose romancing, the dubious analogies,
and the self-interested implication of the speaker. We find, for
instance, that Caleb lapses from the simplest plausibility. We
are never told how Falkland rapidly finds trunks that Caleb
conceals in "a small apartment of the most secret nature"
(II, 8), or how Falkland smuggles the incriminating jewelry
into a locked trunk of which Caleb alone has the keys (II, 10).
How did Hawkins get the knife that killed Tyrrel? We are
fobbed off with the feeblest of excuses, for why he should have
removed it from the street, assuming that he happened to be
passing by, and then have tossed it offhandedly "in a corner of
his lodging" (I, 12) is obscure. I suppose one can weave
hypotheses to cover these seeming lapses in the narrative, or
to explain how Caleb happens to wander toward Mr.
Forester's house when lost in a wilderness of wood and heath,
to arrive at an inn where Mr. Forester by chance has stopped,
and to be there in Forester's company when Mr. Falkland, also
by chance, appears (II, 8). But one does not expect to have to
weave hypotheses in a rationalist's novel; one does not expect
to have plausibility frayed in a book about "things as they are."
Each slipped stitch in Caleb's narrative becomes a guide to
interpreting that phrase, "as they are."

Along the same lines, Caleb—or Godwin—makes an odd
use of footnotes. We learn (II, 11) about Brightwel, "a common
soldier, of a most engaging physiognomy, and two and twenty

years of age," who dies in Caleb's company while both are imprisoned unjustly. A footnote leads every reader to the source for this account: "A story extremely similar to this is to be found in the Newgate Calendar, Vol. I. p. 382." Much of the description of Brightwel, even his name, comes from the *Newgate Calendar*.[7] However, the reader who follows Caleb where he has been invited to follow can infer that the original Francis Brightwel was not a young man cut off in his bloom, because one of his character witnesses had known him for "near twenty years." He did not languish in prison or die there: indicted on August 4, he died on August 22 at his lodgings, after his rapid acquittal. Admittedly he did die of "gaol distemper," but he was not attended by Caleb Williams. His doctor was Sir Hans Sloane, president of the College of Physicians from 1719 to 1735, F.R.S. for sixty-eight years and successor to Newton as president (1727-1741), appointed physician-general to the army in 1722 and first physician to George II in 1727. What appears to be a confirming reference in fact disconfirms Caleb's claims, his righteousness and pathos. He clearly would like us to accept the parallel between the injured Brightwel and himself; and Godwin, even at the cost of weakening his attack on the penal system, clearly would like us to question that parallel.

The crime for which Francis Brightwel was arrested, the *Newgate Calendar* tells us, was committed by that famous pair of early eighteenth-century criminals, Jack Sheppard and Joseph "Blueskin" Blake. In a sense Brightwel died for them, almost as the Hawkinses died for Falkland, and that is perhaps his leading qualification for appearing in *Caleb Williams*, where the story of Jack Sheppard has its peculiar interest. Sheppard,

---

7. My quotations come from the book in which Godwin read both Brightwel's and Sheppard's histories, *The Malefactor's Register; or, the Newgate and Tyburn Calendar . . . from the Year 1700 to Lady-Day 1779* (London, n.d.), vol. 1.

who unlike the real Brightwel *was* twenty-two when he died, was a carpenter's son and a chairmaker's apprentice. After his career as a thief was interrupted by his master's discovery of stolen goods in his trunk, he found himself repeatedly in prison, and repeatedly found ways to get out again. On one occasion, given tools by accomplices to remove his fetters and jail-window bars, he escaped by scaling the walls. On another, when he was put in a strong-room, handcuffed, loaded with irons, and chained to a staple, he unlocked himself from the staple with a nail, picked out mortar with the nail and a bar, and escaped into the rainy evening outside the prison. Disguised as a beggar, with a handkerchief about his head, a torn woollen cap, and deliberately torn shoes and stockings, says the *Newgate Calendar*, Sheppard heard men at an inn talking about his escape: "Conversing with the landlady about Sheppard, he [Sheppard] told her that it was impossible for him to get out of the kingdom; and the keepers would certainly have him again in a few days; on which the woman wished that a curse might fall on those who should betray him."

These are not, of course, all the events of Sheppard's career as the greatest of jailbreakers, but they are some that might ring a bell with an eighteenth-century reader of *Caleb Williams*. Caleb too is a skilled joiner; he too releases himself with a nail from his staple; he too tries to escape by scaling prison walls; he too is handcuffed and fettered in a strong-room from which he escapes with tools given him by an accessory, Thomas the footman; Caleb too loosens bricks with the help of a bar and escapes into the rainy dawn outside the prison (II, 14). The beggar's disguise—handkerchief on head, "a piece of an old woollen nightcap," and purposely torn apparel—also recurs in his narrative. So does the conversation of the men at the inn, and so does the later one with the landlady, to whom the disguised Caleb says that "I did not think it possible he [that is, Caleb himself] should escape the pursuit

that was set up after him. This idea excited her immediate
indignation; she said, she hoped he was far enough away by
this time, but, if not, she wished the curse of God might light
on them that betrayed so noble a fellow to an ignominious
end!'' (III, 5). One can easily see what has happened. As Caleb
writes about his social ruin, he moves from his earlier structure
of moral or patriotic romance—Richardson and civil war—to
an antisocial romance or history. His isolation makes him
pattern himself upon a legendary criminal, such as he himself
is to become in Volume III. We have a still further modification
of Caleb's implicit analogy between himself and two victims in
this volume, Brightwel and the innocent but indicted peasant
(II, 5), and also the Hawkinses in Volume I.

The principle of analogy brings us back to consider the story
of Falkland as Caleb has told it. We have already talked about
the emotional parameters set up by the episodes involving
Clare, the Hawkinses, and the rivalry between Tyrrel and
Falkland. Other flashback incidents have more limited functions. For instance, Falkland has controlled a fire in the village
and rescued Emily Melvile (I, 6): ''By his presence of mind, by
his indefatigable humanity and incessant exertions, he saved
three-fourths of the village from destruction.'' At the same
place in the second volume (II, 6) another fire breaks out, this
time in Falkland's own house, and Caleb takes over his
patron's job of directing work and ''contributing my personal
labour in the public concern.'' As soon as he sees the locked
trunk of Falkland's secret, he forgets ''the public concern''
while the flames extend and surmount the house, becoming
''more violent than ever'' and causing ''a considerable part of
the chimney'' to tumble ''with noise into the court below.''
Whether or not one agrees that the fire is symbolic of a destructive fever in Caleb himself, no one can fail to see that in contrast to Falkland, Caleb abandons his duty as a citizen, and still
more his duty as a servant. He will not try to save his master's

goods. His "station in the family" and "understanding and mental resources" put him in a position of command, but he reneges on his social function, his personal debt, and the image of heroism that he himself has offered us in the flashback story. Falkland, on the other hand, repeats his earlier action by mounting to the roof and being "in a moment in every place where his presence was required," so that the flames are at length extinguished.

Similarly, Falkland twice shows his rational forbearance with an enemy. In Volume I, he treats successfully with Malvesi (2) and unsuccessfully with Tyrrel (4). The count falls to his knees to beg forgiveness, and the squire "collects his venom for a mortal assault." At a parallel place in the second volume (3), Falkland calls in Caleb "to have an explanation." He asks for the same policy of live and let live which he had asked from Tyrrel, and with the same success. Caleb imitates Malvesi in manner, calling himself "wrong," "ashamed," "a foolish, wicked, despicable wretch" who must be punished "in some way or other, that I may forgive myself": "I cannot bear to think what I have done. I shall never again be able to look in the face the best of masters and the best of men." But he imitates Tyrrel in fact, for he spies on Falkland during the peasant's trial (5), feels "a kind of rapture" after it, when he is sure that Falkland did kill Tyrrel, and walks about in the garden, blurting out Falkland's guilt in "paroxysms of exclamation" for all to hear. Then (6) he tries to chisel open the trunk. This analogy, like that of the two fires, works against Caleb's broad hints through the histories of Emily and Hawkins that he is as pure and persecuted as the maiden or honest yeoman. The conventional moral standbys do not really apply to him.

All the characters in the flashback story are essentially black or white, even Tyrrel, who can act decently, and Falkland, whose flaws are hinted at. Nothing there quite prepares us for

the character of Caleb himself, except for a few early paragraphs. I have mentioned his odd transition from his interest
in natural philosophy to what he seems to see as a consequent
love of romances. Morally, the end of the first chapter is more
intriguing, because of the way in which it passes from what
appears to be sympathy to what is in fact self-pity: "My heart
bleeds at the recollection of [Falkland's] misfortunes as if they
were my own. How can it fail to do so? To his story the whole
fortune of my life was linked; because he was miserable, my
happiness, my name, and my existence have been irretriev-
ably blasted." In retrospect, this outburst sounds false. Caleb
himself creates the link, and shares Falkland's misery because
he has insisted on sharing Falkland's knowledge. "What [Falk-
land] endured in the intercourse between us appeared to be
gratuitous evil," writes Caleb. "He had only to wish that there
was no such person as myself in the world, and to curse the
hour when his humanity led him to rescue me from my
obscurity, and place me in his service" (II, 4).

Yet Caleb never realizes the meaning of this observation.
The suffering man has the moral remoteness of a sufferer in a
book, whom one can love, as Caleb truthfully (by his own
lights) says he loves Falkland, and at the same time watch with
an eye for the story and the sentiment. Caleb's romance-
reader's soul is such that after making Falkland, in Falkland's
words, a "subject upon which for you to exercise your
ingenuity, and improve your power of tormenting," Caleb can
think "with rapture . . . at finding myself, humble as I was by
my birth, obscure as I had hitherto been, thus suddenly
become of so much importance to the happiness of one of the
most enlightened and accomplished men in England" (II, 3).
This enlightened and accomplished patron, "so generous a
protector," develops into "a fish that plays with the bait
employed to entrap him," while his loyal servant acts with
only "apparent want of design," well knowing how to introduce the conversation "by insensible degrees to the point I

desired" (II, 1, 2). The man watches the master writhe under
the "gratuitous evil" of his surveillance, his hints and questions put (some of the time) "with the cunning of a grey-
headed inquisitor" (II, 1). And these days of spying, of
goading, of merciless persecution, Caleb calls "a more favour-
able period of my life" (II, 4).

From Falkland's point of view, his course of action is clear.
He cannot trust the young man his tormenter, who has abused
his kindness to increase his anguish for "an alluring pungency" (II, 1), for "all the delight which a young and unfledged
mind receives from ideas that give scope to all that imagination
can picture of terrible or sublime" (II, 4)—or, as far as Falkland
knows, for some other private motive. Once the secret has
been extorted, who can tell what new direction Caleb's "curiosity" may take? Not Caleb himself, who has told us that he
could not quench his zeal. Godwin does not want to argue, of
course, for Falkland's behaving one way or another. What he
does stress is Caleb's failure to see through Falkland's eyes, or
to apply to himself the sort of causal reasoning about character
which he applies to Tyrrel, the Hawkinses, and even Falkland.
He has violated not only "every received principle of civilized
society" (II, 6), but also what Godwin elsewhere, in 1797,
called "the first and most fundamental principle in the intercourse of man with man," which is "reverence."[8] But this
same Caleb expects civilized society and human intercourse to
remain open to him. Falkland, for private ends, works a kind
of poetic justice in closing both.

Like Caleb, Falkland uses analogy for his own purposes. He
acts upon a dictum of Godwin's: "One of the most sacred principles of social life, is honour, the forbearance that man is

8. *Enquirer* 10, "Of Cohabitation." The fine article by Ousby and Ousby,
"'My servant Caleb',", pp. 47-55, makes clear why Godwin might have been
particularly sensitive to Caleb's violation of domestic "reverence" in the early
1790s.

entitled to claim from man, that a man of worth would as soon steal my purse or forge a title-deed to my estate, as read the letter he sees lying on my table."⁹ The letter from Hawkins that Caleb reads, and that Falkland knows him to have read, has slipped behind a drawer (II, 2, 3), but *de minimis non est disputandum*. Caleb's being accused as a thief, his having his own box pried open and Falkland's valuables thrust into it, represents a symbolically accurate punishment. Godwin could hardly have made this clearer than he has, when the informal trial scene before Mr. Forester presents as evidence the valet's account of Falkland's trunk, which Caleb earlier chiselled open, along with Caleb's incriminating little trunks. The actual transfer of one kind of goods, knowledge, is given a fictional correlative, the transfer of another kind of goods, more social, more visible. This is Caleb's own method, in giving public structure to experience through the use of allusion and analogy; and it appropriately traps within an expressive fiction the man who has seen real life only as a titillating romance. If Caleb has discovered the "truth" about Falkland, Falkland has revealed the "truth" about Caleb, in both cases a truth more of social capabilities than of fact. These are truths within Things As They Are, that great social fiction in which the reigning value is egoism, the lust for reputation or for confidential knowledge, truth as a means of possession.

The values upon which Falkland and Caleb act are false, and so they publish truths without a love for truth, for personal ends such as society encourages. One should note that neither they nor Tyrrel gets direct social pressure towards specific forms of egoism. "I was taught the rudiments of no science, except reading, writing and arithmetic," Caleb writes in the first chapter. "But I had an inquisitive mind, and neglected no means of information from conversation or books. My improvement was greater than my condition in life afforded

9. *Enquirer* 14, "Of the Obtaining of Confidence."

room to expect" (I, 1). Falkland's fatal disposition comes from reading Italian romances, not from the society in which he actually moves. "Imagination" and "fancy," according to Caleb, encourage in Falkland a "temper perpetually alive to the sentiments of birth and honour," while philosophy, which was presumably what society brought to his education, "purged" his imagination (I, 2). Even the despotism of Barnabas Tyrrel, broached in Chapter 3, comes from his having been spoiled as a child, and must therefore have been latent within him. Similarly, despite his prefatory comment about "a general review of the modes of domestic and un-recorded despotism," Godwin does not try to be exhaustively specific. He does not touch on corrupted marriages, for example, or on the industrial evils that he was to describe in *Fleetwood* (1805). He points instead to a moral condition that permits "domestic and unrecorded despotism." For Godwin, as for the Fielding of *Amelia* and the Smollett of *Humphry*, these moral conditions exist in society as reflections of what exists in individual men. That is what makes Caleb's individual experi-ence with Things As They Are so crucial, because only through such personal knowledge can he change. The story must be told in the first person, and moral blindness must be central to the whole conception of *Caleb Williams*.[10] Godwin requires the epistemological mode which is the subject of this study.

Caleb's analogies are modified by analogies he cannot detect, his rhetoric modified by inconsistencies hidden from him. When Emily defies Tyrrel, there follow her captivity in the house, her escape, and her imprisonment by the law. The same pattern holds for young Hawkins. After a dispute, Tyrrel

10. McCracken, "Godwin's Literary Theory," shows that Godwin believed that the reciprocity between men and society, in which each cor-rupts the other, could best be dealt with by the study of individuals, their passions and motives, by men who were themselves emotionally engaged. Historical analysis, that is, required a focus on psychology and a deep root in the psychological life of the reader.

makes the Hawkinses "prisoners in [their] own domains" by blocking a road (I, 9); Leonard Hawkins tears open the gates, and as a consequence is jailed under the Black Act. He escapes from jail, just as Emily is bailed out by Falkland, but in vain. Hawkins is hanged, Emily dies of a distemper. Caleb, as we would expect, also follows this pattern: he falls out with Falkland, and becomes a captive as if in "one of those fortresses, famed in the history of despotism, from which the wretched victim is never known to come forth alive" (II, 8). His escape is followed by his recapture and legal imprisonment, and at the end of the volume, by another escape which (we have known from the first chapter on) will end badly. The pattern of triple analogy is radically modified not only because of the allusion to Jack Sheppard but also because of a new depth of moral knowledge which Caleb's behavior with Falkland has offered us. We now can see that the brutal squalor of the prison has direct connections with personal behavior. The capricious keepers who feel "no man's sorrow," the prisoners whose "state was immutable" in their "scene of invariable melancholy"—here is another version of the caprice and callousness of our hero, here is a variation on the continuing misery of Falkland, which Caleb has stoked. By no means does Godwin want to palliate the penal system, but he wants to show us its moral roots. Caleb, of course, claims that the prison is quite alien to his nature: amusingly enough, he insists that the turnkey not exceed a set social function and threatens revenge for insolence (II, 14), although he in his own relationship with his master has proved a bit of a leveller.

Caleb also distracts us from his social criticism with an odd sort of self-contradiction. In lamenting the prison, for example, he speaks as though the dark, the insolence, the prisoners' misery, and the torture of unsure anticipation were absolute evils (II, 11). When he decides in the next chapter to impress us with his resolution and independence, though, he discovers "chearfulness, good humour and serenity" in his dungeon, and announces that he "wanted for nothing": "My fare was coarse; but I was in health. My dungeon was noisome; but I felt no inconvenience. I was shut up from the usual means of exercise and air; but I found the method of exercising myself even to perspiration in my dungeon" (II, 12). The only thing that remains the same in the pathetic chapter as in the triumphant one that follows it is his sense of his "blessed state of innocence and self-approbation." The section on Caleb's escape, already quoted, follows immediately; and it is so much longer than need be that one suspects him of having gone into detail to prepossess the reader in his favor, only to blunder into damning parallels with Jack Sheppard.

Later yet, he once again launches into social condemnation: "Turn me a prey to the wild beasts of the desert, so I be never again the victim of man dressed in the gore-dripping robes of authority! . . . Let me hold [life] at the mercy of elements, of the hunger of beasts or the revenge of barbarians" (III, 1), and he congratulates himself on his enviable enthusiasm in the midst of his woes. Within the next four paragraphs he gets what he asks for. A band of thieves attack him bestially, led by the very Gines whose barbarian revenge is to torment him on and on. They leave him dripping the gore of which he has just spoken, "totally regardless of my distressed condition." Godwin wants to show that social ethics partake of a more general morality; Caleb, that he maintained his enthusiasm and his role as innocent victim. But he dramatizes his suffering excellence only at the cost of making his cries about freedom and authority look like cant. In fact, as the novel goes on and his misery deepens, he meets almost no oppression from legally constituted authority, a force that Falkland never uses.

The uses of allusion, analogy, and the implicated narrator in Volume II, then, not only follow from the practices of Volume I, but also complicate the moral patterns found there.

The conventional pathos of thwarted hopes and unthwarted oppression ends with the rounding off of the flashback story as an aesthetic whole. Emily, Clare, Tyrrel, and the Hawkinses are dead; Falkland is prey to raving and settled gloom: we have here an ending like that of, say, *The Castle of Otranto*, where the characters are parcelled out between death and melancholy. Because Volume II, in contrast, moves into Caleb's first-person narrative, we perceive it much more in terms of psychological process. This new focus makes us react more strongly to Falkland's mental suffering, and points up Caleb's refusal to enter emotionally into Falkland's mind at the very time that he implicitly asks us to enter into his own. Moreover, by principles of modification and incremental analogy, the moral patterns of the book keep growing more complex in terms of affective stresses, especially as we move in and out of Caleb's mind, intrigued or repelled or pushed by skillful allusion toward more dispassionate judgments. To put this another way, our learning englobes Caleb's in Volume II differently from Volume I, as we move from establishing the naive forms of his thought to a deeper knowledge of the consequences, for him and for Falkland, of that naiveté. From his indignation and allusions, we can see that his own shedding of naiveté has made much less progress, or more one-sided progress, than he can know; and we can infer by analogy what the Postscript confirms, that his continued ignorance is to doom him to a still more unpleasant version of the present to which past ignorance has brought him.

III: A CONCLUSION IN WHICH EVERYTHING AND NOTHING IS CONCLUDED

As Volume II modifies Volume I, Volume III modifies Volume II, and the Postscript modifies the rest of the book: the context of understanding in each new part differs from the context(s) before it. This is hardest to see in Volume III,

partly because Godwin imitates the wildness of Caleb's growing fright and desperation by letting the controls of space,
time, and plot drop away. If for no other reason, he must
make us feel the continuity of themes and procedures in this
volume. Thus, for example, the pattern of Volume III is a
simple inversion of the pattern of Volume II, which develops
from a personal confrontation through increasing restraints
to Caleb's imprisonment. Volume III deals with Caleb's
evasion of arrest, then his acquittal in law and his conviction
in popular opinion, to end with his personal confrontation
with Falkland, completed in the Postscript. Thus, too, Caleb's
account of affairs continues to leave verisimilitude shaky.
Falkland's spy, Gines, happens to be the other man whom
Caleb has served to humiliate, and Gines's brother happens
to be the very printer who receives his pamphlet. Two successive nights of bright moonshine surround a grey drizzly day,
a phenomenon that has less to do with isobars than with
Caleb's continuing imprisonment, now by nature, after he
breaks jail. At the moment that the old hag in the thieves' den
aims a hatchet blow at his head, Caleb wakes by chance
(III, 4), and by chance a combination of a hailstorm and over-
sleeping keep him from being caught near the Severn (7). If a
carriage passes, of all those in England it is Falkland's (5); if
men talk, they talk about Caleb, twice in one chapter (5); if
Caleb finds lodgings in London, they are with a miser who
has just lost a son, and who turns Caleb in for fear of becoming expensively fond of him (10). Laura's Italian father happened to know of Falkland's behavior with Malvesi (13). This
is an extraordinary group of coincidences.

Caleb's allusions are another source of continuity, although
he now drops structural parallels, like those from Richardson
or the *Newgate Calendar*, for a looser kind of reference. As his
own experience grows fuller, he needs fewer details from
books to give it shape, but retains the set of mind that led to
the earlier allusions. For instance, despite his complaints

about "the miserable expedients and . . . studied artifice" forced upon him (5), he chooses roles that are expressive rather than simply practical. When he looks "like the son of a reputable farmer of the lower class" (7), he travels safely; but that sort of disguise does not suit his fancy. No, he prefers to be a beggar, an Irishman, a Jew, or a freak, not something inconspicuous. Since each of these four disguises is penetrated, it seems safe to say that practicality runs a poor second to Caleb's urge to adopt the guise of an outcast, economic, political, religious, or physical. Similarly, he finds himself drawn "by a fatality for which I did not exactly know how to account" to write "the histories of celebrated robbers" instead of the moral disquisitions in which he "distrusted my resources" (8). He even decides to write an etymological dictionary, presumably in imitation of Eugene Aram, the scholarly murderer whose case Godwin footnotes for us a bit earlier (4).[11] No wonder Caleb's enemies can cooperate with his choice of roles so easily by making him a legendary criminal, the subject of ballads and broadsides. In an ironic turn typical of this novel, the autobiographer finds himself socially altered into a literary object, famous throughout the British Isles.

11. Godwin footnotes the *Annual Register for 1759*, which has its own place in the genesis of the novel. This volume not only includes the histories of William Andrews Horne and Eugene Aram (with four full columns about Aram's etymological work), it also has a brief biography of Lucius Cary, Lord Falkland. Perhaps most intriguing is the history of one John Ayliffe, which comes between those of Aram and Horne, to complete the ration of criminal tales in the volume. Ayliffe, we learn, was born to servants and was himself a "house-steward," who later in life tried to swindle a benefactor (by forgery) and then accused this benefactor of having preferred a false accusation against him. The case is strikingly like that of Caleb and Falkland, and the language of the *Annual Register* much like that of indignant characters in the novel: "In comparison of this insinuation, his forgery can scarce be considered as a crime. This was such a complication of villainy, with all the aggravations of ingratitude, as can scarce be paralleled" (6th ed., London, 1777), p. 366.

Given this kind of continuity in technique, Volume III may seem to strengthen, not modify, Volume II. None the less, there is a difference, in part because in Volume III we do not learn anything new about Caleb himself, and therefore find it unnecessary to be actively engaged in judging him. We also feel his suffering more, now that it is not the direct result of his tormenting Falkland or part of the bravado of being Jack Sheppard redivivus. The suffering is enlarged by Caleb's use of cosmic images, no doubt self-aggrandizing, but also suggestive of his own guilt, so much so that Godwin seems to have borrowed his tone from Reynolds's *God's Revenge against Murder*.[12] In line with this imagery, Falkland's agent, Gines, is "infernal" and "diabolic." The "God-like Falkland" seems "burnt and parched by the eternal fire that burned within him," which can be compared to "the imaginary hell, which the great enemy of mankind is represented as carrying every where about him" (12). Or conversely, he appears like "that mysterious being, to protect us from whose fierce revenge mountains and hills we are told might fall on us in vain" (6); his pursuit is "like what has been described of the eye of omniscience pursuing the guilty sinner." Between the oppressive egoism of the two antagonists, who see themselves in biblical or Miltonic terms, and the absolute allegory of Good and Evil, Truth and the Lie, which seeps through Caleb's particular narrative, we are led, as Godwin intended, to see the events related to a broader context than in Volume II.

Metaphysical imagery makes common cause with the mass of strange coincidences I listed above. We have seen how Providence works in *Amelia*, once Booth gives up distorting the world for his own benefit and recognizes things as they are; once Bramble makes the same change, he enjoys a secular version of divine rewards. There is no Providence in Godwin, nor does Caleb give up his egoism in Volume III, but the coin-

12. Godwin mentions his having read this book for *Caleb* in his preface (1832) to *Fleetwood* (1805), printed as Appendix 2 to McCracken's edition of *Caleb*, p. 340.

cidences insist on two nonevaluative corollaries of Providence, a sense of destiny and a sense of "second causes." Even to the provisional extent that we accept these overtones in Caleb's version of his life, they have important rhetorical effects. The destiny in which Caleb is netted, illusory or not, subordinates the social criticism to the individual in the novel by making him its center. The malign forces are those which men themselves set at work. That is an idea continued from Volume II, but here, with so much more diverse social criticism, reaffirmed with the emotional logic of imagery. "Second causes" have been a mainstay of Caleb's procedure as detective and romancer, reading hidden meaning into what he sees and hears. Through them, the accidents of the world gain an intentionality, a literary direction, which also binds together the diversity of Volume III and gives a different weight to the clash between squire and servant. It also makes us feel the degree to which Caleb is trapped and thus mitigates our hostility to him.

Perhaps I should say, Caleb and Falkland; there is no question, as we read Volume III, that the action is one of poetic justice. Like a reader deep in a Gothic novel, Caleb has longed to climb into Falkland's skin, and now he must repeat Falkland's experience. He has pursued Falkland·and is now pursued himself. He has threatened Falkland's reputation in private, and later in public (III, 11); he finds his own reputation, and that alone, blasted. He has looked forward to watching over his patron: "To be a spy upon Mr. Falkland! That there was danger in the employment served to give an alluring pungency to the choice" (II, 1). He now encounters the danger, the result of his "choice"; he now has a spy set on him by Falkland and learns the agony of being the object of relentless sport. The system of analogy by which Caleb has worked now includes him, leading to his final identification with Falkland in the Postscript. During Volume III, in fact, the glimpse we have of Falkland (12) suggests the parallel suffering of the two men, and when the feverish Caleb writes "all is not right within me" (15), we expect to see the Falkland whom we do see in the Postscript, the burnt-out victim of Caleb and of himself. His former rage, which made him "haggard, ghost-like and wild, energy in his gestures and frenzy in his aspect" (Postscript), has passed to Caleb, who inherits in turn his legacy of guilt at the end of the book. Caleb does not discover these analogies until it is too late, and then only dimly. What he does discover are certain moral and psychological facts which prepare him, once he can step outside his egoism, to come to the partial understanding depicted in the Postscript. Among these are the meaning of reputation, of suffering, of privacy, and of the reverence due men from each other. I do not think any of these realizations have to be expanded upon, for Caleb tells us about them himself, poignantly, in writing about his own life. In the four roughly even sections into which Volume III is divided—Raymond's lair, the road, London, and the flight from Gines—each of his realizations receives a new treatment in a different setting, so as to form for us a complex and moving moral experience.

One point may be less clear, a point that returns us to the literary mode of the book. In romances, and therefore in the flashback story, as I have said, all characters are good or bad. Caleb is neither, nor is the real Falkland. As the novel goes on, fewer men and women fit in with the sort of literary reduction with which Caleb began. Even Gines and the keeper of the prison have rather more to be said for them than Tyrrel. Gines, Caleb admits, "had his virtues. He was enterprising, persevering and faithful" (III, 2); the keeper shows "constitutional and ambiguous humanity" (II, 14). Raymond's superiority to the vices of his gang still makes Caleb feel "how much he was out of his place, how disproportionably associated, or how contemptibly employed" (III, 4). The "buxom, bluff, good humoured widow," whose "sincere and generous warmth" on Caleb's behalf gives him so much pleasure, likes him only because she has heard he is handsome and clever, which are equivocal virtues (III, 5); Caleb measures her by his private selfish standards, but we are less likely to do so. He sets forth Mrs. Marney, who earns his "transient" sympathy when she is sent to Newgate for having shielded him (III, 10), in wholly favorable terms, although she caters to a rich relation's snobbery by preferring "a very small annuity" to "the exertion of honest industry" (III, 8). Her successor, Mr. Spurrel, however, receives a more elaborate and more mixed character than anyone in the book besides its two heroes, driven as he is "by a sort of implicit impulse, for the sake of avoiding one ungenerous action, to take refuge in another, the basest and most diabolical" (III, 10). These two protectors prepare the way for Laura and Collins (13, 14), another older woman and man whom Caleb calls mother and father, as he has been a sort of son to Spurrel. Both of them, otherwise virtuous, turn their "son" out, as Spurrel does. His rejection at these hands gives a last exquisite twist to Caleb's misery and raises once more the question of the mixed character. Are Laura and Collins socially corrupted because they refuse to admit Caleb's innocence, or even more, the possibility of his reform? How far must each man in society engage in "literary reduction" of what he sees, supposing a certain continuity of character which may not tally with the facts? Caleb has been turning away from such reductions, as I have said, prompted not only by his own feelings but also by his talks with Raymond, who denounces the laws for their blindness to reform and asks if he is "not compelled to go on in folly, having once begun" (III, 3). The Postscript hangs on his deepened realization of character.

We have here a social problem intertwined with an aesthetic one. As in *Amelia*, prediction and judgment become more difficult as the idea of "character" grows more equivocal. This is true in Caleb's experience, as reflected in the way he frames his narrative, and also in our experience of Caleb himself. Morally obtuse as he is, we do not keep making fresh judgments against him, partly because Godwin stops developing such judgments in an intriguing way, partly because we share his pain, self-caused or not. We react to Caleb as he ought to have reacted to Falkland, and as he does react to Raymond, not exculpating him but placing his vice in proper context. That context includes our own bias toward tolerance, as well as the other acts of the "guilty" man, the behavior of society, and the moral consequence of erecting his acts into principle. Throughout *Caleb Williams* these recurrent issues come up as aesthetic response as well as overt subject matter, so that we undergo an education along with the hero, moving toward what Godwin called "reverence" and the principle of utility. Caleb himself enunciates this principle quite early: "I conceived it to be in the highest degree absurd and iniquitous to cut off a man qualified for the most essential and extensive utility merely out of retrospect to an act which, whatever were its merits, could not be retrieved" (II, 5). Raymond repeats it, and so (III, 12) does Falkland; the fire scene in the flashback story (I, 6) symbolizes a version of it, for Falkland saves the village from total ruin only by pulling down an untouched (innocent?) house next to the burning one; and the "amiable, incomparable" Collins sets forth another version of it when his erstwhile "son," Caleb, proclaims his innocence (III, 14).[13]

In a world of total innocence, without crime, folly, or accident, one would have harmony between particular and universal "truth": one could have "reverence." In the world as it is, practicality may demand that we, like Laura and Collins and Falkland, make predictions by analogy from what has gone by, even although innocence may suffer; it may demand that we forego "barren truth" in favor of a more fruitful truth.

13. In support of the principle of utility as enunciated by Collins, cf. Godwin's "Morality is nothing else but a calculation of consequences, and an adoption of that mode of conduct which, upon the most comprehensive view, appears to be attended with a balance of general pleasure and happiness." *Enquiry concerning Political Justice*, ed. F. E. L. Priestley, 3 vols. (Toronto: University of Toronto Press, 1946), 1: 342.

No doubt practicality, in catering to Things As They Are, leaves actions morally ambiguous, just as Caleb, when he starts in this volume to look at the characters of men As They Are, finds them morally ambiguous. The intellectual greatness of this novel, from Godwin's point of view, lies largely in its ability to make us feel, through its form as well as its statements, that moral ambiguity is both unsatisfactory and necessary. Its roots are in our compulsion for many reasons to treat others systematically, as though life went by literary rules. Only "reverence" can help counterbalance the effects of system, by restoring the complexity of feeling and judgment which system reduces or precludes.

Godwin, like Fielding, lets us see the inadequacy of system for predictions and judgments that are vital to his hero; he uses discriminated variety with variables of character and situation. Specifically, we may look at a group of chapters that involve parenthood or quasi-parenthood, III, 8-14. The motif first occurs, conventionally, in the flashback story, with the Hawkinses, Tyrrel and Emily, and Clare and Falkland. It is given weight because of the orphaned Caleb's dependence on surrogate parents, since he has no friend of his own age but Brightwel (a few paragraphs in II, 11, 13). Analogy and the narrative, then, make this group of chapters, involving Mrs. Marney (8-9), Mr. Spurrel (10), Falkland (12), Laura (13), and Collins (14), the alternative to moral and physical isolation. Where prediction and judgment are most needed, they are most difficult: Godwin uses analogical, associative methods to achieve order and frustrate inquiry. Thus Mrs. Marney saves and Mr. Spurrel betrays Caleb from the same emotion, growing love. The same emotion, selfish fear, pushes Spurrel and Falkland to hand Caleb over to Gines, for sharply different fates. Mrs. Marney and Falkland help Caleb to avoid jail, but with different motives; different motives underlie Falkland's and Collins's giving Caleb the same utilitarian argument to spare Falkland's reputation; the emotional prudence of Laura,

whom Caleb calls "mother," and the rational prudence of
Collins, whom he calls "father," lead to the same effective
result, but with quite different emotional force behind the
moral judgments made. The sense of order and entrapment,
familiar from Johnson and Fielding, intensify the sense that
inquiry is baffled, however much information Caleb receives.

Caleb Williams can only conclude when Caleb abandons his
system, as he does more or less overtly: "Why should my
reflections perpetually centre upon myself? self, an overween-
ing regard to which has been the source of my errors!" (Postscript). In surrendering his system of inquiry, Caleb stoppers
the source of his fiction, the projection of a symbolic action.
The murder of Falkland, as Caleb himself calls it, is the last
symbolic act because it is the last act before the moral peripeteia;
and it completes the narrative, for Falkland, like Emily, lives
three days after being arrested in a sickbed, while Caleb
laments that he "has fallen a victim, life and fame, to my
precipitation! It would have been merciful in comparison, if I
had planted a dagger in his heart" (Postscript). Caleb is to
Falkland the assassin that Falkland was to Tyrrel, and Tyrrel to
Emily.

With the abandoning of system and personal fiction, the
novel redefines "truth." Caleb tells Falkland no facts in the
Postscript that he has not already told him in III, 12. Nor does
factual truth, despite Caleb's "youthful reverie" about it (II, 9),
compel more belief than lies, such as Falkland's own about
Tyrrel and Caleb. Laura's naive creed that "true virtue shines
by its own light" (III, 13) is denied by Collins in the next chapter and made empty by the difficulties of judgment which we
have discussed. The "truth" that makes Falkland embrace
Caleb is something other than the kind of truth for which
Caleb's system has been fit: it is the revelation of a personal
ground for action, the intuition of which is the only valid base
for prediction and judgment. Knowledge depends on "sym-

pathy" in Hume's and Adam Smith's sense of that word, as in all five of the novels we have analysed; here the author stresses the epistemological role of "sympathy" between characters as well as that between characters and reader, so as to make Caleb and Falkland more broadly symptomatic of the society in which the reader takes part. That is why a reformer like Godwin should be especially interested in psychological novels; and that is why the novel as an aesthetic structure, which reveals Caleb to us, is itself as a whole the formal anticipation of the Postscript, which reveals Caleb to Falkland.[14]

As we have seen, Godwin's novel resembles Sterne's or Smollett's in the degree to which the failure of personal system represents success in autobiographical revelation. He pursues the same method in the Postscript, for Caleb's speech, compelled like his spying by "uncontrollable impetuosity," paints a state of mind by parting from factual truth. In the same sentence, Caleb calls himself "a cool, deliberate, unfeeling murderer," and contradictorily claims "I have said what my accursed precipitation has obliged me to say." He spends most of his speaking time defending himself and blaming Falkland, only to decide that he is "compelled to applaud" Falkland as "a man worthy of affection and kindness," so worthy that his accuser becomes "the basest and most odious of mankind!" The logical faults create for Falkland, as for us, the state of feeling both calculating and hasty, free and fated. That is a state of feeling Falkland knows so well in himself that Caleb's speech revives in him the primitive rapport among men which underlies the Shandys' and Bramble's final wisdom.

14. Godwin's original ending left Caleb broken, delirious, and impotent after a final rebuff by Falkland and the law. Such an ending, however affecting, would have blurred the moral causality of the novel, and Godwin wisely abandoned it. This ending is reprinted from Godwin's manuscript as Appendix 1 to McCracken's edition of the novel, pp. 327-34; it is discussed by Dumas, and, more coherently and responsively, by Mitzi Myers, "Godwin's Changing Conception of *Caleb Williams*," *SEL* 12 (1972): 591-628.

The end of *Caleb Williams*, like the end of *Rasselas*, of *Humphry*, or of *Amelia*, offers an equilibrium of forces in which the past is reinterpreted, so that a temporal process becomes a settled, quasi-spatial condition. From the vantage point of two centuries' hindsight, making the past present may seem an oddly appropriate thing for this novel of Godwin's to do. He created *Caleb* from fragments of an English past, Richardson's novels and the *Newgate Calendar*, the *Annual Register* of 1759 and *God's Revenge against Murder*. He also used a pattern with which we have grown familiar in the course of this book, a retrospective pattern by his time, for such kitsch as the novels of Mrs. Radcliffe or *The Monk* did not, as far as I can tell, employ it, Austen deserted it after *Northanger Abbey*, and it lingers on quite attenuatedly in *Castle Rackrent*. Godwin used it so successfully that, of his several novels, *Caleb Williams* is the only one still read or remembered.

In every way, *Caleb Williams* is a member of the family of novels described in this book. The use of analogy is typical of .Caleb himself, implicitly, as for example when he gives us the stories of Emily Melvile and the Hawkinses; it is also typical of Godwin as he develops his moral indictment. Caleb himself is not much interested in epistemology, for he is sure that his system of seeing things is right. He does not use the principle of modification. Godwin, who is less sure of Caleb's rightness, does, through analogy (e.g., between Caleb's behavior and Tyrrel's) and allusion (e.g., to Jack Sheppard and Eugene Aram): each of Caleb's formulations is right, but of limited utility as the perspectives of the novel widen. The system of order relates to one central character, of course, since it embodies the behavior of his mind in formal terms. His process of learning, as he moves from boy sleuth to prisoner to prey, establishes the sequence of his narrative; our process of learning, as Caleb moves from naive romancer to naive predator to sufferer, first trapped and blind, then trapped and gifted with the agony of hindsight, establishes a parallel

sequence or dialectic for us. Once again, however, let me note
that the dialectic is not absolutely fated. The first part of the
book could end in melodramatic self-torments on Falkland's
part, if a more cheaply popular novelist than Godwin had had
the writing of it; and Godwin's first ending did cut off any
growth of insight at the pre-Postscript level. Its mode, then,
like that of the other four books, is "presentational" in that no
part of the book is revoked by the conclusion, no part is made
merely an element in a process (as, for instance, in a novel by
Henry James).

Caleb does seem more ordered than any of the other books,
since the visible order is integral to its meaning, and the first
two-thirds of it moreover follow an order of simple narrative.
After his escape from prison, however, Caleb more and more
loses control; and from what we know of the practice of the
other four writers we have discussed, it would be surprising to
find that Godwin had not used some sort of rhythmic pattern
to guide us. In fact he begins this pattern quite early, with the
first dramatic incident that happens to Caleb, Falkland's confession (II, 6). Thereafter, each crisis comes at the point of a
four-chapter interval. His official imprisonment begins when
he is accused by Falkland at his trial (II, 10) and ends with his
jailbreaking (II, 14), which is repeated in his escape from the
old hag with the hatchet at Raymond's (III, 4), four chapters
later. In III, 8, he enters London, "the termination of an immense series of labours," and in III, 12, another confrontation
with Falkland drives him from any hope of security. The
pledge of vengeful pursuit in III, 12, ought to be reversed in III,
16, as Caleb becomes the pursuer, and indeed III, 16—or the
Postscript, which follows III, 15—not only reverses roles but
also conflates the crises we have just listed. Caleb, that is,
participates in a trial and confession, escapes from present and
impending punishment, and arrives at a terminus for a new
mode of life. As the other intervals have shown him either losing his freedom or finding it delusive, so here he is left finally a

prisoner, a free prisoner of his own inner guilt. The reader does not count chapters, and very likely Godwin did not either; but the relentlessness and control of the rhythm are nonetheless felt.

As to other formal devices, that of the fulcrum, as I have called it, hardly needs discussion, since Caleb himself treats the events of the Postscript as revolutionary. The prison or prisons—beginning with the iron chest in which Falkland's secrets are locked, and continuing with Caleb's imprisonment first by Falkland and then by the law, then by nature, Raymond, his life in London, Gines, and finally his guilt— begin as an emblem and grow into a motif; like the water in *Rasselas* and *Humphry*, the bowling green in *Tristram*, and the gambling of *Amelia*, the emblems come naturally from the normal tenor of the book, rather than being sudden or nightmarish interjections into the narrative. Nor, for all the possibilities for melodrama in *Caleb Williams*, does Godwin make much use of sharp contrast or savage juxtaposition. His formal procedures, like his epistemological interests, join his novel to the family that this book of mine describes.

The Historical Hypothesis

We have found that five irreducibly different novels are also each others' kinsmen. That raises the question of what the relationship may mean for literary history. My hypothesis, which I cannot verify here, is that the system described flourished widely in various genres before 1750, but shrank in range as the century wore on.[1] Linear simplicity became increasingly valued as Bach and Handel gave way to Haydn and Gluck, Hogarth and Kent to Fuseli and Hepplewhite, the embroidered silks of George II's waistcoats to the simple stripes of George Washington's. The novel grew streamlined too, to a system of order depending more on causality (linear plot), less on analogical panorama. When the characters no longer had a plenitude to interpret, the system of inquiry changed, with the factitious mysteries of Gothic novels the last attempt to maintain it. The new modes and methods of reading permanently displaced the old, never again endemic, even in the age of

1. There seem to me to be close connections, for example, between the system I find in the novels and that which Ralph Cohen identifies in Thomson, in *The Unfolding of "The Seasons"* (Baltimore: Johns Hopkins Press, 1970); I find this book exceptionally suggestive when read in the context of Cohen's "The Augustan Mode in English Poetry," *ECS* I (1967): 3-32.

sweeping works like *Middlemarch, Vanity Fair,* and the later novels of Dickens.

That, at least, is my hypothesis. To verify it would take another book or two; I hope in this chapter to convince my readers that prima facie evidence exists for it, or some historical hypothesis like it. Any such hypothesis requires that the system have roots in the interests and practice of the eighteenth century. It also requires that the system not be endemic outside set bounds. I will argue that there is good reason to think both requirements may be met. "Roots" will come first, the evidence for historical plausibility beyond the discussion of systems and analogy in the Introduction. Then, passing to "bounds," I will set our system against some novels by Dickens, to try to show that it is not the product of the genre "novel" (or even of the tight little genre "panoramic and analogical novel written by major popular novelist"), and that it is not the product, worse yet, of the means of analysis I have used.

Let me begin by recalling that these are epistemological novels. That may not be their final purpose: despite their authors' didactic claims, the reader's feelings may in the long run be more important than any cognitive learning. Nevertheless, systems of inquiry establish systems of order. Behavior is chiefly important as material for, and as product of, various kinds of practical knowledge. If one is to have knowledge, one must have knowers to make and test inferences, and so we are shown a central character or matrix of characters who pretend to be interpreters of experience. We are invited to join their experimental groups as critical observers who can (and do) learn more, or at a different rate, than they do. Systems of order and inquiry are to be tied closely by a single structural apparatus that can satisfy both, based on the harvesting, analysis, and comparison of facts, and also on the skepticism, proper to scientific epistemology. Its principal tools, which take into account both experiments and skepticism, are analogy and modification. Analogy permits inquiry and creates order when the plot does not; modification limits inferences (or their utility) by contravening too broad an interpretation of them and forcing one to counterexamples.

The novel that results moves by muted contrasts. "Formal realism" offers the characters and us the experimental field: what we see before us is a heterocosm, various and uncertain. The structure is loose, without a hierarchy implicit in the individual experiences. Our progress through it is tied to the order of mind, in that association of ideas binds event to event, character to character. Different casts of mind, sometimes those of different characters and sometimes those of the same character in different stages of enlightenment, regard the same (repeated, analogous) phenomena so as to provide a range of possibilities for the particulars we encounter. Or so the fiction looks, for in fact we have before us elaborately arranged books whose visible order corresponds to the characters' systems but whose concealed structure guides and supports us.

The first step toward rooting this mode in history is simple, for to ask if eighteenth-century works might well have concerned themselves with epistemology is a bit like asking if medieval ones might have had a splash of theology. Almost every important British philosopher from Hobbes to Dugald Stewart, as well as the major continental ones of mid-century, made epistemology a chief concern; and based it, moreover, on a study of behavior and psychology. Nothing could have been more natural than for it to be a chief concern, then, in the only literary form that could explore, and had developed some skill in exploring, behavior and psychology in detail. Fiction was to the present what history was to the past, the vicarious supplement to personal experience; and thus an avenue to the empirical knowledge on which philosophers drew, as well as an exploration complementary to theirs. Epistemology was also of interest to novelists because, if the narrative looked out upon a perceptual world, it also looked in upon one, that of the reader's mind and emotions. An eighteenth-century novel is not, like Mill's idea of a poem, the overheard muttering of an author, but a deliberate act of communication to an audience as clearly conceptualized as the abstracted human of Locke and Hume, Bonnet and Condillac. The reader's interests and needs are versions of the characters'. It stands to reason that the novelists conceived of him and the characters with the same parameters, those set by Locke and his school, in which the mind is essentially an acquisitive faculty.

To move and convince the reader, to benefit him as a creature of passions and reason, was the traditional province of rhetoric; but one of the great achievements of the period was to bring rhetoric in line with philosophy, and thus to draw closer the novelists' conceptions of their art and their subject matter. R. S. Crane notes that "the philosophy of human nature or of the mind," as exemplified by the work of Hume, "resembles rhetoric" in subject matter, division of problems, emphasis on psychological causation, techniques of argument, and interest in "questions of style and of adaptation to readers."[2] In other words, not only did rhetoric—Crane mentions George Campbell's *Philosophy of Rhetoric* in particular—take over the methods of philosophy, but philosophers began to treat subjects that classically had been parts of rhetoric. What philosophers (other than Locke) and what psychological critics our five authors had read or read about, and with what friends they may have talked about such matters in their work, I do not know. I can suggest that prose fiction was particularly susceptible to such currents. It had few fixed rules, it was often too sprawling to be easily managed, and those who wrote it

2. R. S. Crane, *The Idea of the Humanities and Other Essays Critical and Historical*, 2 vols. (Chicago: University of Chicago Press, 1967), 1: 110-11. For a full discussion of the "new rhetoric" and its concerns, the "hero" of which is Locke, see Wilbur Samuel Howell, *Eighteenth-century British Logic and Rhetoric* (Princeton: Princeton University Press, 1971). See also P. W. K. Stone, *The Art of Poetry 1750-1820* (London: Routledge & Kegan Paul, 1967), pp. 13-15.

longed for originality and respectability at once, as the nature of their recurrent comparisons of their own books to the highest genres—the epic, tragedy, and history painting—testifies. Nor did the authors of fiction have to read works of theory to be able to transpose old aesthetic and rhetorical ideals into the affective structures about which there never before had been so much and such extensive thought, and which depended on the same model of the mind which they used in creating characters and plot.

The mingling of formal and philosophical arguments, mediated by notions of psychology, is plain in my earlier discussion of "Butlerian" and "Hartleyan" analogy. No other device carries the same inferential and constitutive weight. But arguments from similar sources justify (or recommend) other characteristics needed by the sort of novel I have just described. The authors of such novels had to represent a reality as broad, as particulate, and as free from manipulation as possible. Breadth and freedom from manipulations are the pledges of objectivity. A particulate reality reproduces the way the (Lockean) mind perceives, by analyzing sensations into simple ideas that can be, and are, differently regrouped to form complex ideas in the manner of atoms and molecules. As a corollary to these principles, authors concealed, or used for specific limited ends, any kind of order that did not come from the characters' systems of inquiry. These principles and their corollary, of course, were in the soil from which fiction grew, whether from picaresque, mock-historical, or various quasi-fictional forms, like Ward's *London Spy* or Brown's *Amusements Serious and Comical*. The nonrational sprawl had been the order of the day. My argument for the historical plausibility of our system, then, assumes that these preconditions for the epistemological novel existed, and that, as with analogy, our interest is in the color these characteristics took from prevailing critical theory. To suggest that color briefly, I will mention for each of the three principles two common tenets of eighteenth-century criticism which support it. More than two might be mentioned, but two will suffice, I think, to put an argument for historical plausibility on a firm base.

Breadth follows from the claims the novel began to make for itself, in comparisons with the highest genres, epic and history painting. These were genres that came bearing heavy burdens of theory with them, dominated by the canon of unity and variety, such as Harris advises (see above, pp. 11–12). Joseph Trapp, for instance, praises the heterocosm of the *Aeneid*, with "almost every Object of the Imagination beautifully described, all Nature unfolded, the great Events, the unexpected Revolutions, the Incentives to Virtue; . . . [and] the most consummate Art, by which all these Things are brought into one uniform Piece."[3] For the eighteenth century, these epic virtues had been reechoed in *Paradise Lost*, a modern work of enormous prestige, which could "shine for ever [with] the great Lights of Antiquity."[4] As Addison announced in *Spectator* 267, the first on *Paradise Lost*, "every Thing that is great in the whole Circle of Being, whether within the Verge of Nature, or out of it, has a proper Part assigned it in this noble Poem," so that "it gives us at the same Time a Pleasure of the greatest Variety, and of the greatest Simplicity." The novel, through Fielding in particular, grafted itself into this line of criticism.

Moreover, as Addison's affective bias ("a Pleasure of . . . Variety, and . . . Simplicity") suggests, the criteria for epic virtues were becoming more accessible to fiction: formal characteristics specific to the genre (verse, supernatural machinery, fiery muses) got less emphasis, and nongeneric, aesthetic characteristics got more. The formula implied by Addison, that of unity (or uniformity) and variety, became the

3. *Lectures on Poetry Read . . . at Oxford*, tr. William Boyer and William Clarke (from Trapp's Latin) (London, 1742), pp. 11-12.

4. Henry Fielding, *The Covent-Garden Journal*, ed. G. E. Jensen, 2 vols. (1915; reprinted New York: Russell & Russell, 1964), 1: 248 (*Covent-Garden Journal* 19; March 7, 1752).

most tirelessly repeated of the eighteenth century. It came into English aesthetics formally with Hutcheson in 1725, ten years after Crousaz had introduced it into aesthetics on the continent, but it had been brewing in criticism well before that. The pleasures of simplicity and order, after all, were stock in seventeenth-century "classicism"; and by the 1690s, "no Man . . . doubt[ed] but that 'tis *Variety* that composes the *Regale* of the *Mind*, as well as that of the *Body*," that a "Book must needs delight, but cannot cloy,/ Having that great Preservative, Variety."[5] The Crousaz-Hutcheson formula came inevitably, demanding the maximum of systematic variety on affective grounds: "Les rapports fort composez ont leur beauté comme les simples, & par cela même qu'ils renferment plus de variété, les Esprits d'une grande étendue s'y trouvent beaucoup plus sensibles."[6] This canon, universally although

5. [Charles Gildon], *Miscellaneous Letters and Essays, on Several Subjects* (London, 1694), sig. A7. George Smith, prefatory poem to Benjamin Hawkshaw, *Poems upon Several Occasions* (1693), p. vii. The principles of unity and variety had been central to English dramatic criticism throughout the Restoration; they form the basis of Neander's defense of English plays and his "examen" of *Epicoene* in Dryden's *Essay of Dramatick Poesie* (1668), for example. The two works of theoretical aesthetics are J. P. de Crousaz, *Traité du beau* (Amsterdam, 1715), and Francis Hutcheson, *An Inquiry into the Original of Our Ideas of Beauty and Virtue* (London, 1725). Their formula is assessed by the major English theoreticians contemporary with our novelists. See David Hartley, *Observations on Man, His Frame, His Duty, and His Expectations*, 2 vols. (London, 1749), 1: 419; Alexander Gerard, *An Essay on Taste* (1759) (3rd ed., Edinburgh, 1780), pp. 29-33 (Part 1, sec. 3); Henry Home, Lord Kames, *The Elements of Criticism* (1762), 2 vols. (7th ed., Edinburgh, 1788), 1: 305-32 (chap. 9); Joseph Priestley, *A Course of Lectures on Oratory and Criticism* [delivered 1762] (London, 1777), pp. 133, 164; Sir Joshua Reynolds, "Discourse VIII" (1778), in *Discourses on Art*, ed. Robert R. Wark (San Marino: Huntington Library, 1959), pp. 146-48; Archibald Alison, *Essays on the Nature and Principles of Taste* (Edinburgh, 1790), pp. 264-87. See also Ronald Paulson, *Hogarth: His Life, Art, and Times*, 2 vols. (New Haven: Yale University Press, 1971), 2: 167-68, 175-83.

6. Crousaz, p. 49. Cf. the comments on Sulzer and Hemsterhuis in Paul-Joseph Barthez's posthumous *Théorie du Beau* (1807) (2nd ed., Paris, 1895), pp. 18-19.

not exclusively accepted by the middle of the eighteenth century, offered novelists a happily vague and encouraging ideal for marrying control and inclusiveness. We have seen, theoretically in the Introduction and practically in the analyses, how it led to analogy and modification as means of expanding upon an initial situation by letting parts generate their alternatives. The tie between this formal procedure and epistemology is already explicit in Crousaz, who explains that "la diversité multiplie & étend ses connoissances [i.e., the mind's], l'uniformité les affirmit & les fixe dans la mémoire." For Hutcheson, similarly, God has given man a sense of beauty based on uniformity and variety to lead him "to *those Actions* which are most efficacious, and fruitful in useful Effects; and to *those Theorems* which most inlarge our *Minds*."[7]

The epic model was old, the system of unity and variety new: together they gave the novel a context, an ideal, and a formal ground that served the purposes of epistemology. Form and epistemology could come together only in a mimetic fiction, and from the criteria of mimesis comes the second of our three principles, freedom from manipulation. Manipulation, of course, is not the same as commentary. Authors could comment on what they presented, in the manner of Fielding, but not intervene in the supposedly natural events the novel imitates. Fielding's novels, and Sterne's, are histories, clarified for us but not contrived. The surface of both men's work is marked by the ideal of ease and negligence, both observing the ancient rule of *ars celare artem* as Joseph Spence, for instance, proclaimed it: "'Tis the greatest of Arts, to conceal the Art you use; and to have it very evident, is the greatest of Blemishes. The Criticks, and *Cicero* in particular, speak with the greatest plainness against any thing of that kind."[8] As a formal device, apparent negligence had always been connected with a partic-

---

7. Crousaz, p. 13. Hutcheson, p. 101.
8. *An Essay on Pope's Odyssey,* 2 vols. (London, 1726), 1: 25.

ular ideal for the novel, verisimilitude. "Ubicunque ars ostentatur, veritas abesse videatur," wrote Quintilian (*Inst.* IX.iii.12), and as Ian Watt has impressively documented, "veritas" was very much the aim of the novel.[9] Thus in Clara Reeve's *Progress of Romance*, Euphrasia remarks that "perhaps there is not a better Criterion of the merit of a book, than our losing sight of the Author," so that the work may seem "a true history"; Hortensius and Sophronia, the other two interlocutors, "readily agree."[10] In the eighteenth century, once again, verisimilitude was an affective criterion, for "even when ideas have no manner of influence on the will and passions, truth and reality are still requisite, in order to make them entertaining to the imagination." Hence "Words," in the "Disposal" of "a Great Poet," "are [the] Things" they represent, "and, the Deception proves so strong, that the Reader forgets he is perusing a Piece of Writing." Or again, "the Appearance of Reality is that which moves us in all Representations, and these have always the greater Force, the nearer they approach to Nature, and the less they shew of Imitation."[11]

The illusion of reality, so that form and epistemology could join, was helped by the third of our three principles, that of a particulate representation, scenes and episodes rather than continuous flow. Nothing could be older in literary practice. In the hands of seventeenth- and eighteenth-century writers, nothing was more effective in pulling the reader's conscious attention from large formal units. The tableau or dramatic

9. *The Rise of the Novel* (Berkeley and Los Angeles: University of California Press, 1957), especially chap. 1, "Realism and the novel form." See also Vivienne Mylne, *The Eighteenth-Century French Novel: Techniques of Illusion* (Manchester: Manchester University Press, 1965), chaps. 1 and 2.

10. *The Progress of Romance, through Times, Countries, and Manners*, 2 vols. (Colchester, 1785), 2: 24-25.

11. David Hume, *A Treatise of Human Nature*, ed. L. A. Selby-Bigge (Oxford: Clarendon Press, 1896), I.iii.10 (p. 121). Ambrose Philips(?), *The Free-Thinker*, 2 vols. (London, 1722), 2: 51 (*Free-Thinker* 63, [1718]). *The Players: A Satire* (London, 1733), sig. A7ᵛ.

scene, realized in sensory vividness, compelled individual belief and generated an individual complex of emotions.[12] We have seen this atomic method at work in each of our five novelists. The method was given priority by post-Lockean rhetoricians from Burke to Alison, because of their interest in the perception of literature—often in connection with painting—as a temporal act. They dwelt on evocative images or description, swift insights into character, affective units like pathetic scenes. This kind of criticism, especially suited to poetry, shows up most strikingly in fiction like *A Sentimental Journey* or *The Man of Feeling*, but the procedures of these novels only carry general practice to extremes. Moreover, associationism gave force to such surface discontinuity; we have seen how our five authors depend upon the reader's mental mechanics to create transitions, pull narrative and thematic elements into episodes, and shape rhythms from repetition. Agglomerative form is natural to the author's mind and ours, so that we can and must, to admire imaginative beauties, "enter into the train of *concealed ideas* which may establish a connection *not less real*, because it may be at first imperceptible betwixt these strong apostrophes and the circumstances immediately preceding."[13]

The case for the historical plausibility of our three principles—breadth, freedom from manipulation, and particulateness—is very strong. Each has at least two, differently based, common tenets of eighteenth-century criticism behind it: epic theory and Hutcheson's formula, ease and verisimilitude, post-Lockean temporalism and associationism. Each is linked by at least one of those tenets to the new philosophic rhetoric, with its formal and epistemological scheme;

12. I have discussed the development of this sort of fragmentation in the affective mode of tragedy during the seventeenth century, in *Restoration Tragedy: Form and the Process of Change* (Madison: University of Wisconsin Press, 1967).

13. John Ogilvie, *Philosophical and Critical Observations on the Nature, Characters, and Various Species of Composition*, 2 vols. (London, 1774), 1: 66.

and each has ample precedent in artistic practice. For their corollary, the duplicity of form, we find no such massiveness of support. It is overt, however, in an especially public sort of art, architecture, where eighteenth-century builders followed the earlier practice praised by Geoffrey Scott, "subordinat-[ing], deliberately and without hesitation, constructional fact to aesthetic effect." "Where the Renaissance builders wanted the effect of a constructional form," says Scott, "they did not scruple to employ it, even where it no longer fulfilled a constructive purpose. On the other hand, with equal disregard to this kind of truth, those elements of construction which really and effectively supported the fabric, they were constantly at pains to conceal, and even, in concealing, to contradict."[14] Eighteenth-century architects separated actual and professed forms not only to create "aesthetic effect" but also to make statements, as mock ruins assert a historical relationship or the monumental sham façade of the elder Wood's Queen Square, Bath, announces a socioeconomic position. In fiction, as in buildings, of course, "constructional form," as Scott calls it, usually coincides with apparent, dramatized form. Still, the coincidence is the result of deliberate choice. Concealment and false fronts are also possible, for diverse ends.[15]

14. Geoffrey Scott, *The Architecture of Humanism: A Study in the History of Taste* (Garden City, N.Y.: Doubleday, Anchor Books, 1956), p. 81.

15. On the sham façade, see Emil Kaufmann, *Architecture in the Age of Reason* (Cambridge, Mass.: Harvard University Press, 1955), p. 33. André Parreaux mentions similar activities in landscaping, of false rivers and bridges, and of a false ruined castle built by Capability Brown with real servants' quarters in it; see *La Vie quotidienne en Angleterre au temps de George III* (n.p.: Hachette, 1966), p. 40. A broadly affective rather than an aesthetic or socioeconomic statement is made by Sir William Chambers's plan to build the mausoleum for Frederick, Prince of Wales, as a ruin; see the Kenwood catalogue for the exhibition "British Artists in Rome 1700-1800," entry 57. One should remember that sham ruins were meant to be formally as well as emotionally suggestive: William Gilpin, for example, says that ruins are not only to create the illusion of formlessness (natural decay) by "great efforts of

These ends include, as we have seen, "guaranteeing" that the represented world is free from the author's doctoring; they include Smollett's deceptive creation of a narrator, and Johnson's and Fielding's sleight of hand to make us accept a character's never shown process of learning and development. They include an illusory exclusion of the author from the text so that the form itself can make a statement about the characters. For example, because *Humphry Clinker* pretends to toss aside form in favor of epistolary catch-as-catch-can, it makes local energy and vividness positive values, from which Bramble, but also Win and Humphry, benefit. The result is to deflect our sympathies from stern systems. The handling of form, that is, moves us to doubt Bramble's rigid notions about hierarchy, his grim inferences from daily life, and his claims about the present age's easy descent to perdition. Caleb Williams's forms of narration say what he wants to say, but betray what he should have wanted to say; and his choice of form characterizes him as plainly as Tristram's does him. Caleb's failure is Godwin's success because of the damning adequacy of his form; Tristram's failure is Sterne's success because of the damning inadequacy of his, for the shambles of that book are as much a sham as is the façade of Queen Square, Bath. In each of these novels, the option of separating constructional and apparent form serves order and inquiry both.

We have moved from historical "roots" back to the texts of the novels. I should like to continue looking at the texts, to define the coherence of their systems of inquiry from what has been said about naturalness and systems of order. All five novels, as we have seen, use a central character or matrix of characters to interpret reality, imperfectly, for us. In all five,

---

art" but also to force one to imagine the forms, the hypothetical originals, which in the case of sham ruins have never existed. One cooperates, as in our novels, with the hints of dramatized form. *Observations, Relative Chiefly to Picturesque Beauty, . . . on . . . the Mountains, and Lakes of Cumberland, and Westmoreland* [written 1772], 2 vols. (London, 1786), 1: 66-68.

we must weigh, choose, and remodel those interpretations without accepting any one alone. None of the narrators, Jery partially excepted, is both helpful and reliable. The two first-person narrators, Tristram and Caleb (and the three who take part in *Amelia*), are as bad as, although brighter and more consistent than, so extreme an unreliable narrator as Ford's in *The Good Soldier*. Fielding's narrator, typically, deceives and, atypically, deserts us. Johnson's limits himself to a single attitude, that of the Solomonic preacher, and leaves us to see its effective limits. In Smollett, the characters' multiple perspectives make up our fly's eye view. Multiple perspectives are forced on us, besides, not only by the narrators' defaulting and characters' blunders, but also by a moral principle. In all these novels, except for *Rasselas* where there is neither empathy nor human evil, the source of evil is the single, limited perspective of radical egoism. For it, the Shandys, the Booths, Bramble, and in a sense Caleb, own and use the healing salve of simple love; we readers do not, and must use our substitute, empathy, seeing things as the characters see them. That necessarily involves mental pluralism. The principle of modification follows logically from the shakiness of the narrators and characters and the need to keep enlarging perspectives to make a wider and wiser inquiry, to seek a finer and firmer order.

The protagonists have single perspectives, "systems," as interpretive means. These are a priori, often literary, always from sources ultimately external to the created world of the book, and always of only limited utility. Caleb casts himself in literary roles and sees Falkland as a literary object. Part of this characterization is that he is a superficial and morally insensitive reader: if, after all, Caleb's allegiance had been more to Richardson's deeper theme, the horror at people's sacrificing others to their own idols, and less to Richardson's surface procedure, with its sharp separation of sheep and goats (so Godwin would have thought) and its skoptophilia, there would have been no novel. For inner justification, Booth's passional "philosophy" draws on stock forms of melodrama and romance such as establish mutual rapport with Fanny Matthews. So does Tristram, who makes the contents of his mind ours through appealing to common idioms, epic, satiric, and novelistic conventions, as well as those of memoirs, often in parody. In addition to the utopian illusion central in *Rasselas,* Johnson sometimes uses the sort of cliché that Fielding uses for Booth, as in the prince's daydream about the abducted maiden (chap. 4) or his sister's mooning for the life of a shepherdess. Sometimes—Pekuah's foray with the sheik, the hallowed and hoary panaceas of Cairo—Johnson separates the clichés from the inner, mimetic life of the characters, although not from their cultural habits of mind. More covertly, since the reader is to feel that form emanates from the characters, he uses tradition—received ideas of the Happy Valley and the pyramid—to express paradoxes of value. Smollett's characters, except for "Wilson," do not have shaping illusions that are literary. Bramble's system is self-derived from nosology, although it fits well with literary behaviorism. But in addition, the ideas of Methodism provide a form that emanates from the titular character, Humphry, and that can be translated into the secular terms of the novel, whether the varieties of redemption or the play between body and spirit. Moreover, the figure of Quixote hovers behind the main character, Bramble, as a correlative to (rather than as an expression of) his mode of mental behavior; this is Smollett's version of the way *Joseph Andrews* has Homer, Richardson, and Cervantes hover behind the narrator, Joseph, and Adams as correlatives to their modes of action.

From the importance of empathy and the limits of characters, we can see why they often deserve and get our affection, but rarely our trust. We exceed them in too many ways. In accord with the use of formal modification, in which the novel keeps varying and broadening perspectives on an initial body of material, the characters have their limits of aspiration set at or near the beginning of the novel. Rasselas can hope only to be an Imlac, Booth a Harrison, Caleb (if "hope" is the right word) a Falkland, and sick Bramble a healthy Bramble. In *Tristram*, where there is no progress, the son stays tethered to the poles of his father and uncle. The conclusion of each book, except for *Tristram*, marks the point at which the character comes as close as he can to this limit of aspiration. Bramble alone of these characters actually goes through a process of learning, for which we are given mere formal equivalents by Fielding and Johnson, not even that—the use of pivot episodes—by Sterne, and only factual learning and growing disillusionment by Godwin. Each book does have a peripeteia, when the protagonist sees the inadequacy (not the absolute error) of his previous state of mind and modifies it; but we, through a genuine, formally parallel process of learning, have already performed the modification. I do not mean that we disbelieve in the characters' learning, not when the novelists cared to make us believe in it, but rather that we do not rely on the characters to ferry us. Moreover, the characters tend not to practice what they preach, and worse yet for them, sometimes to be better men for their inconsistencies. Bramble believes in a hierarchical and holistic world, but behaves like the confused and divisive world he sees and hates; Booth exalts the determinant passions, but behaves like a man to whom value judgments are crucial; Caleb thinks his rights of man sacred, but behaves like a "grey-headed inquisitor." *Tristram* and *Rasselas* express the same subject through paradox, Tristram's belief and disbelief in the systems he employs, Rasselas's both approved and disapproved inability to behave as belief in eternity implies.

We exceed them in another way. Unlike the characters, we have two levels of organization. One is the same as theirs, the represented world. The other is the representation, the work of fiction, which is susceptible to system, covert system. We can see the fascinating interaction of these two in the muted use of emblems and symbols, ambiguous to the characters directly involved with them, but for that reason formally complete to us. Johnson's pyramid, Sterne's bowling green, Godwin's and Fielding's prison, Smollett's bathing—all knot together themes for motifs so as to make the whole more than the sum of what the parts seemed to be. (None of these symbolic objects, of course, is realized in sensory detail or called on to provide unique revelations with ineffable rightness. To advertise the collective and connective job of given objects would be to risk implying a degree of authorial tampering which would interfere with the mimetic freedom of the book.) Each emblem takes part in the principle of modification, by having a double role that makes it ambiguous. Each mediates between the objective world, in which it naturally and inobtrusively fits, and a world of realized values; that is, between the world that a free consciousness can probe and the world as defined by personal needs and desires. Each emblem represents a solution prescribed by society for distempers of imagination, the body, or conscience. Yet in each case something is wrong. Pyramids are the tombs of pride, and prisons, callous monuments to all the other vices. The bowling green shrivels the great warrior into a second-hand sportsman. Natural waters are sometimes deadly, sometimes befouled by natural and unnatural man. Each emblem thereby provides a false social solution to a real problem, but each allows a valid personal solution through spiritual reading. Heaven-pointing pyramids or baptismal rebirth, the Boethian metaphor of the prison as a projection of deterministic self-fettering, the ideals of harmless joy and loyal fellowship in play—inner meanings, not necessarily perceived as such by the characters, enable true values to bloom from the corrupt or incomplete options society extends. For the characters, both literal and symbolic readings of these objects are valid, as might be other precise inferences from them. Characters must make choices from which meaning follows. To some extent we do too, but for us the equilibrium of choices, the suspension of precise strands, offers an aesthetic solution to an aesthetic problem, such as the characters cannot know.[16] Aesthetic problems are systematically resolved, but the real world admits of no resolutions except simple acceptance, if that.

The novels of Sterne, Smollett, Fielding, and Johnson tell us we must accept the world as it is, although the latter two treat it as probationary. Refuge from it may exist only for individuals. Godwin, perhaps Fielding too, has a gleam of reform in his eye, but social reform is, at very best, distant and difficult. A resolution in personal reform, the only kind of resolution in the five books, is made meager by the abundance of pain and vice, portrayed as widespread, not specific to one individual life or mere background to individual triumph. The conclusion of each, in keeping with the multiple perspectives and empirical skepticism that the mode demands, revokes nothing that has gone before it; it enlarges the scope of the presentation, so as to make more cohere in an intuitive whole. In short, the five authors, like the followers of Locke (which is not an idle comparison), try in their content to describe and give principle to representative but unreduced experience "comme un excellent Anatomiste explique les ressorts du corps humain."[17]

Each of the characters, through events he may cause but cannot control, does come to some degree of equilibrium or sense of finality (sporadic for Tristram), in terms of his own life. We, who have all along steered our own ship by the glimmers of their light, arrive at aesthetic satisfaction, our version of their personal equilibrium and the point of our repose. Yet

16. Leo Braudy speculates that "our knowledge of a complete aesthetic world emphasizes the impossibility of ever completely knowing or judging the actual world." *Narrative Form in History and Fiction: Hume, Fielding, and Gibbon* (Princeton: Princeton University Press. 1970), p. 152.

17. Voltaire's comparison of Locke to an anatomist follows a sentence that connects the presentational mode to true history: "Tant de raisonneurs ayant fait le roman de l'âme, un sage [i.e., Locke] est venu, qui en a fait modestement l'histoire." Letter 13 in *Lettres philosophiques*, ed. Raymond Naves (Paris: Garnier, 1956), p. 63.

the world that can be held in systems of order, in which we can have repose, is smaller than the implied world of the books. The conclusionlessness of *Rasselas, Tristram,* and *Caleb,* the implausible end of *Amelia,* the abandonment of just satire in *Humphry Clinker*—these endings show the failure of literary form to give full coherence to the panorama of life. The characters have tried to shape reality through a priori forms, their personalities, their illusions, their maxims; and the authors have shown us how confined, how open to modification the characters are, so as to put us in the odd situation of feeling at once superior and bewildered, superior because we are open to a richer, denser "nature" than they are, and bewildered by our recognizing our failure to see that nature coherently. In all the books but *Humphry,* this role for the reader is an overt implication of the view of man expressed, and in Sterne and Fielding it is an overt theme. We come at last to a final analogy and modification, in which Christian humility and empirical skepticism agree on the measure of man. The characters have all begun by thinking themselves innocent, essentially adequate, and harassed by the world around them; we also think ourselves innocent and adequate. By the end of the books, they know that they have been and (except for Bramble) are, inadequate despite their success in reaching the level of their aspirations. We, despite our reaching formal aesthetic satisfaction, should at least have started to suspect that the same is true of us.

The systems of order and inquiry in our five novels are coherent and historically plausible. I submit that they may well have chronological bounds, and allege the late novels of Dickens as evidence. Dickens has several advantages for this purpose, aside from his later novels' being so well known that they lend themselves to our rapid comparison. These novels are panoramic; they depend heavily on analogy; they offer multiple perspectives. Their author admired eighteenth-century fiction enough to have named a son Henry Fielding

Dickens (b. 1849). He wrote for a popular audience and so stands a good chance of reflecting a more general practice of the mid-nineteenth century. Such a novelist must, and does, share many procedures and interests with his fellows of a century earlier. He does not, however, share their systems of order and inquiry, and as a result his use of their procedures and his expression of their interests takes a markedly different tack from theirs.

Most obviously, Dickens does not build his novels around a central character as the five eighteenth-century writers do. *David Copperfield* and *Great Expectations* are partial exceptions, of course, but even here the form of the novel does not emerge from a central character's shaping of his experience. David and Pip and the Esther Summerson who partners the third-person narrator—she starts out (chap. 3) "I have a great deal of difficulty in beginning to write my portion of these pages"—are retrospective speakers at a distance, unlike the retrospective Tristram and Caleb and Bramble, who are striking while (or because) the iron is hot. In the eighteenth-century works, the form we perceive derives from, and comments upon, the hero who, in his own voice or not, presents his world to us as a closed system whose degrees of validity we test against the larger world implied by the text. David and Esther have no systems, and their progress in learning how to perceive the truth (as opposed to solving specific mysteries) does not bulk large in the novels they narrate; as to *Great Expectations*, Pip's false gentility is developed as an isolable ethical blemish, which does not much affect his relations with such unpretentious men as Herbert Pocket and Wemmick. Values, for the five heroes of the eighteenth-century works, are correlated with general structures of belief, but not the values of Dickens's heroes. When knowledge is imparted in Dickens, it tends to be specific information and to be secondary to the behavior it prompts. For us too every Dickens novel cultivates its mystery: Who was Esther's mother? Who gave Pip the money? Has Mr. Boffin gone bad? We never ask, however, who Humphry's father was, or even who had Booth arrested, or who stabbed Tyrrel (cf. the murder of Tulkinghorn): that sort of hidden information has its place within a scheme of human knowledge. It is never (parts of *Amelia* excepted) what it often is in Dickens, a means of making us uncomfortable enough to hurry under the comforting shelter of fellowship and feeling.

Because Dickens separates systems of inquiry and order in this way, peripeteias in the plot often, perhaps typically, have no close antecedent link to mental action. One may compare, for example, Esther's discovery of her mother or Pip's of his benefactor with Bramble's of his son or Booth's of his heavenly father. Nor do a priori forms, which give order and which condition inquiry, play much part in Dickens. The systems by which Miss Havisham and Magwitch try to model Estella and Pip, or even the stereotypes in terms of which Fledgeby makes Riah seem to be the traditional usurious Jew and Boffin makes himself the traditional miser, are quite different. Those in *Great Expectations* have no referents outside the novel. Those in *Our Mutual Friend* are forms of sport, deliberate impostures in which the fact of external reference is unimportant in itself and forgotten when the impostures are drawn into the thematic fabric of the novel. Although declines, falls, and little empires are enough in evidence to justify Wegg's reading Gibbon to the Boffins, nothing beyond Gibbon's title has much point in *Our Mutual Friend*. Historically, of course, Dickens writes for an audience of the 1850s and 1860s, not attuned to allusive and imitative forms as Godwin's audience was in the 1790s: *The Baviad* and *The Maeviad, The Rolliad, The Lousiad,* and a host of poetical imitations fall within the decade or so before *Caleb Williams*. All four earlier authors themselves were imitators, Johnson of Juvenal, Fielding of the Scriblerians, Sterne of Rabelais, Smollett of Le Sage; and their audience was that of Pope and Gray. I suspect they were much better able than

Dickens to call on readers to enlarge the perspectives of fiction through a keenness to allusion, or both to use and to challenge preestablished literary systems. For whatever reasons, order and inquiry have a different relationship in the eighteenth-century novels and Dickens's.

Dickens uses analogy a great deal, but as his splitting of order from inquiry implies, he does not use it with modification as the eighteenth-century writers do. In his novels, major characters, like Jaggers or Bradley Headstone, stay outside analogical patterns as none does in our five books. Others are encompassed by such patterns, but only formally: we learn little about them and little about their fellow members of the pattern from their being in it. *Our Mutual Friend*, for example, has parental analogies that give the novel coherence but that do not tell us much that we did not already know about the Hexams, the Riderhoods, the Wilfers, the Podsnaps, the Boffins vis-à-vis Rokesmith and Bella, Riah vis-à-vis the relation of Jenny and her father, and so on. The contrary examples in Dickens, like the analogy between Magwitch and Miss Havisham, are far fewer in proportion to the whole than in our five eighteenth-century books.

Dickens makes much less systematic use than do our five authors of the principle of modification. In the eighteenth-century books, virtually no paragons of value exist, except for minor characters like Grieve, the real Wilson, or the elder Dennison in *Humphry*. Even Imlac, as we have seen, has his limits like any other man. In *Amelia*, absolute goodness is an absolute good, but it implies of necessity a destructive naiveté, such as we see in Atkinson and Amelia, even in the prickly Harrison. It also implies a vulnerability which calls its value, within real humans in a real world, into serious question. *Caleb Williams*, except in a flashback story which is itself heavily qualified, admits no paragons: Laura and Collins, trapped in Things As They Are, cannot be just without injustice. The Shandys' Shandeism, finally, makes men fools; it is not simply a quirk, like Betsy Trotwood's or Mr. Boythorn's peppery temper, external to the value the character represents. Dickens, however, thrives on the non-integral quirk, and overflows with paragons. In *Bleak House* alone we have vital, major paragons like Esther, Jarndyce, Ada, Boythorn, the Bagnets, George, Caddy. We even have narrators who are both reliable and helpful, like none in our five novels. The third-person narrator and Esther are unchallenged as the dark cloud and silver lining of *Bleak House*. Similarly, the narrator, with his varied tones, is our mutual friend in *Our Mutual Friend*, and the older Pip leads us unresisting through his younger self's great expectations.

Because of the loss of the central character as means of control, and because of his cruder, less exigent principle of modification, Dickens likes to use polar oscillations instead of the eighteenth-century novelist's muted contrasts. In *Great Expectations*, for instance, we have forge:marshes, forge:Satis House, forge:Satis House:London, and later the polar contrast made clear in Wemmick's two personalities. This is not simply a matter of setting but of psychological ambiance, which can change brutally in Dickens. His symbols and emblems, subject neither to character nor to modification, tend to make objective a fundamentally impersonal dream state. They render as The World what our five novelists render as perspectives or the result of perspectives. Like dreams, Dickens's symbols are often arbitrary, demanding belief because of their vividness, in a manner reserved to human beings, like Smollett's grotesques, in the pre-Gothic novel. Satis House, with its tattered chatelaine and icy princess, imposes itself on the protagonist Pip; the tarry river and "dustheap" of *Our Mutual Friend* have to do with Dickens's own metaphor of picking carrion. Other, less glaring emblems are caricatural, like Fledgeby's Turkish costume (unchristian behavior) or the Veneerings' ornamental camels (aridity of their lives? or the odds against their getting through the eye of a needle? it does not much matter). Because these symbols are evocative rather than expressive of a complex relationship, they can be neutralized, as the sinister ones (Satis House, the black Thames) are by the end of the books. The eighteenth-century ones retain their force as agents of definition, of equilibrium between character and society.

If my arguments are convincing, they show that Dickens differs from our five novelists in systematic conception as well as in details. The details, that is, are symptoms. Of course a comparison with Dickens, who seems to be in the "same tradition" as Fielding or Smollett, is not exhaustive. Other later novelists would differ in other ways. My arguments will be stillborn if readers do not search for counterexamples in the Bröntes or Thackeray, James, Hardy, Lawrence, Steinbeck, or whoever might be thought to make use of an endemic mode. Individual novels since Godwin's, I am sure, adopted the system I have tentatively identified with the eighteenth century. Joyce's *Portrait of the Artist* comes very close to it, and no doubt there are other candidates. But isolated examples, if they are such, do not seriously affect my case. No doubt, too, my historical inferences would be sounder if the pattern examined were ampler and morphologically more precise in terms of base description and variants. None the less, I submit that strong prima facie evidence exists for the chronological bounds as well as the historical roots of a system common, which is not to say universal, in the eighteenth-century novel. Whether "a system" turns out to be my system can only be learned by further analyses and hypotheses about other works than my—or our—five. I hope fellow scholars will find these beginnings of mine sturdy enough to support further inquiries, for, like every other scholarly author, I would be unhappy to be discarded, but pleased, all in all, to be superseded.

Index

266

Lacombe, Jacques: on discrimi-
nated variety, 19 n.
Lactantius, Lucius Caelius Firmi-
anus, 65 n.
Lambert, J. M.: on the *Aeneid*,
104 n.
Landa, Louis A.: on the flyer in
Rasselas, 27 n.
La Porte, Joseph de: on novelistic
rules, 1
Lascelles, Mary: on the structure of
Rasselas, 37 n.
Le Bossu, René: on epic structure,
197 n.
Lee, Henry: on identity, 10
Lee, Nathaniel: Fielding's allusions
to, 193, 194 n.
Le Fevre, Jacques, 98 n.
Le Fevre, Tanneguy, 97-98
Lehman, Benjamin H.: on the
Shandy family, 72 n.
Le Page, Peter V.: on the prison in
Amelia, 175 n.
Lewis, Matthew Gregory: aban-
doned   eighteenth-century
pattern, 240
Lloyd, Evan: on Methodism, 127 n.
Lobo, Jerome, 24, 25, 45
Locke, John: on analogy, 12; on
identity, 10, 11; and philo-
sophical rhetoric, 246, 247, 252,
259; in Sterne, 70, 73-75 pas-
sim, 87, 88
Lockhart, Donald M.: on the com-
position of *Rasselas*, 36 n.
Love, Harold: on abstract order in
Tristram Shandy, 107 n.
Lowth, Robert: place of literature,
69 n.
Lucan (Marcus Annaeus Lucanus):
in *Amelia*, 181, 197, 200
Ludolphus, Job, 25, 26
Lyles, Albert M., 127 n.

McCracken, David: on Godwin's
literary theory, 209 n., 226 n.
Mackenzie, Henry: *The Man of Feel-
ing*, 252
Macky, John, 148 n.
Macpherson, James: discriminated
variety in, 18 n.; in *Humphry
Clinker*, 140
Macquer, Pierre-Joseph, 131 n.
Malory, Sir Thomas: his *Tristram*,
65 n. 68 n.
Manwaring, Edward, 91 n.
Marat, Jean-Paul: on analogy, 15 n.
Marmontel,   Jean-François: on
memoirs, 67, 68 n.
Martz, Louis L.: on *Humphry Clink-
er*, 113 n., 114 n.
Mead, Richard, 131 n.
Metzger, Hélène, 131 n.
Milton, John: his unity and (broad,
discriminated) variety, 18, 248
Modification: defined 6-7, 11-20
Molyneux, William: his problem,
70 n.
Montesquieu, Charles de Secondat,
baron de: mode of *Lettres per-
sanes*, 40
Mozart, Wolfgang Amadeus, 44
Murphy, Arthur: on discriminated
variety in Fielding, 18-19
Myers, Mitzi: on the ending of *Caleb
Williams*, 239 n.
Mylne, Vivienne: on "realism" in
French fiction, 251 n.

New, Melvyn: on satire in *Tristram
Shandy*, 77 n., 78 n.
Newbery, John: on discriminated
variety, 18 n.
Newgate Calendar, The: used in *Caleb
Williams*, 219-220, 227, 230, 240
Newton, Sir Isaac: his epistemo-
logical method, 9; mentioned,
51, 52